# Health Policy Analysis

**John W. Seavey, PhD, MPH,** is professor emeritus in the department of health management and policy at the University of New Hampshire (UNH). Previously, he was the Everett B. Sackett Professor (1996–2012) and senior fellow at The Carsey Institute (2005–2011). He received his baccalaureate degree from Bates College (1966), an MA (1968) and PhD (1973) from the University of Arizona, and a master's of public health (MPH) from the Harvard School of Public Health (1979). At UNH, he taught a variety of courses, but focused on health policy courses at the graduate and undergraduate levels. He served as chair of the department for multiple terms and was the founding director of the UNH master of public health program.

Dr. Seavey's research focus has been on rural health care in the United States and, more recently, on the impact of socioeconomic status on health. His publications include two books and numerous peer-reviewed articles and monographs. He has also served as reviewer for multiple editorial boards.

Dr. Seavey has been the recipient of many UNH awards, among them the UNH Outstanding Associate Professor Award (1991), College of Health and Human Services Distinguished Career Research Award (2003), UNH Faculty Social Justice Award (2005), and Distinguished UNH Professor (2005). He was on the board of directors of the Association of University Programs in Health Administration (1989–1995), where for a part of his term he served as the chair (1993–1994). Dr. Seavey was also the recipient of the New Hampshire Public Health Association's Roger Fossum Lifetime Achievement Award (2011).

**Semra A. Aytur, PhD, MPH,** is an assistant professor in the department of health management and policy at the University of New Hampshire (UNH). Dr. Aytur teaches courses in health policy, social and behavioral health, and biostatistics. Prior to joining UNH, she completed her doctoral degree (2006) and postdoctoral fellowship (2009) in cardiovascular epidemiology at the University of North Carolina, Chapel Hill. Additionally, she has served as a policy and evaluation specialist for local and state health departments. Her research focuses on policy and environmental changes to prevent obesity, diabetes, and cardiovascular disease. She is particularly interested in health disparities and in policies that influence the natural, social, and built environment to promote health equity. Dr. Aytur collaborates with researchers around the country on policy issues related to obesity prevention, physical activity, health promotion, community resilience, and the environment. She specializes in collaborative decision processes designed to promote civic engagement.

Dr. Aytur has received several research grants from the Robert Wood Johnson Foundation as well as from federal agencies to evaluate policy, environment, and systems change pertaining to chronic disease prevention and climate change adaptation. She enjoys collaborating with policy makers, urban planners, transportation planners, and citizens to develop strategies to promote sustainable, health-promoting community environments. Nationally, she has been a member of the National Physical Activity Policy Research Network and the National Forum to Prevent Heart Disease and Stroke. She was recently nominated to serve on the Environmental Protection Agency's Board of Scientific Counselors for Sustainable and Healthy Communities.

**Robert J. McGrath, PhD,** is the Everett B. Sacket associate professor, chair of the department of health policy and management, and director of the master of public health program at the University of New Hampshire (UNH). In addition, he is a senior faculty fellow in the Institute for Health Policy and Practice and the Institute on Disability. He is a former faculty fellow with the Carsey Institute and was formerly the executive director for the New Hampshire Health Information Center at UNH (2003–2009). He received his BS from UNH in 1996, an MS (1998) from the Harvard School of Public Health, an MA (2000) from Brandeis University, and a PhD (2006) from the Heller School at Brandeis. His coursework focuses on quantitative methods for health management and policy, health policy, and health policy analysis.

Dr. McGrath's research focus is in health disparities for children with a genetically derived condition or special health care needs and the family impacts of having a child with such a condition. He also examines the role of data in health and health care decision making. Dr. McGrath has published on health disparities in many journals, including *Pediatrics* and the *Journal of Pediatrics*. His publications also include two books and a number of peer-reviewed abstracts and presentations, and he serves as a reviewer for a number of national health journals.

Dr. McGrath has received a number of federal and private research grants and has worked with many state-based agencies and community partners to promote healthy child development and interoperable health systems toward a better understanding of health.

# Health Policy Analysis
*Framework and Tools for Success*

*John W. Seavey, PhD, MPH*
*Semra A. Aytur, PhD, MPH*
*Robert J. McGrath, PhD*

SPRINGER PUBLISHING COMPANY
NEW YORK

Springer Publishing Company, LLC
11 West 42nd Street
New York, NY 10036
www.springerpub.com

*Acquisitions Editor:* Sheri W. Sussman
*Production Editor:* Shelby Peak
*Composition:* S4Carlisle Publishing Services

*ISBN:* 978-0-8261-1923-0
*e-book ISBN:* 978-0-8261-1924-7

14 15 16 17 / 5 4 3 2 1

The author and the publisher of this Work have made every effort to use sources believed to be reliable to provide information that is accurate and compatible with the standards generally accepted at the time of publication. The author and publisher shall not be liable for any special, consequential, or exemplary damages resulting, in whole or in part, from the readers' use of, or reliance on, the information contained in this book. The publisher has no responsibility for the persistence or accuracy of URLs for external or third-party Internet websites referred to in this publication and does not guarantee that any content on such websites is, or will remain, accurate or appropriate.

**Library of Congress Cataloging-in-Publication Data**

Seavey, John W., author.
  Health policy analysis : framework and tools for success / John W. Seavey, Semra A. Aytur, Robert J. McGrath.
     p. ; cm.
  Includes bibliographical references and index.
  ISBN-13: 978-0-8261-1923-0
  ISBN-10: 0-8261-1923-9
  ISBN-13: 978-0-8261-1924-7 (e-book)
  I. Aytur, Semra A., author.   II. McGrath, Robert J., 1967- author.   III. Title.
  [DNLM: 1.  Health Policy—United States.   2.  Pediatric Obesity—United States.   3.  Policy Making—United States.  WA 525]
  RA418.3.U6
  362.10973—dc23

                    2014002178

Printed in the United States of America by Gasch Printing.

# Contents

# Preface

This textbook is meant to be used in conjunction with one of the major textbooks adopted for a course on health policy or health policy analysis in a number of different disciplines (e.g., public health, health management, nursing, social work). Frequently, a capstone requirement in such courses is a policy proposal for a particular politician or organization, or the completion of a policy analysis on a particular topic. This textbook is intended to walk you through some important aspects of that task by providing you with a framework, resources, and issues to consider. This framework can be used in either an undergraduate course or a professional master's degree program for people returning to an academic environment after a period of professional development.

Policy analysis is not for the faint of heart. It is a very demanding task that requires synthesizing knowledge from multiple disciplines and using many different skills. Some of that knowledge can be learned through textbooks, whereas other knowledge will come with experience in the political and health care systems and through collaboration with others. This textbook does not replace textbooks on public health, political science, economics, community planning, the health care system, or other related areas.

This book will guide you through the process of developing a policy analysis. Each chapter discusses important questions and issues that need to be addressed in your policy analysis. To do this, throughout this book we have woven the example of developing a policy/program addressing the public health problem of obesity in the United States. We could have used any health policy issue and we assume you will likely focus on a different policy. Although we use several other examples to illustrate certain points throughout the book, we repeatedly return to obesity as the main example. By using obesity, we have had to make certain decisions as we walk you through the framework. For example, for this book we have chosen a specific aspect of the obesity problem in the United States—childhood obesity. However, we recognize that even if you were to pick obesity, you might have chosen a different specific issue within the category of obesity (obesity in young adults or the elderly, or the linkage between obesity and diabetes). In addition, we have chosen to focus our policy initiative at the federal level. However, we recognize that you may choose to tailor your policy initiative for a particular state or local community. Because each state/community has different resources as well as unique characteristics in terms of political culture, structure, and process, it is easier for the purpose of this text to focus on the federal level. However, to provide you with an example of state-level activity, we have included information regarding policy analysis in the State of Washington. Again, we could have selected another state, but the State of Washington has been particularly innovative in certain aspects of the obesity issue. This state example is for illustrative purposes only. You should appreciate the fact that the resources, political culture, structure, and process of the policy issue you have selected will probably differ considerably depending on scope and/or location.

This is not a text on childhood obesity or childhood obesity policy. Nor is it a text advocating a particular policy to address that problem. A book of this type cannot cover everything in equal depth. We have had to be selective in what we have covered and the depth to which we have covered particular topics. There are multiple textbooks on topics such as the legislative process, health economics, statistics, and epidemiology that we address quite briefly. We have tried to put these topics into the framework while pointing you to additional sources. We have not created a policy proposal or done a policy analysis per se, but we have addressed multiple issues to demonstrate the types of questions that you will need to address as you go through the text's framework on your own. By following the obesity example, you can apply it to your own policy area. This is less a book about having the answer than it is about raising issues that should be considered in your policy analysis.

To do this we have used a seven-step framework that is covered in the various chapters. These steps include:

1. Policy background
2. Statement of the policy issue
3. Normative values and stakeholder analysis
4. Criteria for success
5. Systematic review of policy options
6. Recommendation
7. Policy strategies

In each of these steps of the framework, we illustrate questions to be addressed by using general policy issues as well as childhood obesity as a specific example. In addition, there are Breakout Boxes that provide more in-depth examples of policy issues and the current scientific literature or evidence that relates to them. As part of the chapter summary, there are also "Some Things to Remember."

In order to provide all students with a uniform level of background, Chapter 1 discusses specific areas of politics, policy, health, policy analysis, data, and analytical studies that will be important as you work your way through the text. This is a relatively lengthy chapter that points to general issues facing health policy analysis. Chapter 2 deals with some mechanics of writing a policy analysis.

Chapter 3 begins the discussion of the framework by starting with the policy background section of your analysis. Policy issues tend to be recycled. All policy issues have some history behind them. Although there might be a new twist or a new element to the policy issue, the issue has probably been dealt with in some political jurisdiction through time. Some of those programs or policies may have been unsuccessful and some of them may serve as models. In addition, policies intersect with each other, and it is important to understand how a policy in one area potentially impacts a policy in another area. For example, health policies impact economics and economic policies impact health.

After Chapter 3, Policy Background, Chapter 4 focuses on the statement of the policy issue within the policy-analysis framework. The statement of the policy issue is a very precise statement that narrows the focus of your area of concern to a specific area and geopolitical unit. This is critical, because it focuses the rest of the analysis. By necessity, this text makes a series of choices for you in order to keep the obesity example moving. However, we expect that you might make very different choices. As we make our choices, make your own, and think about how you would apply them to the questions raised in the text.

Chapter 5 deals with the importance of understanding the role of values in the political process. Here we note the importance of coalitions, advocacy, and compromise in the political process. Understanding value conflict will make you more aware of potential opposition to your policy proposal. This will help you to develop a stakeholder analysis of those who may oppose or support your policy proposal.

Chapter 6 deals with the criteria for success, laying the foundation for policy evaluation and developing specific and measurable goals for your policy to achieve. This is important in understanding exactly what you hope your policy/program will accomplish. The role of political capital comes into play here, as well as your specific objectives in attempting to address your public health problem. The measurement of these criteria will be important as you think about the implementation of policy in the real world.

Chapter 7 covers the systematic review of policy options within the framework. It discusses the various issues that you will confront in evaluating one alternative versus another. It discusses the strengths and weaknesses of incrementalism and the role of evidence-based policy. It describes the various types of evidence you can acquire and how you might evaluate the evidence that supports or undermines your policy proposal.

The final chapter deals with two different parts of the framework simultaneously, because they are so closely linked. The first is making a recommendation. This is a complex process that involves understanding the expectations of the audience (e.g., your policy maker) and using the best available evidence to support your recommendation. Of course, the quality of this section of your analysis depends on how well the other sections have been completed. The second part of this chapter focuses on strategies. It is not expected that your policy analysis will provide a detailed statement on political strategy, because that will change as the policy proposal works its way through the political system. However, you should be able to make a recommendation as to whether this proposal will go through a legislative policy process or another strategy to get it adopted and fully implemented. Throughout the policy analysis, but particularly at this stage, you need to think about how to frame the policy proposal to maximize its political appeal. You should also begin to think about messaging so that your readers, the public, and the media understand the essence of your proposal.

Policy analysis is a very complicated and challenging process, but one that can be highly rewarding. It will require you to integrate a great deal of knowledge that has been previously compartmentalized in one discipline or another. It will require you to gain experience in the field and to ask for assistance from those who have been in the policy arena for a period of time. It is an exciting endeavor, and the true reward comes from seeing the impact of a policy proposal benefitting thousands or millions of people. We wish you well in your endeavors and trust that the political process and the public will benefit from your analyses.

# Acknowledgments

The development of any textbook is a complicated task, especially in the acknowledgment section. There are so many people who are involved in contributing to the substance of any text. Of course, many of those are cited in the various chapters. However, there are many others who do not get formal citations, although they are perhaps more important. First, the authors have been inspired in their thinking by their own instructors in years past, as well as current colleagues who in daily conversations spark insights and help to construct a framework on which to hang the collection of concepts that others have helped to develop. Health policy analysis is a very complicated area due to its interdisciplinary nature. There are other disciplines that could have been introduced, and more detail that could have been provided in specific areas. However, the intent of this text is to show the extensive nature of health policy analysis while at the same time making it a useful tool.

We have benefited from our graduate and undergraduate students, who ask challenging questions and seek guidance as to how to proceed in health policy. Those students help us as teachers to explain concepts and to challenge them to do their best to contribute to health policy. Every class is a learning environment for both them and us.

There are some specific acknowledgments that need to be made as well. We wish to thank Springer Publishing Company and its editorial staff for their support and assistance in making this book possible and for improving it at every step in the process.

We would like to thank the Pew Trusts for permission to modify the Kids' Safe and Healthful Foods Project description that became one of the Breakout Boxes in this text. Special thanks to Public Health Seattle King County and researchers at the University of Washington for guiding us toward specific state-level examples to make the policy process come alive. In addition, we would like to acknowledge Scott Evenson for his adaptation of the Policy Wheel (Figure 1.1) from its original depiction in Ainsworth and Macera's *Physical and Public Health Practice.* We also wish to acknowledge the comments from Sherril B. Gelmon on an earlier draft of this text. Finally we would like to thank Julia J. Farides-Mitchell and Erica Jabolonski for painstakingly checking citations. The authors are responsible for the imperfections that remain.

# One

# Health Policy Analysis

The purpose of this introductory chapter is to provide an overview of important concepts that you will need to remember in doing your health policy analysis. It provides an overview of some of the interdisciplinary knowledge that is required for doing health policy analysis. You may wish to refer back to this chapter as you work through the remainder of the textbook. You may also wish to supplement the material here by accessing other texts within various disciplines.

## POLITICS AND POLICY

David Easton has defined politics as "the authoritative allocation of values for a society" (Easton, 1953, p. 127). Harold Lasswell defined politics as described by the subtitle of his book as "who gets what, when, and how" (Lasswell, 1936). Politics encompasses the need for every society to make binding decisions for all members of a community governed by that political system regarding which values and interests are to be legitimized by the civil government. In this process, there invariably will be winners and losers. It is the political system that has the responsibility of making these decisions. This leads to tension among members of the political community when critical values

1

and interests collide. We will discuss this in greater detail in Chapter 5, which examines normative and stakeholder analysis. For now, what is important to remember is that the political system makes decisions (no matter what its actual political components and procedures might be) as to what is of relative value and makes those decisions binding on its citizens through laws, rules/regulations, executive orders, court decisions, and other official actions taken by the political system. The political system uses its monopoly of the police powers of the state to enforce those decisions.

Public laws, programs, policies, and public expenditures adopted by the political system are all designed to impact individuals, organizations, and other levels of the political system in order to reach the desired outcomes for that society. Of course, one of the important decisions made by the political system determines when individuals are free to act according to their own desires and when they are required to act in the interest of society as a whole. An example of this is the debate as to whether the federal government of the United States should require individuals to purchase health insurance for the good of the whole. The United States Supreme Court settled the legal issues relative to this in *National Federation of Independent Business et al. v. Sebelius, Secretary of Health and Human Services, et al.* (2012), about which it was decided that the federal government *can* impose such an individual mandate for health insurance; the political and policy issues as to whether it *should* have an individual mandate remain outstanding issues for the political system.

There are multiple definitions of policy. Some definitions are more general than others and each has its own advantage. We do, however, wish to provide an understanding as to how the term is going to be used throughout this book. We use the term *policy* to refer to a product or outcome of the political system, the system that is designated to make decisions regarding the collective good. Some scholars categorize policy as "big P" and "little p" policy. "Big P" policy refers to legislation or formal laws, rules, and regulations enacted by elected officials, such as a state legislature or the United States Congress (Brownson, Chriqui, & Stamatakis, 2009; The Community Foundation for Greater Atlanta, 2008). These policies include laws that regulate the resources and behaviors of individuals, organizations, and businesses. Judicial decisions may determine policy through rulings on cases involving various public programs and procedures. In contrast, "little p" policy refers to institutional policies (e.g., organizational guidelines, internal agency decisions, or memoranda) that guide organizational behavior and functions. Although all types of policy have important implications for health, we will focus primarily on "big P" policy for the purposes of this book.

## THE POLICY-MAKING PROCESS

Policy operates in an iterative manor, much as a turning wheel (see Figure 1.1). In this text we are mostly focused on the policy-formulation phase. However, as we will see in Chapter 8, Recommendations and Strategies, we cannot overlook the policy adoption and implementation phases of this policy wheel. Policy can be created anywhere on this wheel.

Policy making is a process that has often been described theoretically and modeled within the political science literature. Theories and conceptual models from the literature can help to better understand the policy process (Bacchi, 1999; Coveney, 2010; Jones, 1984; Kingdon, 2003; Lasswell, 1971; Sabatier & Jenkins-Smith, 1993). For example, one commonly used model is one proposed by Longest, which has four general elements: (1) policy formulation, (2) policy implementation, (3) policy evaluation, and (4) policy modification (Longest, 1998). Figure 1.1 is a modified version of Longest's model of policy making.

Figure 1.1 provides a composite view of several different theories about the policy process. As designated by the circular nature of the

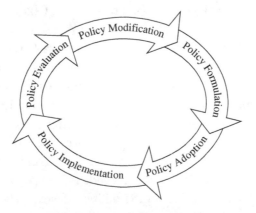

**FIGURE 1.1** Policy wheel.
*Source:* Evenson and Aytur (2010).

diagram, these component parts of the process are quite iterative in practice. That is to say, they do not always flow linearly from one to the other, nor do they have definitive boundaries. In some cases, the activities overlap. However, for descriptive purposes, we describe them generally here. The first step in the policy process is typically policy formulation (policy development). This includes identifying a problem or issue, considering value orientations, framing the issue, proposing one or multiple approaches to addressing the problem/issue, defining the policy objectives, estimating impacts, and then drafting the policy content and strategically moving the policy toward adoption. This phase is the primary focus of this text.

However, this phase bridges with the other phases in the political process. It involves all the strategic and negotiation points one must consider and engage in to get support for a formal piece of legislation. We will focus on some of this in Chapter 8, Recommendation and Strategies. Once a policy has been legislatively passed into law and adopted, the policy implementation phase begins. This involves "who does what and when" to make the program operational. At times, this is distinct from the adoption phase; for example, creating a detailed blueprint for action. At other times, this phase overlaps with the adoption phase and the legislation prescribes specific implementation guidelines. For example, the adoption process could stipulate when various components of the law are to begin and allow time to build the capacity for implementation. In both cases, there should be clear goals and measures of success to evaluate outcomes. These are expanded on in Chapter 6: Criteria for Success.

After some period of implementing programs/policy, progress toward the stated goals and outcomes must be measured. This is the policy evaluation phase. Here it is important that the previous phases be clear and explicit so that success (or lack thereof) can be empirically demonstrated. The final phase, policy modification, is the closing of the policy feedback loop where adjustments to a given policy are made if necessary. Here one might examine costs relative to benefits. Programs and policies are frequently modified due to changing needs and expectations as well as changes in the partisan control of the political system. There may also be calls to repeal the policy if outcomes are deemed negative or to expand the policy to other groups. Adjustments are made continuously.

## HEALTH AND HEALTH POLICY

Health policy is part of the larger field of health services research, an area devoted to the discovery of new information for the improvement of individual and population health. Due to the nature of health, both health services research and health policy analysis are interdisciplinary by nature, using the knowledge of both the biological sciences and the social sciences. The evolving fields of implementation science, decision science, and sustainability science also address health policy analysis (Clark, 2007; Clark & Dickson, 2003).

Health is a complicated concept. The most famous definition of health comes from the World Health Organization (WHO): "health is a state of complete physical, mental and social well-being and not merely the absence of disease or infirmity" (World Health Organization Constitution Preamble, 1948, p. 100). This definition points to the comprehensive nature of health; there is both a physical and mental aspect of health as well as a sense of well-being. The definition tends to be more aspirational, with a focus on what it takes to achieve human potential rather than a description of reality. Individuals and societies transition from one state of health to another over time. Given the WHO definition, "health" may be a very temporary state.

Health is not a given. Societies create conditions that promote both disease and health. As demonstrated by Evans and Stoddart and other similar social–ecological and systems science models, societies produce health or disease through the interaction of multiple variables (e.g., policy, the natural and created environments [the built environment], building medical care systems, as well as individual behavior; Evans & Stoddart, 2003; Huang, Drewnowsksi, Kumanyika, & Glass, 2009; McLeroy, Bibeau, Steckler, & Glanz, 1988; Stokols, 1992; Stokols, Allen, & Bellingham, 1996). Manipulating any one of these variables (e.g., education or the transportation systems) creates greater disease or health for individuals and for society as a whole. Therefore, by implication, societies have the ability to influence their own health through their public policies. The creation and distribution of wealth; the educational system; natural and built environments, including but not limited to the creation of safe living and work environments; and access to the medical care system all play critical roles in determining the health status of a given population or a particular individual. All of these inputs to health are shaped by the actions of both individuals and society through the policy process; the health of a society is not predestined, and public policies play a major role in determining health.

Our understanding of these different inputs to health has changed over time. For example, efforts to increase physical activity and improve nutrition among the general population were historically aimed at changing individual-level health behaviors. Individuals were told to exercise more and eat healthier meals. The focus was on how to get the individuals motivated to change their behavior and to adopt healthy eating patterns. Thaler and Sunstein (2008) refer to this as "the nudge" or "libertarian paternalism." However, such approaches have been found to be minimally effective, costly, and difficult to sustain (Lyn et al., 2013).

As a result, public health professionals have begun to address this problem using a more comprehensive approach referred to as "policy, systems, and environmental change." This approach includes: (a) policy interventions that seek to change laws, ordinances, regulations, or legislation (e.g., a city council zoning ordinance prohibiting fast-food chains within a certain distance of a school); (b) system-level interventions, which promote changes that impact organizations, institutions, or communities (e.g., a school deciding to buy a certain percentage of its cafeteria food from local sources, and training the food-service staff to cook and serve vegetarian meals on certain days); and (c) environmental interventions, which involve changes to the physical environment (e.g., a school constructing bike lanes and bike storage facilities to encourage active transportation to school), often resulting from policy decisions such as zoning and transportation expenditures (Lyn et al., 2013; Michigan Cancer Consortium, 2012). As a result, our increased understanding of the interaction of various factors of health has complicated the policy process because one simple intervention is probably not going to be sufficient. These initiatives are also built on the notion that individual decisions for healthy behavior can be facilitated or frustrated by political decision making.

## HEALTH POLICY ANALYSIS

As a result of this more comprehensive and systematic understanding of the inputs to health, the breadth of "health policy" has increased dramatically.

Policy regarding transportation has an impact on health. Environmental policy has an impact on health. Educational policy has an impact on health. Economic policy has implications for health. The 2010 Adelaide Statement describes this approach as "Health in All Policies" (Krech, Valentine, Reinders, & Albrecht , 2010; World Health Organization, 2010). The Adelaide Statement emphasizes the need to examine policies for these health inputs across different policy areas. It calls on the health sector to be involved in the development of policies in other sectors to maximize health status as well as to ensure health equity. This is a significant broadening of the scope of the health sector within public policy making. The Adelaide Statement describes innovative models emerging from around the world. Of critical importance to the success of this approach will be an aggregation of evidence, including studies of policy adoption and implementation in different geographic and political environments.

Health policy analysis is a type of applied research. Although one might think that our health care system is evidence based and dependent on what research demonstrates to be valuable, that is not always the case. In fact, it is not usually the case. Many health programs and proposals that have been demonstrated to have scientific validity never get broadly implemented and, even more commonly, many existing programs and practices in medicine have never been formally proven to be effective. The Institute of Medicine has estimated that about 4% of health services have strong evidence to back them and that more than half have no evidence or weak evidence to support them (Field & Lohr, 1992). Researchers have identified several aspects of policy analysis that are in need of particular attention (Brownson et al., 2006; Brownson, Chriqui, & Stamatakis, 2009; Schmid, Pratt, & Witmer, 2006). These include: (a) documenting *how* an impact is achieved in a particular context; (b) understanding barriers to successful implementation; (c) delineating multiple outcomes that could be important (including unintended consequences and differential impacts on different vulnerable populations); and (d) developing tools to help prioritize policy choices, including specific criteria to evaluate policy impacts.

The importance of conducting sound policy analysis is highlighted when one considers the problem of chronic diseases such as obesity. Although there is much we know about the cause and consequences of obesity, how the political and health systems should respond to that knowledge becomes the focus of health policy analysis. For example, because elderly and minority populations are at heightened risk of diabetes, how should Medicare and Medicaid policies be developed to minimize the impact of diabetes on individuals, specific groups, and society as a whole (Fradkin, 2012)? Obesity has become a modern-day American epidemic, but logical and scientifically based programs to fight obesity tend to flounder for lack of political action.

There has been a recent focus on the importance of evidence-based medicine and evidence-based public health (Anderson et al., 2005; Brownson, Chriqui, & Stamatakis, 2009; Green, 2006; Kumanyika, Parker, & Sim, 2010; Swinburn, Gill, & Kumanyika, 2005), underscoring the need for systematic evaluation of what works in medicine and public health. Although this is encouraging, evidence-based health care is something that is easier said than done. Evidence-based health systems and policy remain the goal, no matter how difficult the path may be.

## EVIDENCE-BASED HEALTH POLICY

There is a great deal of literature focusing on medicine and the medical care system. Aday, Begley, Lairson, and Balkrishnan (2004) have created a useful paradigm of health policy analysis by dividing the literature into three areas of concern: effectiveness, efficiency, and equity. You will need to think about this as you develop your own policy. Is your program/policy proposal designed to increase effectiveness, efficiency, or equity? We shall briefly explore these concepts so that you have a better idea as to how to structure your policy analysis. We will discuss this in greater detail in Chapter 7, which deals with the systematic review of policy options.

### Effectiveness

The effectiveness literature focuses on demonstrating what works to improve the health of the individual or the population. Certainly, public policies should encourage those treatments that work and discourage those that waste resources or do not improve the health of the population and/or potentially cause harm. The regulation of the medical care industry from the licensure of health professionals, accreditation of health care organizations, and approval of pharmaceuticals are predicated on protecting the public from harmful practices and encouraging those that are effective. Since the days of codeine-laced cure-alls, effectiveness and prevention from harm have been key components of health policies.

Effectiveness needs to be discussed from two different perspectives, population effectiveness and medical effectiveness. Medical effectiveness tends to deal with individual patients and the impact of a specific intervention. These are typically evaluated by conducting clinical trials that take a similar group of people and then randomly assign them to either the prescribed treatment or to a placebo to test the effectiveness of the treatment.

Population effectiveness rests on Geoffrey Rose's population strategy that has become the theoretical basis for public intervention to prevent disease (Rose, 1992). Rose maintained that prevention should not just focus on high-risk individuals, but on the population as a whole. Thus, reducing salt consumption benefits not only those with hypertension, but also those who are prehypertensive. By reducing the average intake of salt for the entire the population, the population as a whole benefits. Although this reduction of the average intake in salt may not make a perceptible difference to some individuals, it is effective for the population as a whole.

In addition to the biological aspects of effectiveness, there are also the health systems and social system aspects of effectiveness. For example, although certain pharmaceuticals have been demonstrated to be effective for diseases on the individual level, the lack of clinical facilities, refrigeration, social support systems, or cultural norms may prevent those same pharmaceuticals from being effective for the population in a developing country.

The focus on evidence-based medicine is not new. However, it gained a great deal of momentum with the pioneer work done by Wennberg and Gittelsohn (1973). Their research focused on the variation in the practice of medicine from one geographic area to another and what could potentially explain such variations. The Dartmouth Atlas documents the geographic variation in the practice of medicine within the United States (http://www.dartmouthatlas.org/). In addition, there is also great variation in health status across the United States. Studies conducted by the Joint Center for Political and Economic Studies have shown that life expectancy in some parts of the United States can vary by as much as 30 years when comparing one zip code to another (Virginia Commonwealth

University, 2013). What tends to explain this variation? What are the consequences of this variation? Given that variation in medical care exists, what is the right level of medical care? Geographic variation has multiple potential explanations. How much variation is warranted and how much is unwarranted is a part of the difficulty of current efforts to restructure payment systems in order to create the right incentives for increased efficiency and effectiveness of medical care (National Institute for Health Care Reform, 2011).

It is important to note several important aspects of effectiveness of medical treatments. Generally, effectiveness of medical care is tied to the biological aspects of disease and proposed therapies. Do statins reduce cholesterol and thereby reduce the risk of cardiovascular diseases? Is the use of statins related to memory loss? To test these questions, the gold standard has been a clinical trial, by which a comparison is done between those receiving treatment and those not receiving treatment. We will discuss the strengths and weaknesses of clinical trials later in this chapter.

In some areas, such as pharmaceuticals, the federal government's Food and Drug Administration (FDA) is authorized to approve or disapprove such medical interventions. Formal approval by the FDA does not end the process of evaluation of effectiveness, because payers (Medicare, Medicaid, and private insurance companies) make their own decisions regarding whether they will categorize the treatment as "experimental" and, therefore, not list it among their covered services.

However, the FDA is restricted in terms of its authority; although it has authority to approve appliances (e.g., implants) and pharmaceuticals, it is not authorized to approve or disapprove medical procedures. There has been medical controversy over the effectiveness of vertebroplasty, a surgical procedure used for people with severe back problems (Wulff, Miller, & Pearson, 2011). As a medical procedure, the FDA was not involved in its approval. There are thousands of these procedures performed each year in the United States, at a cost of $5,000 to $6,000 per patient. This procedure also became accepted in medical practice prior to any clinical trials demonstrating its effectiveness. However, in 2009 the results of two clinical trials were published and both demonstrated that the procedure was no more effective than a sham procedure (a procedure recognized as not providing any medical benefit; Buchbinder et al., 2009; Kallmes et al., 2009). Despite these findings, the procedure continues to be performed and paid for by major insurance providers in the United States.

The analysis of comparative effectiveness has the possibility of initiating a more precise recommendation for the most effective treatment for different subpopulations and the beginning of "personalized medicine." Frequently, the criteria for effectiveness do not take into account the experience and perspective of the patient. This is particularly important in terms of taking into account the sequelae of a particular procedure. For example, prostate surgery may remove cancerous tissue, but due to the slow-growing nature of prostate cancer in general, the patient might die of another disease before he would have died from prostate cancer. However, by undergoing the surgical procedure for prostate cancer the patient may have a diminished quality of life due to incontinence and impotence following the procedure. The effectiveness of such treatment from the patient's perspective is far from clear. As noted by the example, the effectiveness of treatment is more complicated than the removal of cancerous tissue. The Patient-Centered Outcomes Research Institute (PCORI) has been established, not only to do comparative effectiveness research, but to also take into account the patient's perspective, culture, and values (Garber, 2011; Patient-Centered Outcomes Research Institute, 2012). PCORI offers great possibility for dramatically changing medical care in the future and it has the potential to provide the patient with information that will allow greater control over the application of more complex medical technologies (Institute of Medicine, 2012).

One of the modern classics of effectiveness studies is that done by McGlynn et al. (2003) on the quality of care in the United States. It concluded that patients in the United States received a little more than half of what was recognized as quality care. The study sent a shock wave through the medical community and it remains a seminal piece of evidence in the effectiveness of our medical care system.

As seen above, determining what is effective is not as clear-cut as one might initially think. This becomes compounded, given rapidly changing technology. What may appear to be effective today might be outmoded in 1 or 5 year(s). If effectiveness is a major part of your policy proposal, you should access texts in epidemiology and effectiveness research.

## Efficiency

A second major aspect of health policy analysis revolves around the issue of efficiency, the ratio of outputs to inputs. As indicated by Victor Fuchs in his groundbreaking book from 1974, "No country is as healthy as it could be; no country does as much for the sick as it is technically capable of doing. . . . The grim fact is that no nation is wealthy enough to avoid all avoidable deaths" (Fuchs, 1974, p. 17). This recognizes the fact that societies have a limited amount of resources and that spending in one area may reduce the ability for spending in another. Within a health care system one would want to maximize the health of the population in order to conserve resources for other sectors of society, such as education or national defense. This is typically measured by the percentage of the gross national product spent on health care. By this measure, the United States spends by far the highest percentage of any industrialized country in the world for health care (Kaiser Family Foundation, 2011). When a society realizes its resources are limited, one would hope that those medical services that do the least good are the ones to be reduced or eliminated in order to be able to expend additional resources on those services that are more cost-effective. The Institutes of Medicine recently convened the Committee on the Learning Health Care System and identified three main themes, efficiency of an underperforming system relative to its potential being one of them (Institute of Medicine, 2012).

In 2009, Thomson Reuters estimated that between $250 and $325 billion of unwarranted medical services are wasted each year in the United States (Kelley, 2009). The Good Stewardship Working Group developed a list of the top five activities primary care physicians could stop doing in order to improve care and reduce costs (The Good Stewardship Working Group, 2011). They then calculated that the annual savings of not doing these things (e.g., not using brand-name drugs when initiating lipid-lowering drug therapy) could result in a cost savings of $6.76 billion per year (Kale et al., 2011).

The International Federation of Health Plans developed an interesting international comparison of prices for specific medical procedures and pharmaceuticals; for example, a hip replacement in 2010 cost $9,637 in Britain, $10,753 in Canada, $12,629 in France, $15,329 in Germany, and $34,454 in the United States (Klepper, 2004). The magnitude and cause of the inefficiency of the U.S. medical system might be in dispute, but there is a consensus that there is a great deal of waste within the existing system. The amount of waste and inappropriate care was indeed popularized and became a factor in the political discussions for health care reform with Atul Gawande's comparison of the differences in health care costs in two Texas communities (Gawande, 2009).

Of course, one of the major areas of efficiency is the area of disease prevention and health promotion versus medical treatment. Public health advocates generally site that the efficiency of the health system can be enhanced by preventing disease and disability in the first place. Studies using cost–benefit and cost-effective analyses have demonstrated that prevention activities can save money by foregoing medical expenditures (Graham, Corso, Morris, Segui-Gomez, & Weinstein, 1998; Grosse, Teutsch, & Haddix, 2007; Mays & Smith, 2011). This aligns with the well-known proverb that an ounce of prevention is worth a pound of cure. Vaccines are a typical example of this policy focus on prevention. However, here, again, one must be careful not to apply this universally. For example, if a disease is fairly rare and the consequences of getting that disease are not too harmful, providing a vaccine to the entire population, or even a large proportion of that population, may be far more costly for society than providing medical care treatment for the few individuals who actually acquire the disease. Generally, however, disease prevention and promotion are less costly than treatment, especially taking into account the adverse experiences of people having to experience the disease process, treatment, and sequelae.

## Allocative and Production Efficiency

Of "allocative efficiency" and "production efficiency," production efficiency is the more generally understood term. It involves maximizing the ratio of outputs to inputs for producing a given item. For example, one can improve the production efficiency of a medical practice by using physician assistants or nurse practitioners. The latter are typically paid less than physicians and can perform a number of frequently performed tasks at a lower cost. The use of scheduling protocols can improve the flow of patients and, thereby, increase the number of people screened per day for imaging services, thus spreading the fixed costs of the service over more units of service (patients). Specialization, division of labor, and substitution of capital for labor are general strategies that are frequently used for increasing the production efficiency of particular units.

In contrast, allocative efficiency deals with maximizing outputs in society given limited resources; it focuses on the efficiency of one sector versus another. If one wants to produce the most health for a society, improving the production efficiency of a hospital might not necessarily increase the allocative efficiency of the health care system in producing a healthier society. Making hospitals more productively efficient does not solve the inefficiency of treating people after they become sick. The United States has dramatically increased its spending per capita and percentage of gross national product for health care (Kaiser Family Foundation, 2011). Shifting resources from medical care to public health could increase the allocative efficiency of the health care system by producing a healthy population, thus eliminating the need for some of the increased medical costs. Shifting resources from medical care to providing livable incomes for the poor, increased education, or improving the built environment in an inner city might improve the health status of the population at a much lower cost than increasing hospital expenditures, even in efficient hospitals. One can have very efficient hospitals within a health care system that does not maximize the health for the population given the limited resources available and the inputs that are the most important for producing a healthy population. Spending money on prevention or providing more general education to the population may produce much greater health at a lower cost to society as a whole. Whether the United States spends too much of its limited resources on medical care is an open allocative efficiency question.

## Types of Efficiency Studies

The literature on efficiency is divided into three major types of studies: cost-effectiveness studies, cost–benefit analyses, and cost–utility studies. Cost-effectiveness studies catalog all of the input costs (wages, equipment, buildings, time, etc.) in comparison to the results of that effort (lives saved, procedures done, etc.). It is a systematic analysis of the cost of alternative methods to reach the same objective. As a result, comparisons can be done contrasting different procedures to see which is more cost-effective. One of the difficulties of such studies is making accurate calculations in terms of the total costs. Studies may take a very institutional focus by thoroughly cataloging institutional costs, but might forget about the patient's costs. An institution can shift some of its costs to patients, thus making the results look more cost-effective than they actually are, if one includes patient costs as well. For example, the early discharge of patients from hospitals reduces hospital costs and increases its efficiency, but shifts patient costs onto supporting family members who must care for the patient at home. Despite potential technical problems, cost-effectiveness is an important tool in public health policy analysis (Grosse, Teutsch, & Haddix, 2007). You should become familiar with what makes a solid cost-effectiveness study.

A second type of efficiency study is a cost–benefit analysis. It uses the same approach as a cost-effectiveness study in calculating the cost of the procedure. However, it is different from a cost-effectiveness study in that the benefits are measured not in terms of procedures done or lives saved, but in terms of dollars. Thus, the comparison of cost and benefit is dollars to dollars. The complication here is that the number of lives saved needs to be converted to a dollar amount, thus requiring a dollar value to be placed on a life. There are multiple ways that have been used to measure the value of a life. Although some may raise ethical objections to such an approach, in fact, placing a dollar value on life is done fairly frequently, such as when an individual is compensated by insurance for the loss of a limb, survivors are compensated for the loss of a loved one, or when proven life-saving technology is intentionally not used due to its expense. Cost–benefit analyses make such decisions as to the value of adding 3 additional years of life for an 85-year-old person or the potential of an additional 62 years for a 25-year-old. Frequently, foregone earnings are used as an approximation of the earning potential of someone at a given age. Doing this again raises ethical problems. How does one value the life of someone who has not been working but has been doing child care? Is the value of the life of a retired person zero? Despite these difficulties, economists use conventions to address these and other issues. It is important for you to understand the implications of these conventions for policy and to learn to appreciate the utility of cost–benefit studies.

Another type of efficiency study is a cost–utility study. This type of study does similar things as the other two; however, the results are weighted by society's preferences. For example, although a cost-effectiveness study might look at the results in terms of the number of lives saved, the cost–utility analysis would take society's (or the patient's) estimate of the value of the extra years of life saved. Cost–utility analysis takes into account the quality of that year of life saved. How much of a difference do patients value an additional year of life that is pain-free versus an additional year of life in severe pain? This is where economists and epidemiologists have used the concept of a quality-adjusted life year (QALY). Such measures can be controversial from theoretical as well as technical perspectives. Some argue that QALYs diminish the value of life of a "disabled" person. Others might take exception to the methodology by which the QALY is actually calculated. Despite these difficulties, most view these types of studies as useful inputs into programmatic and health program/policy considerations.

Economic analysis is a whole different area of policy analysis. If efficiency is a major focus of your policy proposal, you need to become familiar with the details of the various types of efficiency studies in greater detail than we can possibly do here.

## EQUITY

The third major area of concern for health policy analysis is that of equity; generally, this means promoting fairness within the health system. This includes eliminating disparities in access to health-promoting resources for subpopulations (e.g., gender, sexual orientation, race, ethnicity, income, education, geography). This area of policy addresses how health policies can promote the elimination of unfair differences in health status. Why are certain minority populations differentially impacted by diabetes (Betancourt, Duong, & Bondaryk, 2012)? Blacks have a very different life expectancy than do Whites (Smedley, Smith, & Nelson, 2003). Former U.S. Surgeon General Dr. David Satcher and colleagues calculated that 83,570 of the African Americans who died in 2002 would not have died if Black and White mortality rates were equal. This means that there were 229 "excess deaths" per day, or the equivalent of an airplane loaded with only Black passengers crashing every single day of the year (California Newsreel, 2008). What policies or programs can be enacted that will reduce such disparities? The major national health-planning document Healthy People 2020 (2013b) identifies the reduction in disparities of health status between subpopulations within the United States as one of its major goals. The Centers for Disease Control and Prevention (CDC) recently developed a guide to assist practitioners with integrating the concept of health equity into local practices and policies, such as building organizational capacity, engaging the community, developing partnerships, identifying health inequities, and conducting evaluations (Centers for Disease Control and Prevention, Division of Community Health, 2013). The guide offers lessons learned from practitioners within local, state, and tribal organizations that are working to promote health and prevent chronic disease health disparities. It provides a collection of health equity considerations for several policy, systems, and environmental improvement strategies focused on tobacco-free living, healthy food and beverages, and active living.

Equity is divided into two aspects. One aspect is *procedural equity*, to assure that processes that are in place are fair and do not discriminate. For example, procedures are in place to guarantee that those who receive organ transplants are not those with the most money or who have connections to the medical community, but those who are in greatest need and have a higher chance of survival. The second aspect of equity is substantive equity, to reduce the disparities between survival rates that cannot be explained by biological conditions, such as infant mortality rates for Black children. What policies or programs can be implemented to help reduce the disparity in outcomes among various populations? If equity becomes a major aspect of your policy proposal, you should access major texts in epidemiology and public health and medical ethics.

## INTEGRATIVE FRAMEWORKS

There are several integrative frameworks that enable health program planners, policy analysts, and evaluators to balance criteria when they analyze health programs and policies (Gielen, McDonald, Gary, & Bone, 2008; Green, 1974; Green & Kreuter, 2005; Human Nutrition, Foods and Exercise,

2013; Kumanyika, Brownson, & Cheadle, 2012; Work Group for Community Health and Development, 2013). These include PRECEDE-PROCEED, RE-AIM (Reach, Effectiveness, Adoption, Implementation, Maintenance), and L.E.A.D. (Locate evidence, Evaluate evidence, Assemble evidence, inform Decisions). L.E.A.D. is discussed in more detail in later chapters.

PRECEDE-PROCEED is an evaluation framework that was developed in 1974 by Dr. Lawrence Green. It describes a process that starts with desired outcomes and then works backward to identify the best combination of strategies for achieving those outcomes. The framework assumes that the program participants (or "consumers") will play an active role in defining their own problems, establishing their goals, and developing their solutions. Health behavior is conceptualized as being influenced by both individual and environmental factors, and the framework is broken into two distinct parts. The first, *PRECEDE* (Predisposing, Reinforcing, and Enabling Constructs in Educational Diagnosis and Evaluation), provides an educational diagnosis. For example, predisposing factors include knowledge, attitudes, beliefs, personal preferences, existing skills, and self-efficacy toward the desired behavior change. Reinforcing factors include conditions that reward or reinforce the behavior change, such as social support, economic rewards, and social norms. Enabling factors include skills, availability and accessibility of resources, and other services that facilitate behavior change.

The second part of this framework, *PROCEED* (Policy, Regulatory, and Organizational Constructs in Educational and Environmental Development), provides an ecological diagnosis. This framework has been widely used in public health and behavioral medicine (Freire & Runyan, 2006).

Another framework that evolved from PRECEDE-PROCEED and has gained popularity is RE-AIM (Reach, Effectiveness, Adoption, Implementation, Maintenance; Glasgow, Vogt, & Boles, 1999; King, Glasgow, & Leeman-Castillo, 2010). RE-AIM provides a set of criteria for planning and evaluating interventions that are intended to be broadly implemented, including policy interventions. To facilitate translation of research to practice and policy, RE-AIM emphasizes balancing internal and external validity. It also describes specific ways of measuring the potential public health impact of a program or policy.

The RE-AIM framework can be useful in comparing different public health policies, determining whether certain subpopulations benefit more than others (equity), and identifying areas for integration of policies with other health-promotion strategies (Jilcott, Ammerman, Sommers, & Glasgow, 2007). Application of the RE-AIM framework requires data or knowledge about the target population and the potential settings and organizations (e.g., clinics, worksites, schools) that can implement a policy change. Jilcott et al. (2007) describe how to apply RE-AIM to health policies, including policies that impact health in other sectors (such as urban planning policies that shape the built environment). Glasgow et al. (1999) offer examples based on actual community strategies employed in Colorado over the past 3 years (see http://www.livewellcolorado.org).

Questions to consider for RE-AIM include:

1. Whose health behaviors and health are to be improved?
2. Which stakeholders need to be included in the planning process, and which agencies are responsible for approving or adopting the policy change?
3. Which agencies are responsible for implementing the change?
4. Which agencies are responsible for maintaining the change?
5. What funding needs to be secured to implement and maintain the change?

"Reach" includes the absolute number, percentage, and representativeness of those affected by a policy or environmental change. For example, to apply RE-AIM to our obesity issue, imagine that a city council decides to build a new bike lane to increase active transportation. Which populations are likely to be affected the most? Does the bike lane connect a low-income neighborhood to a park or school, or does it connect a wealthy neighborhood to a commuter rail station?

"Effectiveness" in the RE-AIM framework involves using research methods to study who actually uses the bike lane. This may involve collecting data before and after the bike lane is built. Alternatively, one can sometimes make an educated guess by referring to published studies from similar communities that have constructed bike lanes. As mentioned previously, effectiveness may also involve measuring changes in risk factors (e.g., obesity) and/or disease rates in the target population, although this would involve a longer period of study. This can be achieved by collecting primary data, using secondary data from a surveillance system such as the Behavioral Risk Factor Surveillance System (BRFSS), or referring to published literature for estimates.

"Adoption" in the RE-AIM framework considers which political entity has the authority to decide to build the bike lane and the process it uses (e.g., the city council and the Department of Transportation would be responsible for making decisions about the bike lane, and which funds could be used).

"Implementation" in the RE-AIM framework considers how the policy is actually carried out. For example, are enough funds to build the bike lane actually allocated? Is the project completed? Who enforces use of the bike lane (e.g., are police officers or crossing guards deployed to manage dangerous intersections)?

"Maintenance" has two considerations, one at the setting level and one at the individual user level. For example, who will make sure that the bike lane remains free from trash and debris? Will additional city funds be allocated to maintain it? At the user level, one can measure ridership at different points in time to determine whether people keep using the bike lane or whether use drops off after a period of time.

## NATIONAL EFFORTS OF HEALTH POLICY ANALYSIS

Health policy questions have been with us for a very long time. Perhaps one of the earliest efforts in the United States to methodically address these issues based on evidence was the study done by the Committee on the Costs of Medical Care that produced a multivolume study of the United States health care system and made recommendations for its improvement (Committee on the Costs of Medical Care, 1932). It is not surprising given the current debates on health policy that the recommendations from the 1920s were not unanimous and that there was a spirited minority report.

However, many of the recommendations of that committee would be familiar to current debates on health care policy. One of the consistent recommendations has been the collection of data so as to identify the precise nature of the problem. Within health policy, this is generally called "type 1 evidence." It provides information to document the existence of a problem. An example of "type 1 evidence" would be the incidence rate of a specific disease that demonstrates either its increase or decrease over time. The collection of obesity data has done much to stimulate health policy action in the United States. It demonstrates the existence of a problem. Type 1 evidence does not attempt to explain the cause or the potential solution to the problem. The collection of demographic, epidemiologic, and medical use data has been an ongoing activity of federal, state, and local health departments. In 1956 the National Health Security Act led to the establishment of the National Center for Health Statistics (NCHS). Health data collection remains an important aspect of knowing where we are in terms of improving the health of the population.

### Agency for Healthcare Research & Quality

Through the 1980s and 1990s there was a concerted effort to improve the analysis of the health care system through the establishment of the Agency for Health Care Policy and Research (AHCPR), which later became the Agency for Healthcare Research & Quality (AHRQ; http://www.ahrq .gov/). Here the focus was not just on the collection of data, but the analysis of data to demonstrate that one approach may be more effective, efficient, or equitable than another. This is generally referred to as "type 2 evidence." It requires a higher level of data analysis by taking into account confounding factors and potential spurious relationships. A large number of sponsored research projects are conducted and supported by the AHRQ as well as the National Institutes of Health (NIH) and the CDC to demonstrate the efficiency, effectiveness, or equity of medical and public health practices. These studies are generally carried out by research universities or consulting companies as well as by private foundations (e.g., the Kaiser Family Foundation or the Robert Wood Johnson Foundation). In addition, most levels of public and private funding require formal evaluations of their sponsored projects. The lessons learned from these projects help to inform policy makers of the successes and failures of funded efforts to solve particular health problems. The products of these studies frequently end up in the peer-reviewed literature (journals with blind peer review of submissions) as well as grey literature (studies conducted by government or scientific research groups that are published in limited noncommercial publications and tend to not be peer reviewed).

## Congressional Budget Office

One source of policy analysis that is frequently overlooked is the Congressional Budget Office (CBO; http://www.cbo.gov/). Established to serve Congress, the CBO is a nonpartisan research group established to conduct studies for members of Congress. It is also the official scorekeeper for estimating the cost of legislative proposals. Consequently, its results tend to have a major political impact on legislative discussion and votes. For example, during past and recent debates on health care reform, the CBO's cost estimates of various proposals sunk some proposals and elevated others. CBO studies are done on the cost impacts of various legislative proposals, the number of uninsured, lessons from Medicare's demonstration projects on value-based payment or disease management, lessons from various Veterans Administrations programs, and other programs.

## Government Accountability Office

The Government Accountability Office (GAO; http://www.gao.gov/) is an independent and nonpartisan organization that works for Congress. It is designed to assist Congress in improving the performance and ensuring the accountability of the federal government for the benefit of the American people. It is designed to provide members of Congress with timely information that is objective, fact-based, nonpartisan, nonideological, fair, and balanced. Its studies are generally in response to a hot political topic and are, therefore, done relatively quickly given the limitation in terms of time and data. There are several reports issued daily on various topics. The GAO also provides testimony to Congressional committees. Individual members of Congress can request studies to be done on topics of interest to them for potential legislation. Health topics might cover such things as Medicaid's response to states during economic downturn, the impact of changes in Medicare Part D, and premium changes in Medicare Advantage Programs, among others.

## The Institute of Medicine

The Institute of Medicine (IOM; http://www.iom.edu/) was founded in 1970 and is one of the five national academies of science. It is a private, independent entity that attempts to provide best-evidence reports and information to the public and to decision makers. Much of its work is the result of Congressional mandates. Two of its most seminal works were *To Err Is Human* (Institute of Medicine, 2000) and *Crossing the Quality Chasm* (Institute of Medicine, 2001), which have been the foundation for much of the quality improvement work in the health sector in the past decade. The IOM has been an important source of information for shaping health policy discussions. Because we are using obesity as our primary example, it is important to point to the IOM's publication: *Bridging the Evidence Gap in Obesity Prevention: A Framework to Inform Decision Making* (Kumanyika, Parker, & Sim, 2010).

## Patient-Centered Outcomes Research Institute

As mentioned previously, one of the contributions of the Patient Protection and Affordable Care Act of 2010 (ACA) was the establishment of the Patient-Centered Outcomes Research Institute (PCORI; http://www.pcori.org/). Its mission is to provide people with evidence-based information on the comparative effectiveness of various treatments. It is housed in an independent, quasipublic body. As reflected in its initial draft of priorities, it aims to take a patient perspective versus a purely clinical perspective in looking at the outcomes of alternative medical practices.

Some have viewed outcomes research as the beginning of personalized medical information, the indication that one procedure may be more effective for given subpopulations. PCORI tends to be different from effectiveness organizations set up in other countries, such as the National Institute for Clinical Excellence (NICE; http://www.nice.org.uk/) in Great Britain, in that it is not a governmental agency, it is limited in its ability to use cost-effective analysis or use its findings to recommend policy, and it is chartered to take a patient perspective. PCORI is designed to address one of the major questions in health care: Although both procedures X and Y are effective, is procedure X more effective than procedure Y? The results of these studies will potentially have major implications for the future allocation of scarce resources. Due to the stakes involved for medical care providers, the political pressures on such agencies are high. Whether this new U.S. agency will be able to escape the political pressures faced by previous efforts remains to be seen.

## Centers for Disease Control and Prevention

The CDC's Policy Research, Analysis, and Development Office (CDC, 2013h) spearheads and coordinates policy work, including establishing policy priorities at multiple levels (federal, state, local, global, and with the private sector); conducting policy analysis; developing and implementing strategies (e.g., regulatory, legal, economic) to deliver on policy priorities; and coordinating agency work with the health care system and relevant organizations to advance the CDC's policy agenda. The CDC also assesses policy best practices and helps diffuse and replicate those practices.

The CDC recently funded the Center of Excellence for Training and Research Translation (Center TRT). The Center TRT recently developed an evaluation framework for obesity-related policy interventions that draws on RE-AIM and other processes mentioned previously (Leeman, Sommers, Leung, & Ammerman, 2011; Leeman et al., 2012). Policy analysts who are evaluating the formulation of a policy can use the framework to identify inputs such as data needed to assess political will, develop the policy, and identify stakeholders (formative evaluation). They then identify activities and outputs that are relevant to formulating policy, such as engaging stakeholders, raising awareness, and drafting policy solutions (process evaluation). Intended outcomes are also identified, but these may change as the process evolves. Through the use of "emergent logic models" (logic models that evolve over time), policy interventions can be examined in relation to the iterative policy process that we described in Figure 1.1.

In addition, the CDC (http://www.cdc.gov/) collects data, conducts and sponsors scientific research, administers national health efforts, promotes healthy and safe behaviors, and provides support to state tribal and local health initiatives. For example, the Nutrition and Obesity Policy Research and Evaluation Network (NOPREN), is funded by the CDC to conduct transdisciplinary nutrition- and obesity-related policy research and evaluation in certain states. NOPREN helps to promote understanding of the effectiveness of policies related to preventing childhood obesity through improved access to affordable, healthy foods and beverages in a variety of settings, including communities, workplaces, health care facilities, childcare institutions, and schools (Ascher, Blanck, & Cradock, 2012). Several of the state-level policy research examples showcased in subsequent chapters of this book were funded in part through the CDC's NOPREN initiative.

The CDC is an essential resource for any health policy analysis. Some of the data-collection activities of the CDC are listed in the Data section, which follows.

## Private Policy Research Institutes

There are literally hundreds of health policy research institutes around the country. There are too many to list them all and many specialties in health care have their own major research institutes. Some of these are imbedded in universities (public and private) and some are supported through federal and state grants or private funding. Some health institutes focus on rural health care (e.g., the six federally designated rural health research centers funded by the Health Resources and Services Administration's (HRSA) Office of Rural Health Policy, http://www.hrsa.gov/ruralhealth/policy/rhrcdirectory/index.html) and others focus on particular aspects of health, such as disabilities (e.g., the Association of University Centers on Disabilities, http://www.aucd.org). Some are focused on state health policy initiatives (e.g., National Academy for State Health Policies, http://www.aucd.org). The Rand Corporation (http://www.rand.org) has long been a center for major health care studies and reports. When talking about health insurance, one always has to mention the landmark "Rand Study" demonstrating the impact of cost sharing on patient outcomes (Newhouse, 1993). It remains the only clinical trial on health insurance. Rand continues to publish important health policy research, some of it published in peer-reviewed journals and others by Rand itself. The Henry J. Kaiser Family Foundation (http://www.kff.org/) has been a source of important policy studies on Medicare, Medicaid, the uninsured, and health care reform. Most studies involving Medicare or Medicaid generally cite some information or analysis done by the Kaiser Family Foundation. Policy institutes also reflect the full political spectrum. The Heritage Foundation (http://www. heritage.org/) and the CATO Institute (http://www.cato.org/) have long been identified as a source of conservative and free market health care proposals. The Brookings Institution (http://www.brookings.edu/) and the Center for American Progress (http://www.americanprogress.org/) tend to do more liberal-oriented policy research.

Human Impact Partners (HIP; http://www.humanimpact.org/) is one of the few organizations in the United States that conducts policy analyses with an explicit focus on uncovering and then addressing the policies and practices that make communities less healthy and that create health inequities. Emphasis is placed on policies outside the medical arena (e.g., housing, education, transportation, or urban planning). One important process for considering such policies is a health impact assessment (HIA; Dannenberg et al., 2008). An HIA is a practical tool that uses data, research, and stakeholder input to prospectively determine a policy's potential impact on the health of a population. HIAs also provide recommendations to address these impacts.

The above examples demonstrate the richness of nongovernmental research centers. There are many others that are relevant for particular areas of health policy analysis. For example, if you were focusing on a particular disease, there are organizations at the state and local levels that would be important resources.

## DATA

Despite the ideal for use of evidence-based medicine and public health, evidence is frequently difficult to attain. Data is not always readily available, especially in the United States, where there is a focus on individual privacy and proprietary ownership of data. States generally have specific rules regarding the aggregation of data and the reporting of analyses so as to protect individuals from being identified. Specific health policies (e.g., Health Insurance Portability and Accountability Act of 1996 [HIPAA]) have tried to address these privacy rules for health care.

Much health data in the United States is collected by private corporations (e.g., insurance companies, hospitals, clinics, physicians, etc.).

Consequently, such data is considered to be proprietary data and generally unavailable to the public and to researchers without specific authorization by the owners of the data. In addition, because data tends to not be centralized in the United States, it is collected in different ways by different organizations, making comparisons between health data from different organizations very difficult. This is because organizations may use different definitions of variables, different means of measurement, and different computer software programs. Consequently, combining data from different organizations can become very difficult, even if these private organizations give approval for sharing data.

More recently, conversations among policy makers, practitioners, and private industry have centered on better data for decision making and improving medical care. There have been multiple calls for a transition to electronic medical records. Progress, however, has been slow, largely due to the issue of patient confidentiality and privacy. Creating linked data across multiple sites of patient care becomes problematic when the data systems capturing those data are privately developed and not interoperable, or in other words, cannot talk to one another. In addition, these data are also generally not linkable to population-based census data, so it is difficult to relate these data to important demographic and socioeconomic information.

The federal government, through the Department of Health and Human Services (http://www.hhs.gov/), collects much of the health data that is publically available. This is frequently done through cooperative agreements with state governments. For example, hospital discharge data is collected uniformly through the Uniform Hospital Discharge Data System (UHDDS), although control and analysis of the data may vary from state to state. Other standardized data sets include: Uniform Ambulatory Care Data Set (UACDS), Minimum Data Set for Long-Term Care and Resident Assessment Protocols (MDS 2.0), Outcome Assessment Information Set (OASIS), Data Elements for Emergency Department Systems (DEEDS), and Essential Medical Data Set (EMDS).

The National Center for Health Statistics conducts a number of different surveys. Some of the more popularly used health data sources are:

- National Health Interview Survey (NHIS) (http://www.cdc.gov/nchs/nhis.htm)

- National Health and Nutrition Examination Surveys (NHANES) (http://www.cdc.gov/nchs/nhanes.htm)
- National Ambulatory Medical Care Survey (NAMCS) (http://www.cdc.gov/nchs/ahcd.htm)
- National Hospital Discharge Survey (NHDS) (http://www.cdc.gov/nchs/nhds.htm)
- National Survey of Ambulatory Surgery (NSAS) (http://www.cdc.gov/nchs/nsas.htm)
- National Home and Hospice Care Survey (NHHCS) (http://www.cdc.gov/nchs/nhhcs.htm)
- National Nursing Home Survey (NNHS) (http://www.cdc.gov/nchs/nnhs.htm)
- National Survey of Residential Care Facilities (NSRCF) (http://www.cdc.gov/nchs/nsrcf.htm)

The Department of Health and Human Services has other agencies involved in data collection. For example, the Agency for Health Research and Quality collects data under the Health Care Cost and Utilization Project (HCUP; http://www.ahrq.gov/research/data/hcup/index.html). The Surveillance Epidemiology and End Results (SEER; United States Institutes of Health, National Cancer Institute, 2013) for cancer has been an important source of information on the experience of cancer patients. There are also national and state disease registries that collect information on specific diseases.

Some of the information collected by governments includes the entire population (Census and Vital Records, http://www.census.gov/; Medicare, http://www.medicare.gov/; and Medicaid, http://www.medicaid.gov/ data sets), but most national data-collection systems rely on samples of the population. As a result, analyses using sample populations use extrapolations to the general population. This raises questions of external validity, and the ability of the data to reflect the larger population.

For example, although Medicare data is fairly complete and collected nationally, whether the experience of this subpopulation can be applied to the entire population composed of people aged 18 to 64 is questionable. An example of this is the literature on the geographic variation in medical practice. The only national data system that can address how extensive medical variation exists is data from Medicare. However, whether disparities in Medicare expenditures can be extrapolated to the entire population can be debated. For example, one of the variables that influences medical expenditures is the health status of the population. Whether a Medicare recipient had insurance prior to being enrolled in Medicare could have a major impact on the variation in Medicare expenditures. Those individuals coming from areas with low employer health insurance may experience higher Medicare expenditures once they become eligible for Medicare due to their previous lack of health insurance. Consequently, additional Medicare expenditures in particular areas may have less to do with the "practice of medicine" than with the elderly having been previously uninsured. Each data set has its own inherent problems regarding its ability to make generalizations to the population as a whole.

The primary way to become familiar with the strengths and weaknesses of any data set is to go to the original source of the data set and examine the methodology used in data collection and the definition of data elements. Another way to learn about the strengths and weaknesses of data sets is to examine studies using those data sets, because those studies will generally point out some of the limitations of the data set in their sections on methodology for that study.

Data on various diseases differs greatly. Although some diseases are reportable and, therefore, must be reported to a central data source (typically a state Department of Health, which then reports it to the CDC), most diseases are not reportable and so our knowledge of the number and distribution of those diseases rests on estimates from smaller population samples. In addition, many of these nonreportable diseases are self-reported and, therefore, lack a professional formal diagnosis for verification. As a result, we have relatively precise numbers of people diagnosed with syphilis in a given year (a reportable disease), but much less precise numbers of those people with arthritis. Arthritis is a very debilitating and expensive disease, but its prevalence in the United States or any particular state rests on estimates from population samples. Likewise, the "obesity epidemic" tends to be based on estimates, not actual numbers. Whether or not something is counted may have little to do with its importance for the health of the population. If the disease you are covering rests on estimates, you need to question the reliability of your data. Does the data reflect only those who have been hospitalized for a particular diagnosis, or does it include those living with the diagnosis in the community as well? Are the rates based on incidence (the number of new cases) or prevalence (the number of existing cases)?

A corollary question that needs to be asked regarding data collection is: What level of precision is needed for your policy analysis? As indicated previously, the number of obese people in a particular state or the country as a whole rests on estimates. Who has made these estimates and how reliable is their methodology? Does the organization giving the estimate have an incentive to exaggerate or underestimate the number? Given the sophistication and uniform nature of these estimates, what would be the practical policy impact of having the exact number of obese people in the United States versus the current estimate? Does it really matter whether the estimate is off by plus or minus 1% or 3%? Is money better spent getting the exact number of obese people or funding services to treat the problem? The SEER for cancer has been an important source of detailed information on cancer patients that has been useful in studying the etiology and treatment of cancer. However, the geographic areas included in SEER represent only 28% of the U.S. population (http://seer .cancer.gov/). What would be the cost of getting 80% or 100% of cancer patients? How much additional knowledge would we gain by having more data? Would the additional information be worth the cost? These are important health policy questions.

Another source of data that is currently being used and discussed for health policy development is what are known as all-payer claims data. Many states have either developed or are in the process of developing all-payer claims databases (APCDs). These databases require all insurance companies selling policies in a particular state to provide the same proprietary data in an agreed-upon format to a central state data-collection system. This has allowed those states implementing APCDs time to gain specific information on the utilization of health services by the commercially insured population within their states (Love, Custer, & Miller, 2010) in addition to those insured in their Medicaid insurance systems. This data can be highly useful for understanding disease prevalence in populations, conducting surveillance of populations, and analyzing where and when certain types of care are not being offered to the insured population. However, these data systems are also limited. For example, claims are not typically processed for the uninsured population. In addition, unless the data system is set up to collect patient utilization in adjoining states, the data may not reflect insurance claims for people receiving medical services in other states. Also, most insurance claims data do not include socioeconomic or demographic information on patients, which are known to be major factors related to health disparities.

The ACA has become a recent driver of data discussions. Under the ACA, providers will be reimbursed based on the quality of the care they provide and the health of their service populations. What has emerged from this is a detailed discussion of how to measure the health of the population and how to determine what data is needed to measure quality of care. As a result, the AHRQ, which deals with much of the data issues related to federal law and policy, has begun issuing best practices and instructions on how to "cross walk" across multiple data sources.

Characteristics of the health care system also influence the availability of data. For example, most states used to have relatively complete profiles of the utilization of health services by their Medicaid recipients. That information has been useful in designing Medicaid benefits as well as determining reimbursement levels. As more state Medicaid systems rely on private managed care entities to deliver services, Medicaid data tends to become inaccessible to researchers due to the fact that the data from managed care companies is proprietary. Some states have been able to obtain some of this data by making the agreements with their managed care companies contingent on supplying such data to the state. However, these agreements have to be carefully constructed to ensure the state has access to the data that it needs, especially as its needs change over time. Despite these agreements, receiving static statistical reports from a provider is not the equivalent of having the raw data and being able to aggregate and analyze it at will.

In addition to disease and insurance data sets, there are health surveillance systems run by the CDC to estimate health behavior patterns. For example, the BRFSS (http://www.cdc.gov/brfss/) is an important source of information on behaviors known to be associated with disease. Because this data is collected at the state level, states and large metropolitan areas can be compared to each other on important behavioral characteristics such as smoking, the use of alcohol, or obesity. However, for a particular state it may be more important to look at variations within the state (e.g., urban versus rural or one county versus another county). Some states are now increasing the sample size for their BRFSS survey to be able to compare subpopulations (Whites versus Blacks) or various counties within that state. However, this increases the cost of such surveys. Given tight state budgets, the additional costs may not be politically possible even though the health policy implications can be profound. You may want to examine whether your state's BRFSS reports provide you with the information you need for your policy analysis.

Some states and larger local communities have developed geographic information systems (GISs) and begun using data-visualization tools that allow health data to be displayed and analyzed spatially and longitudinally. Specific neighborhoods can be highlighted as having a high incidence of mortality, morbidity, or automobile accidents. Using these systems can be a very effective way to demonstrate where policy intervention might be most effective. However, such systems and capacities are very inconsistent across the United States. Foundations such as the Robert Wood Johnson Foundation (RWJF) have led efforts to make "place-based" health data more accessible. Some examples include:

- RWJF County Health Rankings, http://www.countyhealthrankings .org/
- Community Health Status Indicators (CHSIs), http://wwwn.cdc.gov/ CommunityHealth/homepage.aspx?j=1
- Health Disparities Maps, http://www.rwjf.org/content/dam/images/ Sandbox/2013%20Commission/Charts/2013DCMetroMap_full.pdf

Although it might appear that there is a great deal of data available, there are problems with almost any data source. The data that is available frequently does not match the problem being analyzed. Age categories may not match, or the definition of a disease using the International Classification of Diseases (ICD) codes may vary (http://www.cdc.gov/nchs/ icd.htm). There will be a release of the ICD-10-CM on October 1, 2014, that might cause some disruption in comparisons of studies using ICD-9-CM. Use of data becomes even more complicated if you need to use more than one data set. Due to monetary constraints, many of these data systems are not collected every year. For example, one of the most important data sources, the U.S. Census, is used to calculate the denominator for disease rates as well as provide important socioeconomic data. The census is conducted every 10 years. This 10-year gap is particularly important for communities that are growing or losing population rapidly or that have significant health problems in minority populations. The lack of timely census information inhibits large-scale studies on the impact of socio-economic variables (e.g., education, employment, and income) on disease. Statistical estimates may be provided for interim periods for some of the census data elements collected, but interim estimates are not provided for all data elements within the census.

An additional problem is that for those data systems that are collected on a regular basis there is always the temptation to change questions or definitions of a particular measure in order to better reflect current understandings or needs. For example, one might want to change the definition of "obesity" or "overweight." However, such changes must be done very conservatively because any change in definitions can lead to the inability to compare results to previous years, thus losing important trend data over time. One has to carefully weigh the loss of longitudinal data against the use of a better definition or a change in a survey question.

Standard data systems may not use the exact measure or variable that you need for your analysis. For example, a survey may collect "individual income" when "family income" or "household income" is really what is needed. The definition of a "family" versus a "household" can be very important. This becomes even more critical when one needs to link two or more data systems, each using its own definition for "family" or "household."

When one is confronted with imperfect data, one must either use a variable that is not quite right, but perhaps close enough, or go to the expense of collecting a new set of data. The new set of data might be better suited for the study, but the time and expense of collecting this new data set would tend to be high. In addition, data collected for a particular study or policy may be challenged as being biased toward finding what was intended. There will be a natural suspicion as to the reliability and validity of the data that you collected for a specific purpose. Using a recognized national or state standard data set also allows others to verify your findings. However, there are times when you may indeed want or need to collect very specific data for your policy initiative, especially if this is a relatively new area of policy analysis.

## ANALYTICAL STUDIES

In addition to difficulties with data, there are difficulties in what is done with data in terms of analysis. A number of frameworks have been created to weigh the level of evidence for health care. Steinberg and Luce discuss the weight of individual methodologies (Steinberg & Luce, 2005). Below is a modified version of their order of the strength of individual studies:

- Randomized clinical trials
- Quasirandomized (group randomized) trials
- Nonrandomized clinical trials
- Prospective or retrospective cohort studies
- Time-series studies
- Case control studies
- Cross-sectional studies
- Case series and registries
- Case reports

The gold standard for medical care studies has traditionally been the randomized clinical trial, especially a double-blinded clinical trial in which both patients and providers are blind in terms of those receiving treatment and those who are not.

However, individual studies, even clinical trials, should not be evaluated in isolation. Weighing the level of evidence is based on multiple factors. Biological connections are important. What are the hypothesized biological or social relationships that make the relationship between the intervention and outcome feasible? Is there a chain of reasoning that makes the relationship plausible? Although clinical trials may be the preferred analytical method, time, expense, or ethical considerations may require other types of studies.

How many studies of the policy issue have been done, and to what extent are they comparable? If there are few studies, the weight of evidence of even of a single clinical trial is less convincing. If studies use different definitions or different protocols for intervention, there may be very different outcomes. On the other hand, if different types of studies (cohort and clinical trials) come to the same conclusion, there may be increased evidence. Is there a consistency of findings in the individual studies over time and using different populations? If studies basically confirm previous findings, there is a greater level of confidence in the results. Due to all these types of questions, systematic literature reviews and meta-analyses literature reviews become important in weighing the level of evidence in favor of or against a particular health policy proposal/ program. Additionally, emerging analytic techniques from the fields of engineering and systems science are now being applied to policy analysis, particularly to enable us to visualize the simulated or projected outcomes of different policy alternatives (Madahian, Klesges, Kelesges, & Homayouni, 2012). All of this will be discussed in greater detail in Chapter 7, Systematic Review of Policy Options.

As indicated previously, clinical trials are generally considered to be the gold standard of evidence. Clinical trials involve the provision of treatment to one group and the lack of the same treatment to another. Both groups of patients are generally randomly assigned as to who receives treatment, and investigators are careful to note any differences in the populations that might explain different outcomes other than the existence or lack of treatment. Due to the random assignment of treatment, other confounding factors will, on average, be equally distributed between the two groups. If both the providers and the patients are unaware of who is receiving the intervention, it is a double-blind study and has increased credibility by removing potential provider bias.

Despite historic reliance on clinical trials, there are multiple problems with them, especially for the development of policy. Clinical trials are expensive and lengthy, and the sponsors of the clinical trials may have a substantial stake in the outcome. Therefore, there may be a potential built-in bias of the clinical trial in terms of seeking a favorable outcome. Another difficulty with clinical trials is the difference between efficacy (the demonstration of what works in a research setting) as opposed to effectiveness (the demonstration of what works in the real world; Steinberg & Luce, 2005). This is especially important in the policy world, where a number of different demographic and social factors in the real world become important factors.

Clinical trials rely on volunteers of both patients and providers to follow rigorous protocols. It may be difficult to get volunteers to participate in a clinical trial if there is a 50/50 chance they will not receive the intervention, especially if this intervention "promises" a chance at survival. Not all volunteers are accepted in clinical trials. Patients have to have a certain level of the particular disease being studied and/or a lack of other diseases to be accepted into the study. These clinical trial participants become "ideal patients" who might benefit from the intervention. In addition, providers need to be recruited as well. These tend to be specialists dealing with the disorder in question who possess a greater level of expertise than the typical physician who may be treating patients in the real world. In addition, these providers are frequently compensated for recruiting participants and for their own participation in the trial. Clinical trials can also involve a relatively small number of participants due to the difficulty and expense of getting participants.

As a result, clinical trials tend to involve ideal patients and practitioners rather than the routine patients and providers confronted in the real world. Although clinical trials provide comparisons between the populations receiving the intervention and the controls not receiving the intervention (internal validity), they generally do not compare those in the clinical trial to those patients who are likely to receive the treatment in the real world (external validity; Steinberg & Luce, 2005). Consequently, clinical trials have been accused of overstating the effectiveness of the intervention in the real world, even without intentional bias. John P. A. Ioannidis has published a number of provocative articles questioning the methodology of most clinical research (Ioannidis, 2005a, 2005b; Tatsioni, Bonitsis, & Ioannidis, 2007). Despite their imperfections, clinical trials remain the gold standard.

However, there is growing consensus that a "mixed-methods approach" is one of the most effective ways to evaluate the impacts of policy change, especially in public health. This means that both quantitative and qualitative information is collected in a strategic manner (Schifferdecker & Reed, 2009). For example, think about how one might study the impact of building a new bike path, as described in the previous RE-AIM discussion. One might use a combination of interviews and focus groups (qualitative methods) with city council members and neighborhood residents to better understand their motivations for wanting to build a bike path. One would also want to query them about any problems they foresee and potential opposition to the bike path. One can use methods such as "content analysis" and document review to study minutes of city council meetings or check whether the city has a published a Bicycle Plan to better understand the process of adopting and constructing the bike path. One can study records of city expenditures to determine how much money was allocated, and use direct observation, engineering devices, or intercept surveys to study ridership before and after the bike path is built. One can collect survey data or obtain secondary data about health behaviors (such as bicycling to work or for leisure) from the target population. One may also collect or obtain secondary data about risk factors and health conditions, such as diabetes and heart disease in the surrounding area. One can conduct more interviews and focus groups after completion of the bike path to determine whether there are any barriers to usage or challenges in maintenance, and participatory action research techniques such as Photovoice can be used to empower residents to describe their neighborhood environment and their perceptions of the new bike path in their own pictures and words (Wang, 1999). All of these data sources can be considered together, or "triangulated," to gain a composite picture of the success or failure of the bike path. Most of these methods are lower on the hierarchy of studies, but they may be the most useful for your particular policy analysis.

It is important to understand the strengths and weaknesses of various types of analytical studies. Your analysis will depend on the integrity as well as the types of studies used to support your analysis.

## Health Policy Analysis

The role of health policy analysis is more critical today than ever. Technology and the basic sciences have opened up more areas of knowledge regarding disease and health. Data sources have expanded, providing greater access to information. Computer systems allow for the analysis of huge quantities of data to provide more precise and sophisticated analytical processes. For example, the previously mentioned all-payer claims data systems being developed by some states provides a new opportunity to analyze health care utilization by the general population. The increasing use of electronic medical records will expand the opportunity to have more accurate and accessible information on individual medical care that can be aggregated for clinical research. The role of government has been expanded in terms of access to medical care, and the Medicare and Medicaid systems have taken on increased roles in developing new forms of medical care and payment systems, such as accountability care organizations (ACOs) and insurance exchanges.

The need for health policy analysis has also become greater as the cost of medical care continues to accelerate, requiring an increasing percentage of the country's gross national product for health care. The increasing disparities in health experience based on geography, race, gender, and ethnicity all need both investigation and mitigation to create a more equitable health care system. The increased focus on the built environment and how it interacts with the health status of populations and individuals adds new dimensions to creating the conditions for a healthy population. Health policy analysis is in a position as never before to make a contribution to the health of individuals and the population.

What follows is a template as to how to construct a health policy analysis to assist policy makers. This template is a framework. As you work through the chapters, some elements of the framework will be more critical than others depending on the audience for which your policy analysis is intended. Working through this framework, the text will use the obesity epidemic in the United States as its main example, although other examples will be given as well.

## SUMMARY

Health policy analysis is an area that requires knowledge and skills from a variety of disciplines and perspectives. In this chapter we started with some clarifications as to how this text uses terms such as *politics, policy,* and *health* as well as summarized models of the political policy process. These concepts will become important and will be expanded when we talk about developing a strategy for making policy analysis meaningful within the political system. In addition, we discussed the importance of evidence-based health policy and the promise and problems associated with implementing such a concept. We also discussed the importance of data and how various data systems become important in the gathering of evidence-based policy. We have noted particular health data sets that might be important in analyzing health policy and will revisit this information in Chapter 7, focusing on the systematic review of policy options. We also reviewed some major national organizations in the United States that are useful resources for those doing health policy analysis.

We further highlighted some important elements and issues from areas that are critical for conducting thoughtful health policy analysis. We will build on these concepts as we go through the policy analysis process, using obesity as an example of the types of things that need to be done.

## SOME THINGS TO REMEMBER

- Politics is the authoritative allocation of values for society, and as such plays a central role in determining societies' relative values.
- Public programs and policies reflect those values.
- The policy process of policy formulation, policy adoption, policy implementation, policy evaluation, and policy modification all exist on a policy wheel. Policy can be developed anyplace on the wheel (Figure 1.1).
- Health is a complicated concept, and our current understanding of the inputs to health requires a multidisciplinary approach to solving society's health problems.
- Health policy analysis is an applied type of heath research; you need to appreciate what works in the real world, with its many complications.
- You will find your policy initiative falling into one of the following categories of health research literature: effectiveness, efficiency, and/ or equity. Understanding the methodological complications of those analytical areas is important.
- Evidence-based policy is the goal, no matter how difficult the path might be.
- There are multiple resources available to assist in policy analysis. Some are partisan and others are nonpartisan.
- Sources of health data in the United States are varied. There are multiple data sets using different definitions and computer systems that make combining data sets difficult. Understand the assumptions and methodologies of all data systems you access.
- There is a general hierarchy of analytical studies. However, you must be careful not to regard that hierarchy as sacrosanct. All methodologies have their strengths and weaknesses.
- Mixed-methods research has been gaining in popularity as a result of the complexity of health.

## KEY WORDS

Agency for Healthcare Research &
   Quality (AHRQ)
All-payer claims databases (APCDs)
Allocative efficiency
Analytical studies
Behavioral Risk Factor Surveillance
   System (BRFSS)
Centers for Disease Control and
   Prevention (CDC)
Clinical trials
Congressional Budget Office (CBO)
Effectiveness
Efficiency
Equity
Evidence-based health policy
Geographic information system (GIS)

Government Accountability
   Office (GAO)
Health impact assessment
   (HIA)
Human Impact Partners (HIP)
Institute of Medicine (IOM)
National Center for Health
   Statistics (NCHS)
Patient-Centered Outcomes
   Research Institute (PCORI)
Policy
Policy-making process
Politics
PRECEDE-PROCEED
Production efficiency
RE-AIM

# TWO

# Mechanics

Before getting into the substance of the policy analysis, it is important to discuss some of the pieces of your policy analysis that are helpful in making it more useful to the readers. Although these pieces are normally completed at the end, it is useful to begin preparing these pieces throughout the process.

You may find yourself writing this analysis for a nonprofit health advocacy group, a legislator, a state agency, a governor's office, a federal agency, a lobbying group, or any of a myriad of other types of organizations developing policy analyses. You may have worked in this organization for years or just begun. In either case, you will need to clearly understand the operating procedures of your organization as well as understand the culture and personalities of that organization. This is important in terms of making sure that your policy analysis fits the expectations of your organization. We will refer back to this many times as we work through various sections of the policy analysis.

In addition to understanding your organization, you also need to understand the motivations behind your organization for pushing this policy issue. At first, this may appear to be quite obvious—the purpose is to address a public policy need. However, there are other motivations that may be important. One of those that will also be mentioned numerous times is political capital. We will use a politician as our primary example here, but the same applies for organizations as well. The concept of political capital is borrowed from economics. Capital is a resource that can be accumulated and then converted for something of value at a later date. Politicians try to collect political capital in the form of public praise, editorial endorsements, campaign contributions, and constituency support, among others. Political capital provides politicians with influence. They can then expend their accumulated political capital to convince others to support their other policy initiatives or gain an assignment to an important legislative committee or other favor. A politician has to be judicious in his or her expenditure of political capital. Using all of one's political capital for one favor means that one may not have any capital left for other causes that come along, unless that effort or others replenish some political capital. Politicians at the end of their careers may want to use up their political capital to pass legislation that is dear to their hearts but would have been too politically costly at an earlier stage. Therefore, policy makers are not only thinking about how to solve a political problem, but how proposing a policy option or joining others might add to their own political capital. One thing you will need to ask yourself is, how much political capital do you think your policy makers are willing to expend to make this policy proposal become law? As a corollary, how much political capital are the policy makers likely to gain as a result of this effort? You need to be conscious of this as you work through the policy analysis. It is important to understand the multiple motivations of your policy makers or organization.

## TABLE OF CONTENTS

A table of contents provides a basic outline of the document. As such, it can be used initially as a map for how the document is going to be written. It may seem like an obvious portion of any document, but it is frequently omitted even though it can be created fairly quickly. Page numbers generally accompany the text indicating where sections and subsections begin. This allows the reader to go directly to the section of interest, either initially or later. The length of the document somewhat determines the amount of detail in the table of contents. If the document is lengthy, one may wish to add subheadings to the table of contents in order to provide more exact locations for significant sections of the report. If the document is short, perhaps only the major sections need to be listed along with the page numbers. The key here is to place oneself in the role of the reader in order to make the document as user friendly as possible.

There are some techniques that can be used to facilitate ease of use. One is to color code key sections of the report. For example, the section on "Recommendations and Strategies" can be printed on yellow paper or in a different electronic format if only paperless reports are produced. If there is a consistency in this pattern, "the yellow sheets" become a shortcut for referring to critical sections of the report that one may wish to return to frequently or separate from the rest of the document.

The key to a useful table of contents is to place oneself in the role of the reader and to make the document as user friendly as possible.

## EXECUTIVE SUMMARY

This section has to be written at the end of your analysis. However, it normally appears in front of your finished policy analysis. One of the facts of life for a politician is the lack of time required to do all that is demanded during the day. Therefore, material that is useful must be tightly organized so as to maximize efficiency. One element of that is an "executive summary."

Depending on the policy you are analyzing, an executive summary might be fairly straightforward or highly complex to develop. Often, it is one of the most difficult parts of an analysis to complete.

Some people mistake an executive summary for an introduction. The latter tells the reader what is to be expected in the document and perhaps some background material to introduce the subject. In contrast, an executive summary condenses the document into a few pages, covering all essential elements of the document.

There is no magic number of pages for an executive summary. Some policy makers prefer no more than five pages, and some prefer no more than one page. Of course, the shorter the executive summary, the more difficult it becomes to write, especially for the author of the document, who has come to believe that every phrase is essential to the logic of the document. This might be the time for you to ask someone else to edit the executive summary and forego the pride of authorship. Providing an outside person to at least take the first cut at what is essential for the reader provides another perspective. You might wish to then add or subtract from the initial draft of the executive summary.

The executive summary has to be sensitive to the policy maker/organization for whom the document is written. Everyone comes to a policy issue with a different level of expertise. Policy makers frequently like to focus on one or two major areas depending on their experience or legislative desires. They may also become involved in areas that are important to their constituents, but not an area of their expertise. So, the executive summary may vary depending on the expertise of the principal audience for the analysis. If the audience is very familiar with the topic, perhaps not all sections of the report need to be summarized. If your analysis is designed for a more general audience, greater detail may need to be provided. This is a judgment call that is made knowing the audience for whom the report is being written.

There are two approaches to an executive summary. This is again dependent on the audience for whom it is directed. Some policy makers prefer an executive summary that is used as a map for reading the report. From this perspective, the executive summary is read both before and after he or she has read the entire analysis. It provides both a map for what is coming and a reminder of what has been read. This type of executive summary can be less detailed because it assumes that the policy makers will actually read or have read the analysis. However, if you are unsure who will read your policy analysis, err on the side of more detail in the executive summary.

The other use for an executive summary is to perhaps serve as the only section the policy stakeholder will read. This places an additional burden on the author of the analysis because the summary must be more comprehensive to avoid any potential misinterpretation. Alternatively, the policy makers may read the executive summary and then only one of the core sections of the report (e.g., Recommendations and Strategies) for additional detail. Understanding the audience or the proclivities of the policy makers is critical in writing a useful executive summary.

Due to the need for brevity, it is important to be as concise as possible. Excessive words must be eliminated while the meaning remains sharp and focused. Some authors prefer to use bullets in executive summaries. However, bullets need to be self-explanatory. Remember that the person reading the executive summary may not have read the report yet and does not have all the background and information that you possess, having done the research and written the report. What may be clear to you as a bullet may not be clear to someone who has not read the details of your analysis.

Some readers are more visual in their ability to comprehend and retain information. Consequently, sometimes a chart or table becomes a meaningful way to communicate information in a small amount of space. However, this creates an additional burden on you because you must make sure that the chart or table is unambiguous and is visually clean. A complicated table in the executive summary that cannot be clearly interpreted or explained is potentially harmful and could lead to costly misstatements by your policy makers who have not read the entire document.

As implied above, much of the executive summary depends on the purpose of the report and the person(s) who read it. The more you know about the people reading the report, the more likely that the executive summary will be on target. Remember that the executive summary may be the only section read just before a press conference or going into a legislative hearing.

As a practical note, we suggest that you continue through the remainder of this book, and then reread this section before writing the executive summary.

## DEFINITIONS/ABBREVIATIONS

You will want to have an appendix in your final document that contains critical abbreviations and definitions for your policy. Although you will finalize this list at the end of your analysis, it is best to keep a working copy as you go through the policy analysis framework. You will find the definitions particularly important in the sections of the policy analysis framework dealing with the systematic analysis of policy alternatives and recommendations.

The first section of any piece of legislation is a list of definitions. There is an important reason for this. Laws need to be as specific as possible in order to carry out the legislative intent of the proposal. It may sometimes seem obvious that people have a common understanding of an important term. However, that is seldom the case, and the court system is filled with cases in which various people have different understandings of what is meant by a certain word or phrase in a particular piece of legislation.

For example, most people have a general understanding of what is meant by a "hospital." However, in the development of a policy on "hospitals" one must be very precise as to exactly what institutions are going to be covered by a proposed policy impacting "hospitals." The definition of a "hospital" for any proposed policy is actually quite complicated. Despite sharing many characteristics, most people would not confuse a college infirmary with a hospital. However, there are outpatient clinics that perform many of the same functions as a hospital. Are they to be included as "hospitals" and thus be covered by the proposed law? Even those institutions that are clearly hospitals may be quite different, and one may not want the proposed legislation to apply to all "hospitals" equally. Some hospitals provide acute care, whereas others provide psychiatric or rehabilitation services. Does your policy proposal apply to all three in the same way? Some hospitals are limited to special populations such as members of the military or veterans. Should they be exempt or included? Some hospitals specialize in one or two diseases (e.g., cancer), whereas others treat all diseases. Some hospitals train physicians and other health care providers (e.g., teaching hospitals) and others merely employ them. Some hospitals are privately owned by investors and some are nonprofit and owned by the community at large. Some hospitals are large and some are "small" (e.g., 50 or fewer beds). Some hospitals have special policy problems, such as urban hospitals that typically serve a more indigent population or rural hospitals that face problems of economies of scale for the provision of certain services. Even among rural hospitals, some are legally classified as "critical access hospitals" and others are not. Which of these "hospitals" are to be covered by your policy proposal? Which of these "hospitals" should be exempted from the provisions of your policy proposal, and what is the justification for their exclusion?

Frequently, there are conventions in terms of what is meant by a "community hospital" or a "critical access hospital" that can be adopted by your analysis. If your policy focuses on increasing public funding for "hospitals," many hospitals might want to be defined as "hospitals," thus increasing the cost of your policy. If your policy is regulatory in nature, many "hospitals" may seek to be excluded from your policy proposal. Lobbyists on both sides will be intently focused on any definition that is adopted. Later, as the policy progresses, legislators or interest groups may support your legislation or refrain from opposing your policy if you merely change your definition of a "hospital."

Definitions are also important in that there are commonly accepted descriptions that people may or may not understand. For example, to return to our major example, there is a standard and accepted definition of "obesity" that has been developed by the Centers for Disease Control and Prevention (CDC). Obesity is defined by a formula comparing height to weight: body mass index (BMI) = height/weight. For adults, being underweight is having a BMI less than 18.5, normal is 18.5 to 24.9, over-weight is 25.0 to 29.9, and obese is 30.0+ (CDC, 2013d). This is the standard definition of obesity, and it is important to use that definition unless part of your policy proposal is to revise what is considered to be the standard. It is also important to know that this CDC definition of obesity does not apply to children. The standard definition of BMI has been considered less reliable for children because they experience growth spurts. Consequently, there is a different definition of obesity that is used for children based on the age of the child and the 95th percentile on a CDC growth chart (CDC, 2013b). You may feel like the standard CDC definition should be changed. For example, some researchers prefer to use measures of waist circumfer-ence to measure abdominal adiposity, which is associated with risk for diabetes and cardiovascular disease (Harvard School of Public Health, 2013). No matter which definition you use, you must be clear as to which one you are adopting for your proposal. Opposition or support for your policy proposal may depend on which definition you choose.

Equally important for child obesity in this definition is the definition of a "child" versus an "adult." Is a 17-year-old person a child or an adult? Or is adulthood for child obesity defined as being enrolled in a primary or secondary educational system? Studies will generally be done using stan-dard definitions; some studies might use a different definition and thus its results may not be comparable. If you are comparing one state to another, do the two states use the same definition of "childhood" as well as "obesity"?

Because obesity deals with both intake and output, it is important to also know what is considered to be "physical activity" in terms of inten-sity, duration, and frequency. For example, how often (three times per week) does one have to swim and for how long (20 minutes or 50 laps) to qualify as "exercise"? The Compendium for Physical Activity provides formulas for estimating the metabolic equivalents (METs) for common physical activities (Ainsworth et al., 2000). Do all the sources you used in your analysis use METs as a uniform measure of exertion?

All of these concepts and terms need to be defined as precisely as pos-sible so that your policy proposal is clear and to avoid needless oppo-sition to your proposal based on a misunderstanding. For example, an organization for the elderly may oppose your proposal if the definition of "exercise" is not based on appropriate CDC guidelines or medical recommendations. Being as precise as possible is important to avoiding potential political struggles down the road that could have been avoided in the first place if you had only been clear and precise in your definitions.

There are also definitions for concepts that might not be well known, but that are commonly used in the debate over your policy issue. For example, recent literature on obesity has focused on the importance of the "built environment" (e.g., streets, sidewalks, zoning, etc., that contribute or create barriers for physical exercise or access to important resources). Although this term is understood within the public health and research communities, it is not a common term within political circles. As a result, a definition of the "built environment" would be helpful for a politician or bureaucrat who might not be familiar with that term. Such definitions would help to avoid having your policy makers caught during a debate or news conference not knowing the implications of a word or phrase being used.

Abbreviations are also sometimes critical in the dialogue on policy. Governments are filled with acronyms and abbreviations. The National Health and Nutrition Examination Survey (NHANES) is one of the major data sources used for obesity research (CDC, 2013e). It is typically referred to by its initials, NHANES, and not its full title. In addition to knowing what the initials stand for, it is also important that your policy makers know essential facts about the data set, if that should become a major element in your policy proposal. The fact that NHANES is a national data sample, that it is a continuous survey covering the noninstitutionalized population of the United States, that it contains clinical indicators of disease in addition to individuals' self reports, and that it is released every 2 years are important descriptors one would want to know in order to defend studies using it as a data source or using NHANES data as a way to measure the success of your proposed policy. NHANES is a credible data set. It is important that people reading your analysis know what NHANES represents. The Behavioral Risk Factor Surveillance Survey (BRFSS) is another critical source of obesity data. It provides important data on things that are not usually measured by the medical system (e.g., diet, patterns of exercise, and smoking). However, because it is based solely on self-reported information, it may not be considered as credible as NHANES data. We will talk more about the credibility of data in later chapters. The important point here is that policy makers should have easy access to a list of important terms and definitions.

In addition to specific obesity terms, it might be important to define general statistical terms that are commonly used and become important for your analysis. For example, confidence interval (CI) and adjusted relative risk (ARR) are commonly used terms pertaining to estimates used in measuring obesity or relating obesity to other diseases. CIs provide the boundaries of probability to a given number. Defining ARR and knowing what a relative risk of 1.29 means can give someone comfort in presenting data that supports your policy. You do not need to provide your policy makers with a tutorial on statistical interpretation, but merely to make sure your readers are comfortable using the information in your analysis. Many policy makers may have never taken a course in statistics or may have taken one so long ago that it is not part of their normal thought process.

## OTHER APPENDICES

In addition to the list of definitions/abbreviations, there are other documents or explanations that you might wish to make available to the readers but that would distract from the flow of your policy analysis. For example, you might want to provide a detailed description of a model program you found in another geopolitical area. You can refer to it in the text and then provide more detail for those who wish to have more information. You might want to provide more detailed information on a critical study or a fuller explanation of a particular methodology. Some readers will use these appendices and others will not. If something is critical to understanding the policy analysis, it belongs in the body or your document. The appendices can provide additional information or clarification.

## SUMMARY

This chapter dealt with some of the basics that you will need to take into account as you are writing your policy analysis. Although products such as the executive summary are generally produced at the end of the process, gathering the elements as you work through the policy analysis will help you in the end.

## SOME THINGS TO REMEMBER

- Make sure you have an understanding of the culture, resources, and personalities of the policy maker/organization for whom you are writing the policy analysis.
- Understand the role of political capital in how your policy makers may view the resolution of this policy issue. How much political capital is your policy maker willing to expend to see this proposal become reality? How much political capital will he or she gain as a result of this initiative?
- Prepare an executive summary that meets the needs of your policy makers/audience in terms of its brevity, comprehensiveness, and ability to sell the story of your policy proposal.
- Map out a table of contents as a guide as to how you are going to write the analysis as well as to guide the reader to locate critical sections for quick access.
- Keep an ongoing list of critical definitions, abbreviations, and terms that are important to the construction of your policy proposal so as to avoid any misunderstandings in terms of what is actually being proposed and who will be impacted by the program/policy change.
- Use standard definitions when possible.
- Make sure your reader can make maximum use of the data and statistical analysis presented.
- Add appendices as needed to provide additional details that supplement the material in the body of your analysis.

## KEY WORDS

Table of contents
Executive summary
Definitions
Abbreviations
Body mass index (BMI)

BMI percentile calculator
Metabolic equivalents (METs)
National Health and Nutrition
    Survey (NHANES)

Three

# Policy Background

This is the first section of your policy analysis. In this section you need to provide background material for the policy issue that you have chosen. We will use obesity as an example here. The length and depth of this section is somewhat dependent on the intended audience of your analysis. If the intended reader is an expert in this policy area, this section might be quite brief. However, we shall approach this section of your policy analysis as though it is to be read by a general audience. Consequently, it will provide more background information on obesity rather than less.

## HISTORY

It would be highly unusual to explore a policy area where there was no history. In fact, most policy issues and proposals get recycled over and over again. The history of health care reform is but one example. There have been various proposals for health care reform for more than 60 years. It is important to recognize the past, especially in policy, because policy is both built on and trapped in the past. Most legislation in the United States is based on incrementalism, the notion that most policy changes are small changes of existing policy rather than comprehensive policy changes (Lindblom, 1980; Longest, 2009; Weissert & Weissert, 2006). For example, health insurance in the United States got its major push after World War II, with tax provision that rewarded employers who provided health insurance to their employees (Starr, 1982). As a result, there is a 60-year history of employer-based health insurance that has become a central characteristic of our health insurance system. It would be difficult to change that aspect of the health insurance market due to existing stakeholders who have an economic interest in keeping it intact. Large insurance companies have developed as a result of this initial policy and employee expectations have been built around this employee benefit. Personal and business income tax rulings are built around employer health insurance. As a result, single-payer health insurance system proposals have faced major obstacles from concentrated interest groups wishing to protect the existing insurance structure.

This focus on incrementalism is partly due to our political structure, which makes it difficult to pass major legislation. Due to the political structure of the United States, there are multiple political avenues available to those with an intense interest to block any piece of legislation within the legislative process. Opponents have an easier time blocking political action than those who need to pass a legislative proposal through the multiple legislative committees in the two branches of the legislature plus the executive and the bureaucracy. It may take only one key obstacle (e.g., a committee chair or a key party leader) or a political tactic (e.g., the need for unanimous consent in the U.S. Senate) to block a legislative initiative. Therefore, legislative proposals are generally constructed to minimize the disruption of the status quo in order to gain sufficient political support. This need for compromise diminishes if there is a political party or group that dominates all the political levers of power (e.g., both houses of Congress and the Presidency), but divided government (where one party controls one branch and the other party controls another branch) at the national level tends to be the norm, especially more recently. If you are proposing policy in a state that is decidedly blue (Democratic) or red (Republican), there may be less of a need to for political compromise and less need for incrementalism. However, even there a major non-incremental policy pushed by the dominant party might lead to voter rebellion in the next election and a loss of majority status. In addition, a non-incremental policy will still face the opposition of major stakeholders that will be negatively impacted. Knowing the history of legislative action is critical in understanding the parameters of potential change within your particular interest. Change can and does occur, but it tends to occur slowly. As we will note later, this does not mean that your policy proposal needs to be incremental in nature.

The policy issue you chose has probably been dealt with before in the same political setting. If not, it has probably been dealt with in another geopolitical unit (e.g., another state, the federal government, or another country), from which lessons can be learned. In fact, obesity has been an issue for a number of years. Consequently, one of the first things that you should deal with in this section of your analysis is a brief history of how the issue has been dealt with over the years. It is important in this section of the policy analysis to demonstrate how other jurisdictions have dealt with the issue and what lessons can be learned from those experiences. Some of those policy efforts might have been very successful, some dismal failures, and still others a mixed success. Due to differences in political systems and political cultures, there may be very innovative programs in other countries. It is important to explore what seems to have worked or not worked in other political jurisdictions.

It is also important to understand that since those past policies occurred in different political systems and cultures or in different times, what might have "worked" in another political setting may not work now in yours. For example, Europeans are more likely to support a government program on obesity than people in the United States, who are more wedded to the concepts of the free enterprise system, limited government, and individual freedom. Transplanting policies from one jurisdiction to another is always fraught with the obstacle of trying to convince policy makers that despite all the differences in geopolitics, the policy could still work in a different environment. Rhetorical phrases, such as "this is not Europe," can be used to politically decimate your proposal. Despite these precautions, it is useful to look elsewhere for policies that are innovative and worth analyzing, adopting, or modifying. The differences between geopolitical units in terms of culture, political process, and so forth, just might not be that important.

You will need to have an appreciation as to what legislation has been introduced in the past. One of the great resources for previous legislation at the federal level is the Library of Congress (http://www.loc.gov/index .html). It provides a number of services online and in person. If you are located in the Washington, DC, area, it is an essential stop for this portion of your analysis. The Federal Legislative History Section of the Library of Congress website (http://www.loc.gov/law/help/leghist.php) provides a vehicle to investigate legislative history. In order for you to use it, you will generally have to know some of the specific legislation in the past. From your knowledge of the policy area or from an introductory article, you might have the public law citation (e.g., P.L. 113-101, the first number represents the Session of Congress passed and the second number represents the order passed, in this case the 101st law passed by the 113th Congress, which began in January of 2013). Since a Congress sits for 2 years, some citations will indicate whether it was in Session 1 or Session 2, each Session beginning at the start of January and adjourning at the end of each year. After the law is passed it becomes incorporated into the U.S. Statutes at Large and will have another annotation, for example, 17 Stat. 272. If you do not know the statute number or Public Law number, you might have a reference regarding a proposed piece of legislation that did or did not become law. A useful reference for finding statutes is Westlaw (Westlaw Professional Legal Research, n.d.). Those bills that may or may not have become law but were introduced into Congress are also cited by using the house of origin ("H.R." for House of Representatives, or "S." for Senate) and the number of the piece of legislation. Alternately, you might know the policy proposal by its popular title.

Thomas (http://thomas.loc.gov) is an online service of the Library of Congress that provides free access to legislative history. Beginning with the 104th Congress, Thomas provides full-text access to public laws, House and Senate bills, House and Senate Reports, and the Congressional Record. Major research universities are generally designated as depositories for government documents and have reference librarians who are familiar with federal government documents. You should make use of these reference librarians, since the cataloging of government documents is different from normal library cataloging, and government documents are generally located in a separate section of the library.

Committee Reports are especially valuable because they contain testimony before one of the committees with jurisdiction over the bill from administrators, proponents, and opponents of the proposed legislation. You must be conscious of the fact that the testimony may be tilted in one direction or the other since the Chair of the Committee representing the majority party may very well have stacked the testimony based on her or his position on the proposed legislation. Congressional hearings are not unbiased, but they are a valuable source of arguments being used by proponents and opponents and may provide some evidence-based testimony.

If the legislation is currently being discussed in Congress, you can follow it through Thomas as it makes its way or stalls within Congress. If you are working at the state policy level, some states have similar legislative services that can be useful in tracking legislative history.

If you need to access federal regulations as opposed to federal laws, a useful website is the U.S. Government Printing Office's Electronic Code of Federal Regulations (http://www.ecfr.gov), which includes a search engine for locating relevant administrative regulations. You can also access the daily *Federal Register* by year or date of issue (http://www.gpo.gov/fdsys/browse/collection.action?collectionCode=FR) through the U.S. Government Printing Office. Hard copies of the *Federal Register* are usually available in public and university libraries, especially those designated as federal depositories.

At the state level, there is a website for state and local government (http://www.statelocalgov.net) that allows you to enter the name of a state and access its government web page. For example, if you typed in "Washington," you would see a link to its legislative, executive, and judicial branches. Under the "legislative branch" link, you would see many useful features, including a "Bill Tracker" tab. You can use the Bill Tracker to search for a particular bill by its number, or to search by key words such as "food," "nutrition," "obesity," and so forth. Many states have similar bill-tracking features built into their government web pages.

Other major resources for the legislative/policy history are the people who are familiar with the policy issue. They exist within the bureaucracy as well as the various lobbying groups and nonprofit organizations focusing on that particular issue. Individuals within those organizations can point you to landmark legislation or current or recent policy proposals. We cannot list here all the recent legislation surrounding obesity. However, as part of this history, it is important to acknowledge such things as the partisan division of the Supplemental Nutrition Assistance Program (SNAP; http://www.fns.usda.gov/snap), as well as legislative efforts such as the Healthy, Hunger-Free Kids Act of 2010 that was directed at improving child nutrition (http://www.fns.usda.gov/cnd/governance/legislation/cnr_2010.htm).

There are also many nonpartisan associations, such as the National Conference of State Legislators (http://www.ncsl.org/), that are focused on sharing research and policy ideas adopted by various states. Issue-specific organizations (e.g., a state public health organization or a state hospital association) sometimes provide information on ongoing legislation within their political jurisdictions. All of these are helpful in finding what is currently being considered or has been recently adopted in your or other political jurisdictions. There are a number of foundations that have encouraged the adoption of model programs and conducted extensive evaluations as to their effectiveness. For example, the Robert Wood

Johnson Foundation (RWJF) has been a valuable source of funds for state and local communities to experiment with policy options, as has Bridging the Gap—a research institute focusing on "policies and practices for Healthy Youth" (Bridging the Gap, 2012, 2013; RWJF, 2013a).

## THE OBESITY ISSUE

Using our obesity example, one would need to provide some information on why obesity is a major social problem that should be addressed by policy. This sets the tone in terms of the seriousness of the issue and the need to spend public resources to address it. Although obesity has occurred throughout the ages, the problem of population-wide obesity is a relatively new phenomenon. What was a human evolutionary advantage, storing fat, has become a recent medical diagnosis and epidemic.

The Centers for Disease Control and Prevention (CDC) has a series of very visual state-based maps tracking the progression of obesity since 1985 (CDC, 2013f). An Organization for Economic Co-Operation and Development (OECD) study has indicated that the United States is the most obese country among OECD countries, with 36% of adults being obese and 35% of children being either overweight or obese (OECD, 2010). In 2010, 16.9% of U.S. children and adolescents were obese (Ogden, Carroll, Kit, & Flegal, 2012). Conversion of these percentages means that in 2009–2010 there were over 78 million U.S. adults and 12.5 million U.S. children and adolescents who were obese. These factual data provide a context for the policy debate in the United States in terms of both its magnitude and its historical context. This is an example of descriptive evidence, or type 1 evidence, as discussed in Chapter 1. If you are focusing on the state level, your state will have its own set of historical data on obesity that could provide a context for policy efforts at the state level. Your state may be in better shape than the national obesity problem, or it may be worse.

Pointing to major historical milestones can be important in the development of policy, as well as to acknowledge important participants in the development of those policies. This can be important for acquiring supporters for your effort. For example, the concern over obesity in the United States is sometimes dated back to 1952, when the American Heart Association identified obesity as a risk for coronary heart disease that could be modified through both diet and exercise (Nestle & Jacobson, 2000).

State heart associations or other health groups can be powerful political allies in the support of your proposals.

From an historical perspective, *The Surgeon General's Call to Action to Prevent and Decrease Overweight and Obesity, 2001* is one of the landmark documents in the fight to confront the epidemic of obesity in the United States. Both Dr. David Satcher and then Secretary of Health and Human Services Tommy G. Thompson under President George W. Bush called for achieving five overarching principles (Satcher, 2001):

- Promote the recognition of overweight and obesity as major public health problems.
- Assist Americans in balancing healthy eating with regular physical activity to maintain a healthy or healthier body weight.
- Identify effective and culturally appropriate interventions to prevent and treat overweight and obesity.
- Encourage environmental changes that help prevent overweight and obesity.
- Develop and enhance public–private partnerships to help implement this vision.

The fact that obesity is principally a behavioral issue and that it was emphasized by a conservative Republican administration as well as a Democratic administration has important policy implications in coalition building and framing of the issue of obesity. One can point to a number of governors, liberal and conservative, who have pointed out the need to address the obesity problem. There may not be a consensus in terms of the solution to the problem, but there is at least a bipartisan acknowledgment that the obesity problem exists and that some type of public policy must be developed to address it.

The 1980, 1990, and 2000 U.S. Public Health Services national health objectives all recognize obesity as a major national problem. The 1998 National Institutes of Health report, *Clinical Guidelines of the Identification, Evaluation, and Treatment of Obesity in Adults: Evidence Report*, provided extensive evidence-based research on the risks of obesity as well as evidence-based guidelines for treatment by health providers (National Heart, Lung, and Blood Institute, 1998). One of the goals of Healthy People 2000 was to reduce the prevalence of being overweight to no more than 20% of adults and 15% of adolescents ("Healthy People 2000," 2009). Instead, the number of overweight increased from 25.4% to 34.9% for adults, increased from 7.6% to 13.7% for children ages 6 to 11, and increased from 5.7% to 11.5% for adolescents (Nestle & Jacobson, 2000). Children who have at least one obese parent are three to four times more likely to be obese due to genetics and unhealthy diets/lifestyles than those without obese parents. (Whitaker, Wright, Pepe, Seidel, & Dietz, 1997; Sassi, 2010). These data do not include those classified as overweight. These data are important for providing a context for the problem and educating readers as to the growing nature of the problem.

Healthy People 2010 lists both physical activity and overweight/obesity as two of the 10 leading health indicators. Objectives for obesity include ("Healthy People 2010," 2000):

- Increase to at least 60% the prevalence of healthy weight body mass index (BMI) 19 to 25 among adults.
- Reduce to 15% or less the prevalence of obesity in children and adolescents.
- Increase the proportion of schools that teach essential nutrition topics such as balancing food intake and physical activity in at least three grades.
- Increase to at least 85% the proportion of worksites that offer nutrition education and/or weight management programs for employees.
- Increase to at least 75% the proportion of primary care providers who provide or order weight-reduction services for patients with cardiovascular disease and diabetes mellitus diagnoses.

The problem with these Healthy People objectives is that there has not been an accompanying list of strategies as to how these objectives are to be accomplished or a list of agencies/organizations that are accountable for making sure these objectives are met. The 1980, 1990, and 2000 U.S. Public Health Services national health objectives all recognize obesity as a major problem. The goal of Healthy People 2020 is to "Promote health and reduce chronic disease risk through the consumption of healthful diets and achievement and maintenance of healthy body weights" ("Healthy People 2020," 2013a). For childhood obesity, the goal is to reduce obesity by 10% compared to the 2005 to 2008 levels ("Healthy People 2020," 2011; HealthyPeople.gov, 2013). All of this historical data is significant in that it provides evidence that despite an early recognition of the policy problem, the past and current efforts have not been successful in reaching established goals.

## POLICY SIGNIFICANCE

One of the things that you need to remember in the development of a policy proposal is that there are a number of issues (the political agenda) that are contending for policy makers' attention at any given time. For example, the 112th Congress was presented with 12,299 pieces of legislation; they enacted 284 laws, and passed 721 resolutions (Govtrack.us, 2013). No political body can solve all the issues that are before it. There are limits in terms of time and resources that can be expended on any one problem. As a result, political bodies establish priorities as to what can be addressed. Frequently, leaders of the legislative body (the majority and minority) or the executive branch establish their own legislative/policy priorities. One of the challenges of any policy analysis is to explain clearly and concisely why it is important to address one issue over other competing policy needs. This is where the analysis needs to present data indicating the extent of the problem, the growth of the problem, the cost of the problem, or other related characteristics that make addressing the issue a critical action at the present time.

This is more complicated than it initially sounds. For example, if one measures a problem in terms of the number of deaths, then one can gather mortality data to demonstrate where a disease stands on the list of diseases causing death. However, not all deaths are necessarily equal. Some diseases (pneumonia) strike the elderly, who are near the end of their natural life span. Other health events (accidents) strike the young and result in greater loss as measured by the number of years of life lost. Presenting data in a meaningful way will help convince policy activists that your issue is critical. Understanding the different ways that disease/disability can be measured will be important in making your case and deflecting critics. Deaths are not the only way to measure the importance of a health issue. Understanding the human impacts of a disease or problem can be another way to demonstrate the importance of an issue. The cost to the public sector, for example, the impact of treating obesity for the Medicaid population, can be an effective vehicle for attracting a policy maker's attention to the obesity problem.

For example, although few people die from obesity, obesity is linked to an increasing number of diseases. Obesity is linked to diabetes, osteoarthritis, cancer, hypertension, stroke, pregnancy complications, asthma, and psychological problems, as well as heart disease. As such, it is a major contributor to death and chronic disease in the United States. In 2010, obesity surpassed smoking as the nation's leading cause of preventable death. The shift in the relative impact of obesity and smoking is related to both a reduction in the number of Americans who smoke (coinciding with stricter policies about smoking in the early 1990s) and an increase in the past 2 decades in the number of people who are obese (America's Health Rankings, 2013; CDC, 2012c; Danaei et al., 2009).

The increase in childhood obesity, which at 17% is triple the rate from just one generation ago, is of particular concern, because obesity in children tracks to obesity in adults (CDC, 2013c; Singh, Mulder, Twisk, van Mechelen, & Chinapaw, 2008). Efforts to reduce obesity in childhood may have a significant impact on not only the reduction of childhood diseases (e.g., adolescent onset of type II diabetes) but also a reduction in the incidence of disease later in life. As a result, a great deal of attention has been paid to the increase of childhood obesity in the United States.

However, children are not the only concern. Older adults can also suffer from obesity. One third of older adults were obese based on data from 2007 to 2010 (Fakhouri, Ogden, Carroll, Kit, & Flegal, 2012). This increase has major cost implications for the cost of Medicare. Which area of concern is more important—childhood obesity's cost in the future, or obesity's current impact on the cost of Medicare? Again, there is no simple answer to that question, but it is something that must be addressed in order to build your case for establishing the importance of the problem you are attempting to address and demonstrating its need to be addressed by the political system.

The costs of obesity can be measured in many ways. It has been estimated that as many as 400,000 deaths and $117 billion in health care costs are attributed to obesity each year (Bassett & Perl, 2004). Costs can also be calculated in terms of indirect costs, such as rising health care insurance premiums or increased taxes due to the costs for programs such as Medicare and Medicaid. One study estimated that obesity accounted for 10% of all medical costs (approximately $147 billion) in 2008, and that obese people's medical care spending was $1,429 greater than normal-weight people in 2006 (Finkelstein, Trogdon, Cohen, & Dietz, 2009). Obesity-related diseases were cited as being responsible for 27% of the increase in U.S. medical costs from 1987 to 2001 (Thorpe, Florence, Howard, & Joski, 2004).

There has been a rise in the number of insured people classified as obese and a rise in the number of obese individuals receiving medical care.

This has resulted in an increase in the cost of private insurance. In 1987, obese adults with private health insurance spent $272 more per year per person (about 18% more) on health care than did normal-weight adults. This raised private health care spending by 2%, or $3.6 billion in 1987. By 2002, the relative differences in medical care spending among overweight, obese, and morbidly obese, and normal-weight adults had increased substantially. Spending among obese adults averaged $1,244 higher per person (about 56%more) than for normal-weight adults. This raised private health insurance by nearly 12%—more than $36 billion—in 2002 (Thorpe, Florence, Howard, & Joski, 2005, p. W5-321).

The life span of an obese person is reduced by 8 to 10 years compared to a person of normal weight. Although an obese person has higher annual health expenditures, over a life span an obese person actually has lower lifetime health expenditures due to an earlier death (OECD, 2010). Although this is logical, it is not readily transparent when talking about the "cost of obesity."

It has been estimated that 11% of Medicaid expenditures for adults is spent on obesity (Finkelstein, Fiebelkorn, & Wang, 2004). This requires either taxation at the state and federal level to support these costs or reduction in coverage for other Medicaid services or clients. Health insurance usually treats being overweight as a behavioral problem and does not typically cover obesity unless it is treated as part of a comorbidity. Medicaid in many states does not cover obesity. For example, states will differ as to whether they cover nutritional counseling or drug therapy for obesity. Although they do not cover preventative measures, most insurance policies and Medicaid do tend to cover bariatric surgery for obesity. Understanding the complexity of existing policies is important background information and a potential reason for the need for a policy analysis.

One disease that has been closely associated with obesity is diabetes in both children and adults (Weiss et al., 2004). Once developed (90% of diabetes is type 2, or adult-onset diabetes), there is currently no cure for diabetes; there are merely treatments designed to control it for the rest of that person's life and to minimize the physical impacts of the disease. Preventing or delaying the onset of diabetes is an important factor in reducing morbidity, mortality, and the cost of medical care. Diabetes has increased dramatically in the United States. During 1995 to 2010, the age-adjusted prevalence of diagnosed diabetes in the United States increased in all geographic areas, with the median prevalence for all states, the District of

Columbia, and Puerto Rico rising from 4.5% to 8.2% (Geiss et al., 2012). Explaining how obesity is related to other diseases could be an important part of the background material. For example, there have been studies of school-based interventions for the reduction in obesity and diabetes (The Healthy Study Group, 2010), and studies linking both diabetes and obesity with socioeconomic status and neighborhoods (Ludwig et al., 2011).

Depending on what aspect of the obesity problem is being addressed, some or all of this data may be important. Access to government statistical data can be gained through web pages of agencies involved with collecting and disseminating such information. For obesity, the Centers for Disease Control and Prevention (http://www.cdc.gov/) and the U. S. Department of Health and Human Services (http://www.hhs.gov/) would be key resources. Federal data can also be obtained through FedStats (http://www.fedstats.gov/), which provides data from more than 100 federal agencies and organizes data by geographic areas, including some data by Congressional District. Access to data collected by the Department of Commerce's U.S. Census Bureau (http://www.census.gov/) will be important for many different policy areas.

If it is clear that the focus of your policy proposal is going to be on childhood obesity, then the data presented and the argument can be more focused. For example, if you were working for the Children's Defense Fund (http://www.childrensdefense.org/) your policy background would most likely be focused on children. However, you will still need to demonstrate why focusing on children is important compared to other subpopulations. If you wanted to focus on adult obesity, a different set of data and laws would be important for the policy background.

## LEGAL AUTHORITY/FLEXIBILITY

One of the initial tasks that you need to determine is whether "big P" policy, or public policy, is the appropriate or useful way to address the problem. Some problems may be adequately or appropriately addressed through private nongovernmental actions and, therefore, "little p" policies, or policies at an organizational level, may be sufficient to address the problem. Perhaps voluntary actions taken by an informed public may be sufficient to solve the issue, such as employers putting exercise equipment at work sites or changing foods available in workplace cafeterias, without any government regulation. However, the existence of the problem or the growing scale of the problem itself might be an indicator that past efforts (public and/or private) have not been successful in resolving the issue.

If a public policy approach does seem to be appropriate, it is also important for you to provide some background in terms of the legal and practical ability for a particular level of government to actually be able to have an impact on the specific problem. Due to the structure of our government, some levels have greater legal authority or financial ability to deal with an issue than do others. The federal government might be able to provide money through a grant program to fight obesity in school-aged children, but it may lack authority to initiate a specific policy or program in all schools throughout the country.

The Constitution's Commerce Clause is the major constitutional provision that provides the federal government with the legal authority to regulate interstate commerce and, as a result, health care. One of the major issues of the recent debate over health care reform was whether the federal government had the authority under the Constitution's commerce clause to require an individual mandate for health insurance. The federal courts have consistently ruled since the 1940s that the federal government has a clear legal authority in terms of issues involving interstate commerce. Regulation of foods for health and safety, and drugs for efficacy and safety, are examples of the federal government's legal authority to regulate interstate commerce.

If your policy proposal focuses on school-aged children, the legal authority might shift to state governments, because they tend to have greater historical and legal authority for dealing with childhood obesity through their control of the public school systems. Because children (preschool to grade 12) are typically within a public school system, a local school board or city government has a great deal of influence over the dietary and exercise patterns of those children within the system. In this case, the federal government can play a less direct role. However, because the federal government traditionally provides financial support to voluntary childhood and school nutrition programs in state and local communities through the U.S. Department of Agriculture, it can have an influence over such programs. However, its legal authority to make specific changes may be more limited than a state's Department of Education or a local school district that can create mandates.

In dealing with other population segments with obesity, legal authority may be less well established. For example, the City of New York's mayor attempted to ban super-size sugary drinks, but the attempt became mired down by legal challenges. In 2013, a New York state appeals court rejected Mayor Michael Bloomberg's attempt to limit the size of sugary beverages sold in the city (*In re N.Y. Statewide Coal. of Hispanic Chambers of Commerce v. N.Y. City Dep't of Health and Mental Hygiene*, 2013). The court stated that New York's Board of Health "overstepped the boundaries of its lawfully delegated authority when it promulgated the portion cap rule to curtail the consumption of soda drinks. . . . It therefore violated the state principle of separation of powers" (Barclay, 2013).

That decision was a setback for the city's Board of Health, which had met significant opposition from the food and beverage industry for years as it attempted to change unhealthy food habits through portion-size regulations. Specifically, Bloomberg intended to require food service establishments to cap sugary beverages at 16 ounces. Mayor Bloomberg described the court's decision as only a "temporary setback" and vowed further appeals, especially since more than half of adults in New York City are obese or overweight. Dr. Thomas Farley, New York's Health Commissioner, justified limiting soda consumption on the grounds that although eating 17 teaspoons of sugar at a time is difficult, "it's very easy to drink a 20-ounce soda with 17 teaspoons of sugar" (Barclay, 2013). The legal authority to act is a critical element in the development of any policy proposal. Examining the status of settled law is an important step if one wants to minimize expensive legal challenges and costly delays in the implementation of a policy.

Due to the existence of Dillon's Rule (local government's power is derived from the state's sovereignty and not from its electorate), local governments have very limited powers of their own (National League of Cities, 2013). Local governments may have to seek state authority or permission in order to act. State laws may indeed prohibit local governments from acting in certain areas in order to create statewide uniformity. This is sometimes done by specific state statute in order to have uniformity throughout the state, or it might be due merely to a lack of authorizing legislation for local governments to act in a specific area. Ultimately, the courts will decide legal authority to act based on precedent and constitutionality.

Different sections of government have different inherent powers. It is important to recognize these differences. For example, the executive branch has the ability to issue or revise "rules and regulations" without having to go through a new legislative process. A governor may or may not have the authority to issue an executive order that will resolve the issue, depending on the powers of government spelled out in law or the state's constitution. An attorney general may file suit against another agency or private sector organizations in order to stimulate action. A legislative committee can use its investigative or oversight powers to force various policy issues onto the executive branch. We will discuss these in greater detail in Chapter 8, on Recommendation and Strategies.

In addition to the legal component, there is also a practical side to solving a social problem. Even if New York City had the legal power to control the size of sugary drinks, there is the practical side as to whether a city ordinance would be effective. Would consumers merely go to a neighboring town to get supersized drinks and skirt the law? New York City has a large population and covers a substantial geographic area. As a result, it might be able to make the case that such a city law could have an impact, even though New Jersey is across the river. However, a small town that might wish to limit the sale of sugary drinks to blunt the obesity epidemic in its children might find its ability to have an impact on obesity quite limited and its negative impact on businesses in the town to be substantial. Children or parents could merely go to the next town to buy what their town prohibits. This is where scale (population and geography) matters in policy.

## MODEL PROGRAMS/POLICIES

The RWJF is but one example of a foundation that has initiated community health initiatives throughout the country. The RWJF has a special focus on childhood obesity. It publishes issue briefs that summarize what has been learned from its multiple initiatives on childhood obesity throughout the country (RWJF, 2012). Most foundations require an evaluation component built into their grants in order to determine what went well and what needed additional effort or modification. Some foundations such as the Kellogg Foundation have more of a geographic orientation. All national foundations establish priorities of interest that might change from year to year or stay relatively stable for a period of years. It is important to research such foundations for examples of their policy-related initiatives. Many of these projects end up being published in peer-reviewed journals (see Breakout Box 3.1), but many do not, and yet are equally insightful and valuable.

## BREAKOUT BOX 3.1

### Obesity Prevention in Early Child Care and Education Settings

Early childhood is a formative period for many important lifestyle behaviors, including diet and physical activity, but little obesity prevention research targeting this age group has been conducted. Early child care and education (ECE) programs are important settings for obesity prevention because child care centers provide care for an estimated 30% to 40% of children under the age of 6 years (Ogden et al., 2012; Singh et al., 2008; Ward, Vaughn, & Story, 2013). Children spend, on average, 30 hours per week in these settings. Thus, ECE settings are a promising avenue for interventions targeting young children (birth to age 5), but the limited research provides limited evidence on which to base policy decisions and practice guidelines to improve healthy eating and physical activity, and ultimately healthy weight development (Ogden et al., 2012).

Systematic reviews of obesity interventions in ECE settings are available, but include only 18 studies that were published in the last decade (Larson, Ward, Neelon, & Story, 2011). Although many of these studies demonstrated positive effects on behaviors, only two out of five studies that assessed weight changes showed positive effects. Two nationally representative studies that have evaluated the nutritional quality of foods offered in child care settings identified concerns relating to the percentage of energy from saturated fat, average sodium levels, and the number of fruit/vegetables items provided by meals and snacks. With respect to physical activity, only 14% of child care centers provided the recommended 120 minutes of active playtime, and one third provided more than 90 minutes. Research suggests that many caregivers may benefit from additional technical assistance and training regarding feeding practices and modeling feeding behavior for children. For example, a recent study found that more than 50% of caregivers received no annual training on nutrition, and only 47% provided nutrition education to children by reading books or playing games with nutrition themes (RWJF, 2012).

Public and private organizations across the nation are working to encourage adoption of policies for ECE programs that promote healthy eating and physical activity. Two of the most significant examples of recent reports are Caring for Our Children's *Preventing Childhood*

*(continued)*

## BREAKOUT BOX 3.1 (*continued*)

*Obesity in Early Child Care and Education Programs* and the Institute of Medicine's (IOM) *Early Childhood Obesity Prevention Policies*, which examine the evidence and provide guidance on obesity prevention policies for young children. For example, the IOM recommends that ECE facilities serve toddlers and preschoolers small, age-appropriate portions and permit children one or more additional servings of foods that are low in fat, sugar, and sodium as needed to meet the caloric needs of the individual child. Additionally, the IOM recommends that formal nutrition information and education programs be conducted at least twice per year under the guidance of a nutritionist/dietician. Head Start facilities are required to provide opportunities for indoor and outdoor active play, adequate space and equipment to promote active play, and opportunities to develop gross and fine motor skills.

In 2011, a panel of experts discussed key issues around measurement of diet and physical activity, policy and environment measurement, intervention approaches, policy research, and capacity development. Following their deliberations, they selected top research priorities for early childhood obesity prevention. The highest-rated priority issues included assessment of the quality of children's meals and snacks, use of financial incentives, interventions that include health care providers, the role of screen time, and need for multilevel interventions. The expert panel highlighted the difficulties in measuring policy and environmental change. Instruments like the Environment and Policy Assessment and Observation (EPAO; Ward et al., 2008) and the Wellness Child Care Assessment Tool (WellCCAT; Falbe et al., 2011) have established reliability and validity, but they require intensive training and access to materials. Minority populations, including African Americans, American Indians, and Hispanics, suffer disproportionately high rates of obesity and are important targets for future ECE interventions; however, interventions must be culturally tailored to meet the needs of these populations. Recent interdisciplinary studies have shown promising results in this regard (Hollar et al., 2010).

The panel stated that future policy research in the ECE setting would benefit from consensus that traditional study designs and outcome measures may not be appropriate for this age group and setting. For example, randomized trials are often not ethical or feasible in this setting, and high turnover rates of children in ECE can make the

(*continued*)

**BREAKOUT BOX 3.1 (*continued*)**

traditional cohort design impractical. Cost-effectiveness information is also needed. Another recommendation was to use child care programs as access points to help create linkages to families, pediatricians, and other sources of support for obesity prevention. This type of coordination is recommended in the Affordable Care Act as part of the National Prevention Strategy ("National Prevention Council," 2013).

**Thought Questions**

As a policy analyst, how might you help a policy maker to better understand:

1. The current state of the evidence in ECE settings
2. Why preventing obesity in ECE settings is important
3. Why policy and environmental change in these settings are difficult to measure and evaluate

There are also a number of state/community foundations (many financed by the sale of nonprofit health care organizations to for-profit, investor-owned organizations) that serve as a source of program experimentation at the state/local level. These are generally less well known but may be particularly important because they fund local policy initiatives and therefore have credibility as homegrown policy responses that are compatible with the local political culture, political structure, political process, demographics, laws, and so on. Consequently, these experiments may be more politically acceptable to policy makers within that state. Nonprofit organizations such as the American Heart Association publish useful policy examples (Lintelman, 2013). You need to look at the multiple nonprofit associations in that geopolitical unit that are oriented on the issue that you have chosen.

One of the common policy problems that must be addressed is the notion of uniqueness. Every state and local community likes to think that it is unique and that what works in a neighboring state or one across the country cannot possibly work in its unique community. Consequently, the more similar the setting of a policy initiative, the easier it might be to overcome community opposition based on the uniqueness argument. Neighbors, however, can also be rivals. Some states may disparage policy initiatives in those neighboring states, even though those states are more alike than others. If you use policies from another political jurisdiction, you need to pick comparative examples very carefully and understand the political culture, structure, and process of your comparative geopolitical unit as well as that of your own.

## RELATIONSHIPS TO OTHER POLICY ISSUES

Policy issues cannot be thought of in terms of discrete boxes. Due to the nature of policy, policies in one area by their very nature entangle other policies. Transportation policy impacts all types of commercial and social relationships, including health. A highway cutting through a city can separate populations, leading to demographic isolation, racial segregation, and loss of services. This has consequences for obesity. The growth of suburbia in the United States is generally attributed to the development of the interstate highway system and banking policies that encouraged single-home housing. That, in turn, has resulted in an automobile-oriented focus that is related to obesity problems. The need to drive for goods and services, the lack of sidewalks, and the lack of frequently scheduled mass transit due to a disperse population complicate the issue of obesity. The obesity problem cannot be solved without involving many different policy areas and different sectors of government. It is this intersection of public policies that is important to recognize as one develops any particular policy. To what extent will your policy proposal be made ineffective due to existing policies in transportation, zoning, education, and so forth?

As described in Chapter 1, there is a growing international movement to consider "health in all policies" (HiAP; Collins & Koplan, 2009; "Healthy Places," 2013; Rajotte, Ross, Ekechi, & Cadet, 2011; World Health Organization, 2010). For example, in the United States, the state of California recently established an Executive Order on HiAP. California's HiAP Task Force, established in 2010 by Executive Order S-04-10, is made up of 19 different state agencies, departments, and offices. This provides a venue for state agencies and departments to advance multiple goals in order to support healthier and more sustainable community environments (California Executive Order No. S-04-10, 2010; The Strategic Growth Council, 2013a). The Task Force was charged with identifying

priority programs, policies, and strategies to improve the health of Cal-
ifornians while advancing the goals of improving air and water quality, protecting natural resources and agricultural lands, increasing the
availability of affordable housing, improving infrastructure systems,
promoting public health, planning sustainable communities, and meeting the climate change goals. (The Strategic Growth Council, 2013b)

Using the HiAP lens harnesses the power that different government agencies and departments can bring through their diverse areas of expertise.
They can identify co-benefits and can bring people from different sectors
together to address complex social and environmental issues.

For obesity policy, one would need to examine agricultural policies,
food processing policies, food labeling policies, transportation policies,
community development policies, educational policies, and recreation
policies, among others that play a role in solving the obesity problem for
children. In addition, addressing obesity has health insurance and medical
cost implications, national defense implications, economic implications,
Medicare implications, and so forth. Consequently, any policy is affected
by other policies and in turn affects other policies. That, of course, is what
makes the development of policy so complex.

One area that is becoming increasingly important for obesity is the
built environment. The presence of sidewalks, parks, safe walking routes,
and access to public transportation are among many built environment
factors that influence population levels of physical activity (Aytur, Rodriguez, Evenson, Catellier, & Rosamond, 2007). The natural environment
(cold weather) has its own implications for obesity. However, policy decisions that shape the built environment can overcome some of the problems associated with the natural environment. For example, free outdoor
community skating rinks may build social capital as well as provide
exercise during the winter months. The existence of "food deserts" (the
lack of grocery stores providing inexpensive fresh food) in inner cities
can be overcome with thoughtful zoning and community development
grants. These policy areas need to be explored, since they provide useful
means of attacking the problem in a multifaceted manner. Innovation
generally comes from recognizing the synergy between policy areas as
well as recognizing unintended consequences and transforming them
into intended consequences (e.g., to use existing zoning laws to intentionally eliminate food deserts). The synergy between policy areas has

its downsides. If everything is connected to everything, one can become overwhelmed with the potential harmful impacts and become paralyzed due to an inability to take everything into account. This also creates difficulties in terms of evaluating policies and demonstrating a significant impact of policies, because so many factors are involved (see Breakout Box 3.1). This can lead to policy stalemate, which often leads to deference to the status quo. At some point, one has to draw the line and say that we have taken into account what we currently perceive are the major policy interactions. If there are others, we will deal with them at a later time.

It is also critical to realize that policies have both intended and unintended outcomes (those not generally anticipated). Unintended consequences can be both positive and negative. There may be some unexpected positive or unexpected negative results of the policy/program. If one is focusing on the implications of an education policy (lengthening the school day for increased exercise), one may forget to examine the unintended consequences of that policy on family dynamics and the need for parents to arrange for transportation or alter work schedules. In addition, some policies will have positive impacts for some groups of people and negative consequences for others. Are you sure of who is going to benefit and who is going to be disadvantaged by the proposed policy?

## POLICY AGENDA

One of the issues that you need to address in this section of your policy analysis is why this issue should reach the policy agenda at this particular time. As indicated previously, there are multiple problems to be solved with only limited time and resources available. Why has this issue emerged at the present time? If it is an issue that has been unsuccessfully dealt with on other occasions, why is now the time to act? Has the nature of the problem grown in scale? Have the political dynamics changed to alter the prospect for successful resolution? This is sometimes referred to as the existence of political will or expediency. Sometimes the answer is that an incident (a tragedy or personal experience) has occurred that has generated public interest. For example, an automobile accident killing a young bicyclist might generate public support for finally dealing with the issue of having bicycle paths that are separated from vehicle traffic. A new strain of a deadly virus might increase sensitivity to public hygiene. The death of a local celebrity due to malpractice might create a firestorm about hospital safety. The major question to answer is, why now? What has changed in the policy environment to place this higher on the policy agenda?

These policy triggers can provide a narrow window of opportunity for a policy proposal to gain traction. However, the window of opportunity can close very quickly. Powerful stakeholders may begin to lobby against any changes in policy, and public attention might go to the next big event. As a result, policy makers need to be ready to take advantage of the opportunity before the policy window closes. This notion was first posited by noted political scientist John Kingdon in his 1984 book in which he proposes a policy model based upon the alignment of three "streams": the problem, the policy, and the politics (Kingdon, 2010). He argues that the convergence of these three streams opens a window of opportunity for change. Laws are frequently named after an individual who has suffered as a consequence of the lack of legislation. Building on a tragic incident, policy is frequently introduced to respond to the emotions of the day.

Reports from the CDC can describe the extent of a health problem, but the general public does not usually read these reports, and such data lack the personal face to make them meaningful to policy makers and voters. Statistical deaths (the number per 100,000) are generally not very persuasive. However, one of the most effective visuals of the obesity epidemic has been the series of CDC maps showing the percentage of obese persons, state by state, over time for adults and youth (Centers for Disease Control and Prevention, 2013g; National Resource Center for Paraprofessionals, 2011). Visually, they make a very strong statement as states turn different colors and as old colors disappear and new colors are added as the progression of the obesity epidemic continues. However, it is generally the human face of the problem that makes the problem or the policy much more meaningful to policy makers and voters. In politics, the number of dead or diseased may have less significance than the death of one publicized individual in a local community.

What is it about this period of time that allows you to think this issue is ripe to be addressed now rather than next year or the following year? Has there been a significant shift of public opinion? Has there been an incident that raises the issue's salience to lawmakers or the public? Sometimes the political clock is a determining factor. If the policy is potentially controversial, it may be too close to an election to tackle the problem and make political enemies. That same legislation might be more politically viable right after an election in order to allow time to pass and emotions to cool before the next election. An election that results in the naming of a new chair of an important legislative committee that has blocked previous legislation or the turnover of the party in control of the legislature may be the trigger for promising policy activity. Some state legislatures create a biennial budget and leave general legislation to the second session. The basic issue here is to address the question, why now?

Policy makers do not always think their policy proposal is ready to pass. Sometimes a legislator may introduce a piece of legislation knowing that it will not pass, but hoping that it will stimulate establishing a commission or a special committee report that will stimulate further interest in the issue. The introduction of a policy may be just an educational effort to get other policy makers thinking about the issue and thinking about alternative solutions. Policy makers might introduce an idea as a trial balloon, expecting that it will probably be shot down but nevertheless testing the water for political acceptability. Such trial balloons are useful in finding out where major opposition groups might be or what issues might need to be overcome in order to eventually get legislation passed. In addition, there are legislators who feel that although there is no possibility for policy action, the issue is so important to them that it must remain on the political agenda. If there is no bill, there will be no action. A bill might serve as a placeholder until the time when the proposal may be received more positively. The political environment can suddenly change; if a proposed policy/program is readily available to be submitted, it can respond to that sudden window of opportunity.

The policy agenda is full of competing and complementary policy options. Providing a broad context of the importance of your policy within this agenda provides an important context for your policy makers.

## SUMMARY

This section of the policy analysis is focused on providing a context for the policy proposal that will eventually be recommended. It provides the basis for stating that this particular policy is an incremental approach to what has occurred in the past or offers a different approach than in the past. You will need to discuss the history of past policy actions. You will need to address whether a public policy is the appropriate vehicle to address the problem. This section gives you the opportunity to explore the ways other political jurisdictions have dealt with the same issue. It provides an opportunity to explain the legal and practical ability of a particular level of government to deal with the issue. It provides an opportunity to explain how political conditions are now ripe for enacting a policy addressing this issue, and, as a result, why it is politically expedient to use valuable resources (staff time, political favors, and money) now, when it was not the case earlier. This section will have major implications in the development of strategies that will be discussed in the last chapter of this text.

---

### SOME THINGS TO REMEMBER

- This section should provide a broad context of the policy issue.
- Does this issue need to be addressed by "big P" (public policy) or should it be addressed by "little p" (organizational policy)?
- Policy issues tend to recycle. Therefore, research how the issue has been treated in the past in the same or a different geopolitical unit.
- Seek out sources that provide a context of the historical treatment of the issue. Examine past legislative efforts to address the issue.
- Provide a rationale for why your policy issue is so significant that it should be on the active political agenda for the expenditure of political capital.
- Be prepared to respond to a policy trigger that can jump your policy onto the political agenda for action.
- Look for examples that can add a human element to population data.
- Provide evidence as to the legal and practical authority of a political jurisdiction to address the problem. With weak legal authority, your policy proposal will be in expensive legal trouble no matter how noble it might be.
- Even with the legal authority to act, is the policy practical in scale and geography to be able to address the issue?
- Provide examples of model legislation or model programs that have been tried in other political jurisdictions. Be careful of the argument of geopolitical uniqueness.

## KEY WORDS

Incrementalism

Intended consequences

Unintended consequences

Type 1 evidence

Legal authority

Practicality

Built environment

Health in all policies (HiAP)

Model programs

Policy agenda

Policy triggers

Policy significance

# Four

# Statement of Policy Issue

The previous section of your policy analysis framework is meant to be fairly general and to provide background material for a macro understanding of the issue and the legal authority and practical considerations to act. In contrast, this section of your analysis is very specific and can be relatively brief. However, this section requires a great deal of thoughtful preparation. It is here that you must narrow the scope of the analysis to one aspect of the policy issue that is going to be addressed, from the general issue of obesity to a specific aspect of it.

## POLICY ISSUE STATEMENT

It is unlikely that any policy is going to address the full scope of the obesity issue, the background portion of the analysis has already explained the complexity of the obesity issue and how it is interwoven with other policy areas. Consequently, although the analysis to date has been on the issue of obesity in general, it is in this section that you will make very explicit choices. For example, you might focus your policy on obesity in children, obesity in adults, or physical activity as opposed to nutrition. This explicit statement of the policy issue is going to provide the focus for the rest of the analysis.

In this section you need to be thoughtful and selective. You might want to focus on the part of the obesity problem that has the greatest impact on health—reducing diabetes, heart disease, or other diseases. Alternatively, you might want to focus on that part of the obesity problem that has the greatest impact on quality of life. You might want to focus on the part of the obesity issue that has the greatest impact on the cost of medical care in the public sector. You might want to focus on the part of the obesity issue that is the most practical or the easiest to gain a political coalition for policy adoption. You might want to focus on a particular age group, such as adolescents. You might want to examine a particularly innovative program that you have learned about or that has gained wide popularity in the press. You might want to pursue obesity from the perspective of the "built environment." You might want to think of the obesity problem as an incremental problem, building your initiative on top of another previously enacted policy. You might want to pursue the obesity issue from a personal interest perspective, for example, bicycle riding, hiking, slow food, or surgical procedures. As explained in the previous section, you might take advantage of a policy trigger that has pushed a specific aspect of the obesity issue higher on the political agenda. For example, although the obesity issue is not generally triggered by a single event, a bicycle accident may be the trigger for a community to invest in safe bicycle lanes and thus may have an indirect impact on obesity in a particular community. All of these perspectives are legitimate and many may be interconnected; the problem is you must choose among these and other aspects of the obesity problem.

Although the above implies wide-open possibilities for focusing the issue to a more specific one, you are likely to be constrained by the person or agency for whom this policy analysis is being written. The legislator who you are working for may have a special interest in childhood obesity or the agency that you work for may be focused on the implications of obesity and insurance coverage. It is also important to remember that there may be other people in the health care arena with areas of knowledge and expertise that can assist you in focusing on a particular topic that is ripe for policy action (see Breakout Box 4.1). Congressional staffers, organizationally based policy persons, lobbyists, and others might have valuable insights and information that can assist you in crafting a statement of your particular policy issue.

In this section you need to clarify the primary area of focus for your policy initiative. There are likely to be fewer potential political opponents if you narrow the scope of the policy to a small-scale initiative. On the other hand, the narrower the policy, the less impact the policy is likely to have on "the obesity epidemic" as a whole. It is important to remember here that there is no "right" answer, but still you must make choices. In Breakout Box 4.1, notice how a broad coalition of public health, environmental, education, and farming interests in Washington State worked together to pass the Local Farms–Healthy Kids (LFHK) Act in 2008. Through their collaborative efforts, they helped the state legislature to recognize several issues that were of importance to various interest groups across the state. These issues are reflected in the language of the bill (see Breakout Box 4.1) and contributed to its adoption.

## BREAKOUT BOX 4.1

### The Washington State "Local Farms–Healthy Kids" Act: Policy Issue Statement (State Level)

In 2008, Washington State enacted the "Local Farms–Healthy Kids Act" (LFHK; SSB 6483; Washington State Legislature, 2008) in order to increase access to healthy foods and expand markets for local agricultural products (Washington Environmental Council, 2013; Washington State Department of Health, 2013). Among its many provisions, LFHK established a state Farm to School Program within the Washington State Department of Agriculture to increase procurement of locally grown foods by connecting schools with farmers and providing technical assistance. Funds were appropriated to implement the legislation, including funding to establish a grants program to allow schools to purchase nutritious, locally produced snacks. Additionally, the Act expanded funding for the federal Supplemental Nutrition Program for Women, Infants, and Children (WIC) and Seniors Farmers Market Nutrition Programs, and created pilot projects for food banks to purchase fresh food directly from Washington farms. Programs included in the legislation aimed to make it easier for low-income families to obtain Washington-grown food. A Farmers Market Technology Improvement Pilot Program also enabled farmers markets to accept

*(continued)*

## BREAKOUT BOX 4.1 (*continued*)

electronic payment cards, including electronic benefits transfers (EBTs) to increase usage of food stamp benefits at farmers markets.

LFHK established Washington State as a national leader in promoting policies to provide healthy, locally grown food to people who need it most. A broad coalition of environmental, farming, education, and public health interests worked together to push the legislation through (Johnson et al., 2013). Through their collaborative efforts, they helped the state legislature to recognize the following principles, which became the foundation of the policy issue statement:

1. "The legislature recognizes that the benefits of local food production include: stewardship of working agricultural lands; direct and indirect jobs in agricultural production, food processing, tourism, and support industries; energy conservation and greenhouse gas reductions; and increased food security through access to locally grown foods.

2. The legislature finds there is a direct correlation between adequate nutrition and a child's development and school performance. Children who are hungry or malnourished are at risk of lower achievement in school.

3. The legislature further finds that adequate nutrition is also necessary for the physical health of adults, and that some communities have limited access to healthy fruits and vegetables and quality meat and dairy products, a lack of which may lead to high rates of diet-related diseases.

4. The legislature believes that expanding market opportunities for Washington farmers will preserve and strengthen local food production and increase the already significant contribution that agriculture makes to the state and local economies.

5. The legislature finds that the state's existing procurement requirements and practices may inhibit the purchase of locally produced food.

6. The legislature intends that the Local Farms–Healthy Kids Act strengthen the connections between the state's agricultural industry and the state's food procurement procedures in order to expand local agricultural markets, improve the nutrition of children and other at-risk consumers, and have a positive impact on the environment."

You can read the full case study about LFHK in Johnson et al. (2013).

It is important to realize that even large, comprehensive policy proposals do not generally address the entire policy issue. In the LFHK Act, the focus was primarily on children's health and nutrition, although the bill does contain provisions for other demographic groups. To use a national example, the recent effort focusing on "health care reform" (e.g., the Affordable Care Act [ACA]) focuses mainly on access to insurance by those currently uninsured, rather than actually reforming the medical care system regarding effectiveness, quality, or cost. Although the ACA does touch on some of these other aspects of reform, it is basically an insurance reform initiative. The authors of the ACA had to make conscious choices about which elements of the medical care system they wanted to change or could change and which elements they would not address directly in that particular proposal.

The concept of incrementalism implies that one would tend to attack a portion of the problem as a means of gaining political support and avoiding wholesale opposition to a policy by stakeholders favoring the status quo. We will address the strengths and weaknesses of incrementalism when we discuss the systematic review of policy options in Chapter 7. However, you may wish to push for a nonincremental, broader policy proposal. That choice increases the risk of not getting the proposal enacted. This is generally a trade-off between getting something accomplished or holding out for a more comprehensive policy or ideologically pure proposal. Narrowing the focus of the policy issue is a critical and potentially controversial element of your analysis. Some will say that you have ignored the real problem of obesity in diabetics or the elderly. Others will insist that cost is the main issue. It is in this section of the analysis that you will consciously decide not to address certain aspects of the obesity problem even though you agree that they are important. You may also very well have to expand or further contract the scope of your policy proposal later in the political process in order to gain political support for its adoption. We will discuss this further in the book when we describe various strategies. At this point, you need to focus on a particular aspect of the obesity issue. There may be other obesity legislative proposals competing with yours. To what extent can these proposals be combined? To what extent is the scope of your proposal superior to others?

This section of the analysis can be relatively brief. One can readily make a case that attacking childhood obesity is a priority as the evidence from your policy background section indicated that childhood obesity tends to track to adult obesity, and that the political system has more control over the behavior of children than it does for adults. Alternatively, one might argue that supporting access to healthy foods for the entire population (as shown in the Washington State example) or providing safe places for physical activity will have a greater impact on the overall obesity epidemic. The literature discussion in the policy background section needs to support your narrowing of the policy issue. After selecting this particular focus, you may have to revisit your policy background section to add additional general information on the specific topic that you have chosen.

Your literature section has provided evidence that supports the idea that focusing on childhood obesity would have a major impact on the health status of the population, especially as it matures. However, such an argument tends to imply that the impact of such a policy or program might not occur for 10 or 15 years, when many of the politicians will no longer be around to reap the political rewards (gain political capital) from this policy initiative. Instead, there will be immediate increases in public costs (and the potential loss of voter support/political capital) for the hope of future rewards (voter support and a healthier population). The fact that childhood obesity also increases the onset of related childhood diseases, such as type II diabetes, may have more immediate epidemiological and political returns. Notice that there are two types of returns here in terms of your potential policy; one includes the returns of solving the problem (reducing childhood obesity and the incidence of diabetes in children and adults), and the other is a political return for the policy maker (political capital). These political capital returns can be positive and/or negative.

Sometimes a program that is the most effective for solving the problem is politically inexpedient. Sometimes what is politically expedient is only marginally effective in addressing the policy issue. Helping children tends to be politically popular. In this section you are making conscious decisions as to which areas will be addressed and which shall be ignored or dealt with at a later date.

If you decide to focus on one specific segment of the population, this does not mean that you are ignoring related policy areas. This is where information from the previous section on the policy background might re-emerge. Knowing the linkages and the interwoven nature of the issue will help you as you move forward and potentially engage partners from multiple policy areas, such as agriculture, transportation, zoning, and food protection. At this point, however, the initial statement of the policy issue is your current best estimate at suggesting the appropriate scope of your policy effort.

## WHAT DOES A POLICY ISSUE STATEMENT LOOK LIKE?

As indicated previously, this section must have a precisely worded statement that provides two important pieces of information. Although it can be physically incorporated in the policy background section of your analysis, it is best for it to stand alone so that it is clearly visible and can be found easily in skimming back through the analysis. One could place this statement in a box, such as in Breakout Box 4.2, or make it a separate section of the analysis depending on the level of support that you wish to provide for the narrowing scope of your policy proposal.

First, it should concisely describe the substantive focus of the policy initiative with a brief rationale as to why this is the focus. Second, it also needs to provide a description of the political unit or units that ought to be addressing the issue. The political unit can be the United States, a particular state, a county within a state, or a municipality/political decision-making body within a particular area (e.g., a local school board). You need to make a choice here, because the politics and the legal authority of the level of government will be important in the evolution of the policy proposal.

The statement needs to be brief in order to bring focus to the rest of the analysis. After this section, there can be no doubt as to what your focus will be. How the issue will be addressed is still yet to be decided. However, this statement will have major implications for all the subsequent sections, such as developing the criteria for success, the systematic review of policy options, and framing of the issue in the recommendation and strategy section of your analysis. Although this might be the shortest section, it is perhaps the most critical step in the process.

Let us assume that the policy issue you wish to address is "reducing childhood obesity in the United States" (see Breakout Box 4.2 for an example of a policy statement). Notice that you have a particular aspect of the obesity problem (children) as well as a geopolitical area (United States). You could narrow this further by stating that the target population is school-aged children or only elementary school-aged children. You could have narrowed the geographical scope to a particular state, county, or local unit of government. In focusing on childhood obesity in the United States, you could have chosen not to focus on a particular school district and its governing board or a state board of education. Instead, you have broadened the geopolitical focus to include the entire country. By selecting the United States, you have consciously taken a bigger geopolitical unit in order to have a potentially greater impact on the problem of obesity in the nation. Because the federal government does not have direct control of school-aged children, you have also complicated the mechanisms by which the policy can be implemented due to the lack of direct federal legal authority to act. Federal action is likely to rely on voluntary state participation, with substantial funding being provided by the federal government to support a country-wide initiative. These are all trade-offs that you have consciously made.

Your policy statement does not diminish the importance of other aspects of the obesity problem (adults or the elderly) or other geopolitical points of focus (the city or the local school district); you have merely directed this proposal to a specific policy and geographic area. You might address other areas of the obesity problem later. As indicated previously, the policy makers for whom you are writing this analysis may actually determine or heavily influence the geopolitical context. For example, United States Senators are not generally involved in their own state or local policy efforts; they focus on national legislation. This does not mean that federal legislation will not involve a state or a local school district, as much federal legislation uses the federal government's taxing/grant-making powers (categorical or block grants) to stimulate state and local government policy by providing money to incentivize a national response to a problem at the local or state level. These federal grants generally come with various strings attached to get states to meet federal objectives. Federal block grants to states tend to provide more state control over expenditures than do categorical grants for specific federal programs. The selection of a geopolitical unit in this policy analysis merely means that for your policy proposal the authorizing legislation will be at the federal level as opposed to the state or school-board level. What policy is going to be proposed and how it is to be implemented has yet to be decided; it may indeed involve state or local action. It is also important to remember both the legal and practical limitations of a geopolitical unit to act.

The issue of federal leverage over grants to states has become more complicated since the U.S. Supreme Court (USSC) decision in *National Federation of Independent Business et al. v. Sebelius, Secretary of Health and Human Services, et al.* (2012), in which the majority opinion indicated that states could not be forced to adopt the Medicaid requirements of the ACA legislation under penalty of losing all their federal Medicaid monies. This allows states the ability to refuse to participate in the ACA Medicaid expansion without the threat of losing federal money for the other parts of their Medicaid program. Although the Court has long recognized the ability of the federal government to put restrictions on the use of federal money by state and local governments, including the threat of the withdrawal of funds, the Court for the first time decided that the threat of losing all Medicaid money crossed the line in terms of a federal "compulsion" of the states to adopt the ACA Medicaid expansion. However, the Court refused to provide any criteria as to how to determine when the line of "compulsion" had been crossed. The issue of when federal requirements become "compulsive" is a whole new arena of policy and court battles yet to be fought, and one you may potentially have to deal with when considering legal authority in future analyses.

The political climate and political culture of the geopolitical unit is also something to consider. For example, elections and political leaders make a difference in terms of the acceptability of various policy initiatives. Think of the more recent convention of categorizing states as either "red" (Republican) or "blue" (Democratic) states. Specific policy proposals will be more viable in some areas than others. Understanding the political climate of the country, a state, or region is important in deciding which geopolitical unit you feel is most conducive to your policy initiative.

To provide you with an example, we present a sample policy issue statement in Breakout Box 4.2. Note that this is only one of many that you could have derived for obesity.

## BREAKOUT BOX 4.2

### Policy Issue Statement Example (National Level)

Childhood obesity is a serious public health concern in the United States. Currently, over 30% of children in the United States are considered overweight or obese (Ogden, Curtin, Lamb, & Flegal, 2010). Although recent reports suggest that the obesity epidemic is slowing slightly in 19 states, particularly among low-income preschoolers, obesity remains a serious public health concern for the nation (Robert Wood Johnson Foundation, 2013c; Whiteman, 2013). The Healthy People 2020 goal is to reduce childhood obesity by 10% compared to the 2005 to 2008 rates ("Healthy People 2020," 2013a; Wang, Orleans, & Gortmaker, 2012). However, obesity rates increased or remained the same in more than half of the states.

Obese children are at a much greater risk of chronic disease and cognitive disorders than children of normal weight, resulting in higher care costs (Tresandre & Chatterjee, 2009). Because childhood obesity is highly correlated with adult obesity, comprehensive national interventions are necessary to address the epidemic of childhood obesity.

### Thought Questions

1. After reading Breakout Boxes 4.1 and 4.2, compare and contrast the different issues that are reflected in the hypothetical national policy issue statement on obesity versus the excerpt from the "Local Farms–Healthy Kids" (LFHK) bill in Washington State.
2. Describe at least three interest groups whose issues are reflected in Washington's bill. In what ways do you think the relative importance and influence of these interest groups might change at the federal level compared to Washington State? How might they differ in your state compared to Washington State?
3. Which of the Washington State LFHK Act's provisions do you think might pose difficulties in implementation over time? What types of barriers may be encountered?

## SUMMARY

The important aspect for this section is to provide focus to your policy initiative. First, you need to decide what part of the larger issue of the obesity problem you intend to address. This might be a result of its importance to the overall problem of obesity, your concern for a particular subpopulation, the desire to eliminate health disparities, or some other consideration. In addition, you needed to select a particular geopolitical/political unit for addressing the issue. This involves weighing the legal authority, the geographic area of the political unit, as well as the political climate and culture. The next sections of your policy analysis will all be predicated on this clear and concise statement of the specific policy issue.

## SOME THINGS TO REMEMBER

- In this section you will narrow the focus from the larger issue you have chosen to something more specific. This is not to imply that other aspects of the issue are not equally important. It is merely that for this particular policy initiative you are going to focus on a particular aspect of it.
- The statement will also define the geopolitical unit that will be authorizing your policy proposal. Implementation of the policy/program is a separate issue, often involving a different set of policy participants.
- The policy issue statement will entail multiple conscious trade-offs.
- The policy statement is a relatively brief statement that stands out for easy reference.

## KEY WORDS

Policy issue statement

Incrementalism

Interest groups

Political capital

Policy scope

Categorical grants

Block grants

Geopolitical unit

Political climate

# Five

# Normative Values and Stakeholder Analysis

In this policy analysis framework we will treat normative analysis and stakeholder analysis together because they are so tightly linked. However, one could also address them separately when writing the policy analysis.

## THE ROLE OF VALUES

Having created a statement of the policy issue focusing on childhood obesity in the United States, you now need to do a normative analysis. David Easton developed one of the most often-used definitions of politics in his seminal work, *A Framework for Political Analysis*. In that work he describes politics as "the authoritative allocation of values for society" (Easton, 1953, p. 129). Individuals have multiple and conflicting values, and within every culture different individuals will both share values and hold different values. This is especially true of the United States, because we are a nation of immigrants from multiple cultures and different religious traditions. One of the challenges of living in a collective society is to develop a process designed to resolve these conflicts. A society in which all individuals can act solely on their own personal values is anarchy. The political system is the social construct that has been created to establish value priorities that are binding for members of that geopolitical system.

To add to this complexity, any value when maximized will conflict with another value—society may value life but then authorize the taking of life in the name of national defense, national expansion, or antisocial behavior (capital punishment). No right or value is absolute, no matter how much we might like to think that there are absolutes. There are always ifs, ands, and buts. The socially constructed political system is charged with the responsibility of sorting out these value conflicts for society. Incentives are built by the political system to encourage individuals to behave according to those value priorities.

In making these decisions the political system may take the form of a representative democracy, a monarchy, a military dictatorship, or any other form of political structure and decision making, but all political systems perform this necessary function. Certain political decisions regarding these values allow for more or less individual freedom and more or less social control, but at some point some individual freedom is sacrificed for the good of the polity or state. It is not that everyone within that society must hold or agree with these political values of the state (or even its majority). However, the authoritative powers of the state (the police powers of the state) will be used to enforce those decisions. People breaking laws enforcing these value decisions will be fined, imprisoned, or be subject to some other form of state-sanctioned punishment.

For example, in the United States, freedom of speech or freedom of religion does not require anyone to speak out or to have any particular religion. One is free to have no religion or any particular religion. On the other hand, the police powers of the state will be used to punish someone who attempts to take away those freedoms of speech or religion from someone else. However, because no value can be unlimited, the freedoms of religion or speech are not unlimited. Human sacrifice might not be allowed as part of religious freedom, even though previous societies might have endorsed and practiced such behavior. Freedom of speech is generally respected, but as noted by Justice Oliver W. Holmes, Jr., in a unanimous Supreme Court decision, "falsely shouting fire in a crowded theater" is not protected free speech (*Schenck v. United States*, 1919). Those who do will be subject to penalties imposed by the state. The United States values the free-enterprise system of economics, but it also places multiple types of restrictions on behavior that are unacceptable (insider trading,

establishing monopolies, fixing prices, degrading the environment, producing unsafe products, etc.).

These value positions of society change over time and between geopolitical systems. What is of value in one country or state may not necessarily be acceptable practice in another. People in one country may be
shocked at values enforced in another country. It is not that a state's values
are ethical, fair, or even rational; it is merely that the police powers of the
state will be used to enforce them. Violators will be punished by the state.
Human slavery was long protected as a value by federal, state, and local
governments in the United States until a constitutional amendment was
passed. Women were not provided with the same rights as White males.
As a political system we now reject slavery. However, equal rights for
women remains a contentious issue in the United States today. Women are
frequently disadvantaged by law and by practice in the United States. The
failure to adopt the Equal Rights Amendment proposed in 1972 means
that women's rights must be confronted issue by issue and political jurisdiction by political jurisdiction. For example, the enactment of The Lilly
Ledbetter Fair Pay Act of 2009 (Pub.L. 111-2, S. 181) amended the Civil
Rights act of 1964 to promote equal pay regardless of gender, and over-
turned a Supreme Court ruling (*Ledbetter v. Goodyear Tire & Rubber Co.*,
2007) that made it very difficult to claim gender wage discrimination. The
values of society are continually evolving, and one of the major roles of
the political system is to modify or reinforce the existing value system
that is in place.

These values of society may allow individuals freedom to do things, prevent people from doing things, or require them to do things they may not
wish to do on their own volition. For example, the individual mandate under
the Affordable Care Act (ACA) is one such restriction on individual freedom
(requiring the purchase of insurance) because policymakers felt that health
coverage for all is ultimately for the good of society as a whole and necessary for the law to work. There are those that might disagree, but until the
law is changed, it remains the law of the land. Behind every policy is a set of
principles, values, or social understandings that are generally the basis for
support or opposition by various segments of the population. Some policy
issues are more controversial and divisive within society than others.

David Hume attributes social moral conflict to the scarcity of resources
and limited generosity (Gutmann & Thompson, 1996). This points to the

underlying tension of economics and the political system. There is a natural tension between the political system (democracy) and the economic system (capitalism). There is a continual economic struggle between privatization and socialization. The function of the political system is to provide an alternative power system from that of the economic system (Schattschneider, 1960). Scarcity of resources is certainly a major source of disagreement over policies. However, Gutman and Thompson have added two other reasons for social value conflict: the incompatible specific values and an incomplete understanding of values held by various sectors of the community (Gutmann & Thompson, 1996).

Compromising on values is often necessary, even if it is sometimes a difficult political act. Politicians and citizens often support certain "ideologically pure" political values even though they are seldom pure in reality. Fiscal conservatives may bend that principle when, by their votes, money goes to people or organizations within their own district or for projects that align with their other value priorities. Liberals may bend by voting to reduce social services to a disadvantaged population in order to reduce the deficit. As mentioned previously, any value taken to the extreme will be confronted by another value, and some type of value compromise is required.

Therefore, there is a need to resolve value differences in order to maintain social order. Within a representative system of government, it is generally taken for granted that compromise is an accepted norm within the political system. Some within the current political climate have characterized compromise as a weakness. However, the role of compromise has remained important in keeping the political system alive.

> In politics, disagreements often run deep. If they did not, there would be no need for argument. But if they run too deep, there would be no point in argument. Deliberative disagreements lie in the depths between simple misunderstanding and immutable irreconcilability. (Gutmann & Thompson, 1996, p. 16)

When compromise becomes impossible, the political system threatens to rip itself apart in civil strife. The political system attempts to resolve these differences before resorting to armed conflict. As Abraham Kaplan states,

An absolutistic morality cannot take hold on democratic politics, for politics in a democracy is essentially pluralistic, tolerant, compromising. . . . In democratic politics, compromise must be seen as more than an avenue that leads to the good; politically speaking, it is a good itself. . . . The work of the politician, however, is nothing but compromise; that is it means to say that politics is that art of the practical. (Kaplan, 1963, pp. 50–51)

Gutmann and Thompson (1996) make the case for deliberative democracy, stating that, "When democratic citizens morally disagree about public policy, what should they do? They should deliberate with one another, seeking moral agreement when they can, and maintaining mutual respect when they cannot" (p. 346). Although deliberative democracy is frequently discussed theoretically, the degree to which it is practiced has become a matter of debate. For example, local municipal planning processes (determining where new urban development and infrastructure will occur) generally have a "public participation" process, during which the public is supposed to have a right to comment and participate in the process.

In practice, the nature of "participation" can range from systematic exclusion of certain groups by more organized, powerful groups to token participation (e.g., one town meeting held at a time when many residents cannot attend), to extensive efforts to engage with different community groups (including vulnerable populations; Arnstein, 1969; Aytur, Rodriguez, Evenson, Catellier, & Rosamond, 2008; Day, 2006). The issue of freedom of speech and limitations on political campaign spending culminating in the U.S. Supreme Court decision of *Citizens United v. Federal Election Commission* is a debate as to how to best maintain a deliberative democracy (*Citizens United v. Federal Election Commission*, 2010).

As indicated above, every policy has at its core a set of principles or values that are important to understand in order to judge the political acceptability of that particular policy. By being as clear as possible about the underlying values of a given program/policy, you can begin to understand the potential division that the policy represents. This understanding of the underlying normative values will also help you to define the various stakeholders that will be critical as you move through the policy process (Clark, 2002). Before focusing on the issue of childhood obesity, it might be useful to list some general values that are important for multiple policy issues. Some of these (in no particular order) might include:

- Physical safety
- Individual freedom
- Religious freedom
- Community development
- Equity
- Equality
- Efficiency
- Limited government
- Family
- Child development
- Reducing social and/or economic disparities
- Education
- Free enterprise
- Health security
- Privacy
- Healthy communities
- Sustainability

You could add to this list of values. All of these values and many others may be held by various segments of the geopolitical system and at various levels of intensity. There are periods in the life of a geopolitical system when one value may become more dominant than others. For example, one can point to the al-Qaeda attack on 9/11 as a period in time when U.S. citizens and politicians were willing to sacrifice individual privacy for national security. Today there is some reordering of the worth of these two very different values. This value conflict was and remains debated regarding a number of policy issues relative to airport security, video cameras in public and private spaces, and monitoring of the Internet and other electronic media, among others. Where does the balance lie between safety and individual rights? Situations can change, and so does society's perception of where that balance between various values lies.

A classic text in health policy by the economist Victor Fuchs describes the dilemma in the conflict between individual freedom and individual responsibility in relation to health (Fuchs, 1998). He presents this dilemma by using a parallel between being in a jungle in which there is the survival of the fittest versus being in a zoo in which animals are artificially protected from environmental factors for preservation. Societies and political systems try to place themselves along this continuum regarding peoples' freedom. For example, some geopolitical units might believe that individuals are responsible for their own health, whereas another might believe that individuals are not equally able to do so on their own and thus might need assistance from society to attain a healthy life. Consequently, we have societies providing different levels of public health and laws assisting/guaranteeing some level of access to medical care. The political fight over the ACA is one of values and not insurance exchanges; that is the reason the battle over ACA remains so contentious.

Every policy has at its core a set of values or principles that it is attempting to reinforce or alter. We will briefly discuss some of the values surrounding the issue of childhood obesity. At first glance, it would appear that confronting the problem of childhood obesity is a public good that everyone would favor. Children are highly valued. Children should be healthy in order to achieve their human potential. Children are generally given heightened societal protection due to their vulnerability and dependency. Children are generally seen as "innocents" who are not able to make informed decisions regarding their own well-being until they become "adults." For these reasons and others, policies protecting children are generally regarded favorably.

However, one of the major conflicting values regarding childhood obesity is where the line is drawn between parental authority and social authority. Parental authority is given a great deal of leeway in the United States. Various laws protect the rights of parents to control the behavior and activities or their own children. However, parental authority is not absolute; policies promoting child welfare include protection of children from physical abuse, unsafe homes, underage employment, and other activities defined by society as being harmful to children. Where is the line between parental authority and childhood obesity? Parents can be very protective of their ability to raise their child as they see fit. It is in society's interest to have healthy children. For example, healthy children need less medical care (e.g., Medicaid) and are more likely to develop into productive members of society. Where do society's interests come into play with obesity?

To begin to understand these value conflicts is to begin to understand where opposition to obesity policy may emerge. Where does society start to change a child's behavior in order to reduce the obesity epidemic in the United States? Parents might resist being told what their children can eat or how often they must exercise. On the other hand, eating healthfully and being physically active have been shown to also influence other positive outcomes for society, such as educational achievement. Overcoming or accommodating potential opposition is often critical in terms of developing a policy that has the sufficient political support for its passage, acceptance, and enforcement. In Chapter 4 we introduced the "Local Farms–Healthy Kids" (LFHK) Act that was passed in Washington State in 2008. In Breakout Box 5.1, we step back to examine the policy development process. Specifically, how did various stakeholders come together to pass the legislation? In Breakout Box 5.2, we examine another local policy, the menulabeling regulations in Seattle/King County, to compare and contrast the stakeholder interests and advocacy groups involved. In each case, a diverse group of stakeholders came together as allies. Values and goals had to be clarified, and compromises had to be forged. Breakout Box 5.3 highlights a federal regulation, the United States Department of Agriculture (USDA) Smart Snacks in School rule. Once again, pay attention to the inherent value conflicts, the compromises that are reflected in the policy, and the way that scientific information can be used to bridge barriers.

## BREAKOUT BOX 5.1

### "Local Farms–Healthy Kids" Policy Development in Washington State

The "Local Farms–Healthy Kids" (LFHK) policy development process was especially noteworthy because only 9 months elapsed from the first discussion of the idea to the LFHK bill's passage (Johnson et al., 2013). A broad coalition of public health, environmental, farming, and education interests formed a coalition to push the legislation through. The process began when a statewide antipoverty advocacy group convened the first meeting in July 2007 to discuss ways of supporting farm-to-food bank programs. The diverse group of attendees represented advocacy

*(continued)*

## BREAKOUT BOX 5.1 (*continued*)

groups, a social service organization, and a large metropolitan health department. As dialogue progressed, the group's focus broadened beyond food banks to bringing local food to institutions, particularly schools. At a second meeting, the group solidified its focus on farm-to-school efforts. The policy director of the Washington Environmental Council (WEC) volunteered to present the issue to the Environmental Priorities Coalition (EPC), a coalition of leading environmental advocacy organizations in the state, for consideration as one of their priority issues for the state's upcoming legislative session.

Because the WEC and EPC had historically focused on issues related to climate change, land use, and water rights, there had occasionally been tension with the interests of farmers. However, the WEC policy leader immediately recognized a way to find common ground. Specifically, the policy director noted that the farm-to-institution effort offered a way to collaborate on an issue that was broadly popular and less contentious. The EPC approved the farm-to-school issue as one of its four priority issues for the 2008 legislative session.

For the remainder of 2007, stakeholders from multiple sectors worked together to draft the legislation. Advocates made a strategic effort to identify and address concerns of potential opponents during the writing process. For example, bill authors struck or negotiated politically sensitive terms (e.g., "organic," "conventional") and made sure to reference all key stakeholders. The final bill included a broad array of strategies designed to benefit vulnerable populations as well as the environment and local farms.

In January 2008, state policy makers introduced an LFHK bill in the Washington State Legislature, where it was assigned to the Senate Committee on Agriculture and Rural Economic Development. Messaging efforts highlighted the bill's benefits for Washingtonians in terms of improving economic vitality for farmers while increasing access to healthy foods for children. Primary responsibility for promoting the bill was given to two experienced lobbyists. The lobbyists recruited a lead legislator for the bill in each legislative chamber, and made a successful push to recruit a considerable number of legislators from both Republican and Democratic parties as cosponsors. Advocates secured 51 cosponsors in the House (out of 98 total members) and 33 (out of 49) in the Senate. The LFHK passed in March 2008 with only one dissenting vote.

## BREAKOUT BOX 5.2

### Menu Labeling Policy Development in King County, WA

In the United States, some local health departments have rulemaking authority to regulate restaurants and other food environments (Pomeranz, 2011). For example, in King County, Washington, the Board of Health passed a menu-labeling regulation that required chain restaurants with 15 or more locations nationwide to provide information about calories, saturated fats, carbohydrates, and sodium to customers starting January 1, 2009. King County was the second jurisdiction to require menu labeling (New York City was the first).

To examine the policy processes associated with the passage of restaurant menu-labeling regulations, researchers at the University of Washington used qualitative research methods such as document review and key informant interviews with 12 key stakeholders (Johnson, Payne, McNeese, & Allen, 2012). Participants included a representative of the Washington Restaurant Association, three public health practitioners, four members of the Board of Health, and four restaurant owners.

The researchers found that stakeholders could be grouped into two main categories, or "advocacy coalitions": a public health coalition and an industry coalition. Advocacy coalitions are groups of policy actors brought together by their common values and beliefs to advocate for a common policy outcome (Sabatier & Jenkins-Smith, 1993). For example, within these two coalitions, the researchers identified shared values and beliefs about the appropriate role of governmental regulation in protecting population health and the need for environmental change. Policy actors in both coalitions generally shared concerns about the increasing prevalence of obesity and diabetes. They recognized that approximately one third of total calories consumed in the United States come from food eaten away from home, and they also recognized the need for restaurants to be profitable.

However, the process was adversarial at times, as national and state restaurant associations strongly opposed the initiative initially. Industry coalition members believed that menu-labeling regulations may harm the economy, that voluntary mechanisms are more appropriate than regulations, and that it is unfair to "single out" restaurants. In contrast,

*(continued)*

## BREAKOUT BOX 5.2 (*continued*)

public health coalition members believed that it is appropriate to use regulations when necessary to protect the health of the community, that population health is a priority, that environmental change is needed to make it easier for people to make healthy choices, and that citizens are entitled to nutrition information.

Value conflicts played out in three major areas: industry freedom versus the consumer's right to know, educational versus regulatory approaches, and the importance of environmental change versus a reliance on individual responsibility to make healthy food choices. Representatives of both coalitions came together to hear each other's point of view, and eventually they were able to reach compromises on parts of the regulation (e.g., details about the public display of menu information, and the scope of the requirements). Over time, members of the two coalitions learned from each other and began to trust one another. Members agreed that establishing trust and building relationships throughout the process was a key factor in the policy's ultimate success. Public health staff played a key role in developing scientific briefing papers and providing technical assistance about policy implementation issues. The Board of Health and the restaurant association worked together and eventually developed a menu-labeling policy that was acceptable to both sides. Subsequently, members continued to collaborate in order to revise the regulations so that they would comply with national menu-labeling legislation under the Affordable Care Act.

## BREAKOUT BOX 5.3

### Smart Snacks in School

Children consume up to half of their calories at school each day. On June 27, 2013, the U.S. Department of Agriculture (USDA) issued a set of nutrition standards called the Smart Snacks in School rule (USDA, 2013). It applies to foods and beverages sold in public schools. The last time the USDA updated snack and à la carte food standards was 1979. Congress directed the USDA to update the standards as part of the bipartisan *Healthy, Hunger-Free Kids Act* of 2010 (Pub. L. No. 111-296;

*(continued)*

## BREAKOUT BOX 5.3 (*continued*)

U.S Government Printing Office, 2013). The *Healthy, Hunger-Free Kids Act* requires the USDA to establish nutrition standards for all foods sold in schools—beyond the federally supported meals programs.

Because kids have access to less-healthy snack food and beverage options, improving school snack foods could have a dramatic effect on their diets. Once implemented, the standards are intended to ensure that snacks in vending machines, school stores, à la carte lines, and snack bars are healthy. A food must be a fruit, vegetable, protein, dairy, or whole grain; have fewer than 200 calories; and be low in fat, sodium, and sugar. The standards apply to all foods sold before, during, or up to 30 minutes after the school day. Research conducted by the Pew Charitable Trust (www.Pewhealth.org) shows that the majority of U.S. secondary schools currently do not sell fruits and vegetables in stores, snack bars, or vending machines (The Kids' Safe and Healthful Food Project, 2011, 2013a, 2013b; The Pew Charitable Trusts, 2013; Taber, Chriqui, Perna, Powell, & Chaloupka, 2012).

However, there will be some exceptions to the rule. The standards apply to food sold during the school day, not to food sold during evening or weekend activities such as football games or band concerts. The rule gives states the authority to make exemptions for infrequent fundraiser events, so state leaders will need to make those determinations. If parents, teachers, and students want some occasional departures from the standards, state and local leaders have the option of allowing that. However, some schools have found that they can make just as much money, if not more, with nonfood fundraisers. Schools or districts could choose to apply the standards to all after-school activities, but that is not required by the USDA.

A barrier for many school districts in implementing the standards is the concern that there may be a negative impact on school budgets. However, a recent health impact assessment (HIA; Health Impact Project, 2012) found that schools that implemented healthier standards for snack and à la carte foods generally broke even or increased food service revenue. This allowed a more acceptable framing—namely, when fewer unhealthy snacks are available, students are more likely to purchase a school meal—a change that benefits both children's health and school budgets. Additional research has demonstrated

(*continued*)

## BREAKOUT BOX 5.3 (*continued*)

that students in states with strong school nutrition standards gain less weight than those without such guidelines (Taber et al., 2012).

**Thought Questions for Breakout Boxes 5.1 to 5.3**

1. USDA Secretary Tom Vilsack justified the Smart Snacks rule by stating, "Parents and schools work hard to give our youngsters the opportunity to grow up healthy and strong, and providing healthy options throughout school cafeterias, vending machines, and snack bars will support their great efforts." What values do you see reflected here? How might this message appeal to liberals and conservatives, parents-rights groups, and health advocates?

2. Consider who the stakeholders would be in this case. Do you find evidence of compromises made that might reflect the power of some of these stakeholders?

3. How is data used to defend against possible attacks on this policy?

4. After reading about the policy development process for the LFHK legislation in Washington State, how would you develop a similar policy in your state or local jurisdiction?

   a. Which key values describe your position on the issue? What are the values of the policy makers or organization for whom you work?

   b. With which partners would you want to collaborate? Are there any existing coalitions with which you might work?

   c. Which policy makers and staffers would you reach out to?

   d. Can you foresee any value conflicts with other groups? Which groups are likely to oppose the policy?

   e. What is the prior legislative history in your area? (e.g., Have there been attempts to pass similar policies? Were they successful?)

5. Describe some barriers you might face in your state/local jurisdiction as you attempt to pass the policy.

6. Choose one barrier from your list, and describe ways that you could begin to address that barrier.

7. Menu labeling will be required in all states as part of the Affordable Care Act. However, there are still questions about how effective such regulations will be in terms of changing dietary behavior in the population. We will examine some initial evaluation studies in Chapter 6, but take a moment here to note your thoughts about the impact that menu labeling might have in your state. How would you define "success?" What would you measure?

Social authority over children is also an important aspect of the social system. Society through the political process has already decided to take away children's freedom by compelling them to attend either a public, private, or homeschool setting until they reach a prescribed age or level of education. Mandatory elementary and secondary education is seen as a public good. The state has prescribed a particular curriculum to be covered and sometimes even determines what texts must be used. Both children and parents face penalties for violating these policies.

One of the elements that may make childhood obesity an attractive area for policy intervention is that schools already have "control" over the activity of the students during a substantial portion of weekdays during the school year. Therefore, making adjustments in this school environment could be very incremental and may be a more readily acceptable policy option.

However, one has to recognize that the amount of time in school is already accounted for by current activities. A program intended to fight obesity might focus on increased nutrition education, but that might mean cutting back on coverage of other material or alternatively extending the school day, both of which have important and potentially both positive and negative consequences. It might also mean a school system has to find additional competent individuals to teach nutrition or train existing staff in how to apply these nutrition lessons. Both of these have consequences for the cost of education and potential need for additional revenue or changing priorities in existing spending. Consequently, a new policy on childhood obesity may result in opposition from teachers and others who value the "basics" in education and oppose spending time on things that they feel parents should be teaching their own children. Opposition might arise from taxpayers due to the increased costs involved. School administrators who do not want to lose the money coming from companies that are allowed to put their soda machines inside the school may oppose the removal of soda machines from schools. Opposition by teachers and school administrators may become a critical dynamic. Increasing the amount of physical exercise within the school day might also raise concerns about the purpose of public education, cost, reducing the schedule focusing on the basics, and potential conflicts with the school's organized sport teams. How are the disabled to be accommodated by a policy on increased physical activity in the school day? By addressing these value conflicts, you will begin to see that confronting obesity in the school system is more complex than you initially thought it to be.

Students are only controlled by the school system part of their day. Changing what happens in school might have some impact on behavior and obesity, but it is not likely to change all behavior. If you focus on a school-based program, will that be sufficient to have a substantial impact on obesity? If students rush to the convenience store next to the school, will that dilute the impact of what has been done within the school? Outside the controlled environment of the educational system, children are subjected to a variety of influences. Children watching television are influenced by advertisements designed to make products appealing to them. Fast-food chains develop playgrounds and toys in order to increase sales volume. Pressure by children to buy particular products builds market demand for those products. In addition, as children age, they acquire their own purchasing power. Large and small stores will resist laws restricting marketing practices in the name of free enterprise, corporate profits, and "lost jobs." These values will prompt some to resist social regulations/laws infringing on their ability to sell their products and services to children. Some of these claims will be legitimate and some of these claims may have little substance. Which of these claims have legitimacy? Which of these legitimate claims can be overcome through accommodation or compromise?

Despite the assumption that having healthy children might be a fairly universal value for a society, it is important not to assume that dealing with childhood obesity even in a school setting is without value conflict. If there is a focus on food and obesity in public schools, what happens to children who are already obese? How will one control bullying within the school? Will a focus on not being obese impact the existing problem of eating disorders in public schools?

No matter what the policy area you are analyzing, there will be important value considerations to take into account. These will both support and work against your policy initiative. It is important to be straightforward in addressing these considerations because the penalty for not doing so will be being surprised by the level and intensity of opposition to your policy initiative or not taking advantage of natural allies who can assist you in the political process that follows. Either of these can be fatal to the enactment of your policy initiative. We will discuss this more in Chapter 8, on Recommendation and Strategies.

We have already suggested some of the values at stake here. You might be able to add to the list of values below:

- Healthy children leading to healthy, productive adults
- Reduced medical care costs
- Healthy environments for improved learning
- Parental freedom
- Reducing disparities in obesity by race or gender
- Sanctity of the family
- Focus on the academic mission of schools
- Increased educational costs
- Free enterprise
- Freedom of choice
- Victim blaming and bullying
- Limited government

What you need to do is list these values and discuss how they might play out in the political process that follows, much like we did in this chapter. It is also important for you as an analyst to be clear of your own values or those of the organization/person sponsoring this policy analysis.

## Stakeholder Analysis

Stakeholders are those who are intensely interested in the outcomes of policy debates in a particular area. Because people have limited resources (time, money, and attention span) they often prioritize their political activities. They may choose to ignore important policy issues in favor of other issues that they perceive as having a more direct impact on them. They will prioritize their own activities and resource expenditures based on values that are most important for them. Parents will be more sensitive about school issues than those who do not have children or who no longer have children in the school system. By focusing on the value conflicts as described in the previous section, one can begin to identify who the major stakeholders are for this particular policy proposal.

Stakeholders only have political power if they aggregate and create organized groups. Those groups that are large and more tightly organized tend to have more political power because they can focus their resources (time, money, political action, lobbying, etc.) at critical points in the political policy process. Those groups whose members are more affluent can better afford to pay dues and make significant contributions in support of the legislative agenda of that organization. Other groups might have vast resources to spend on mass media campaigns for or against a proposal. Other groups might have an effective communication system or networks by which thousands of e-mails can deluge a legislator's office in a matter of hours.

Some stakeholders, especially those with great resources, will be actively monitoring legislative initiatives submitted to legislative committees and will become aware of any efforts that might impinge on their activities. Technology has allowed these monitoring activities to engage in almost instantaneous and daily communication with identified supporters. Some organizations have extensive policy sections with people hired either on retainer or who are full-time employees who will readily assist policy makers to write legislation, provide data, or lobby political participants. Other stakeholders may initially be more passive about the issue and need to be prompted to action. Some may not consider the issue to be of critical importance but may be willing to support other groups that have supported their causes in the past. Coalitions of stakeholders might be briefly created over a particular issue and then fall apart once the issue has been resolved. Other coalitions may be more permanent. Some individuals may be so moved by the policy issue that they create a new grassroots organization specifically for that issue. It may appear as a genuine voice of the citizens. Alternatively, some organizations may be created to look like grassroots organizations of local constituents but are actually funded by large commercial organizations to look like a genuine grassroots organization. One of the characteristics of the current political climate is the rise of Internal Revenue Service (IRS) Section 501 (c) (4) "social welfare" groups, that gain tax-exempt status and can actively lobby and support political causes during elections, but are not under any obligation to report who has provided financial support to that organization. These are just some examples of the types of stakeholders who exist or will emerge as the policy process evolves. Because most policy is recycled, many of these groups may have experience in how to mobilize their support or opposition to policy proposals.

The task here is not to be overcome by potential obstacles, but rather to recognize where potential opposition and support may develop throughout the policy-making process. National companies and organizations with large resources can quickly overwhelm a school district, county, state, or even the federal government. Large agricultural lobbies will protect national agriculture subsidies, making certain foods artificially cheaper for schools than more healthy alternatives. It is critical to analyze who and how stakeholders are being impacted by your potential policy.

It is important to also remember that all stakeholders are not equal. You may have millions of individual stakeholders on your side, but one small but highly organized and politically connected stakeholder could stand between you and success. The first characteristic of stakeholder power is the nature of its organization. To be effective in the political process, stakeholders must be organized. There might be millions of people who will be impacted by a given policy proposal, but unless they are organized, and organized effectively, their voice will not be politically effective. For example, health policy issues frequently impact the elderly, but it is due to organizations such as the AARP and National Committee to Protect Social Security and Medicare that that voice becomes meaningful in policy debates. Similarly, the poor and disenfranchised, although large in number, are typically left out of policy debates due to their lack of organization and resources.

Although being an organization itself is important, it is the effectiveness of that organization that has the greatest meaning. What is the penetration of that organization among the group it is purportedly representing? What is the ability of the organization to mobilize its members for action? What is the ability of the organization to fund itself for continuous lobbying activity? What is the reputation of the organization regarding the credibility of its past statements and positions? What is the ability of the organization to fund or conduct research and policy analysis? What technology does it have to assist in a policy debate? What political connections does the organization have with existing policy makers? What is the organization's ability to negatively affect politicians who disagree with its positions? All these elements begin to form the power of stakeholders. In short, what is the value of this stakeholder's support or opposition?

In developing a policy initiative, it is important to understand who these important stakeholders might be and how they will respond to your policy initiative.

Stakeholders will come to the policy debate with a different set of resources. Some may have data. Some may have money. Some may have political contacts. Some may have a substantial number of members in key legislative districts but not have a great deal of money. Some may have lists of people with similar interests. All of these characteristics tend to influence what these stakeholders can contribute in terms of resources for the policy process to come. This is often reflected in the compromises made in the final policy (see Breakout Boxes 5.1 and 5.2).

Success stories can be found across the nation in which communities have organized themselves around a shared vision of "community health" and have successfully made changes in many different sectors to improve health. New Orleans, Louisiana; Cambridge, Massachusetts; Fall River, Massachusetts; Manistique, Michigan; Minneapolis, Minnesota; and Santa Cruz County, California, have been named national exemplars in this regard (Robert Wood Johnson Foundation, 2013b).

There is one set of stakeholders that is more important than others— those who potentially oppose your policy proposal. Their importance is due to the nature of the political structure and process in the United States. Because a division of political power is a major characteristic of our political system, it is much easier to defeat legislation than it is to pass it. Passage of legislation requires a great deal of sustained effort. Defeat in one legislative committee within one chamber of the legislature is sufficient to end your policy proposal. If one party controls one chamber of the legislature and an opposing party controls the other, stakeholders will concentrate on the one that tends to favor their position in order to block the legislative proposal. Unlike you, your opponents need only one chamber or one powerful committee chair to win the policy debate. Who are the key stakeholders who have the ability to block your policy from being adopted? On the other hand, getting your policy proposal adopted is a much more difficult task. You need to develop support in multiple legislative committees and two legislative chambers (except for the state of Nebraska) in order to get your policy proposal passed in the legislature. In the United States, those opposed to legislation tend to have the advantage compared to those wanting to enact legislation. This is by design; the political system of the United States was not designed to make laws easy to pass. As will be discussed in Chapter 8 on Recommendation and Strategies, there are strategies that can help you get your policy proposal adopted by the political system.

Even the most powerful stakeholder does not have the resources to devote to all policy issues. Given multiple interests, stakeholders will prioritize their issues and the policy arenas in which they are prepared to defend those interests. However, a nationally oriented stakeholder may want to attempt to defeat even a minor policy initiative in a small state in order to prevent a policy from gaining a foothold of legitimacy. Consequently, a state policy initiative that may initially appear to be relatively insignificant can attract the opposition of significant national organizations. On the other hand, a national stakeholder may pick and choose which states are the most critical for supporting or defeating a piece of legislation. The national organization might also bypass a policy proposal it opposes due to the presence of more important or pressing issues being debated in the political system. It may be that the issue is not of critical importance or it may be merely that there are more critical issues to be dealt with at the present time. The stakeholder may devote some resources, but not an extensive amount of resources to a particular issue. Because large, organized interest groups may represent a variety of types of organizations that are impacted very differently by a proposed policy, the organization may not be able to resolve its inner conflicts in favor of taking a unified position on that policy. For example, within a business chamber of commerce, restaurants are more likely to be impacted by a policy of obesity than are manufacturers and are more likely to urge political action to favor them.

You will need to examine the values that are being impacted by obesity and then identify the stakeholders. One of the values we identified earlier was parental control. At the local level, some parents may be very influential people within the community. However, because you have selected the national level as your policy focus, those individuals will be less influential unless they organize at the national level. In fact, there is a national group that is proposing a constitutional amendment on parental rights (Parental Rights Organization, 2013). One would want to evaluate the potential impact of this constitutional amendment, its likelihood for passing, and what this organization's position might be regarding obesity. There are groups such as the National Parents' Rights Association as well as other groups that may decide to take a position on childhood obesity (National Parents'

Rights Association, 2013). Alternatively, there are organizations such as the American Public Health Association that feel childhood obesity is an important public health issue and have specific policy recommendations on that topic (American Public Health Association, 2013a, 2013b). You want to evaluate the ability of these various organizations to have a political impact.

Fast-food chains will be very much impacted by any federal legislation regarding advertising or restrictions on menu items. The recent requirement by the ACA to require menu nutrition information has potentially increased sensitivity among fast-food chains, which have a great deal of monetary resources as well as geographically diffused local franchise owners who can be politically activated very quickly. Farmers assisted by federal corn subsidies will not want those subsidies impacted as a result of an attack on obesity and corn syrup. Convenience store owners will resist attacks on their ability to sell profitable items or locate in a particular part of town. Major soft drink manufacturers and distributors will also resist policies that might lead to a reduction of sales. On the other hand, local farmers and public health advocates may be able to form coalitions and craft compromises with potential opponents, garnering enough political support for policy adoption (as was the case in Washington State). Major grocery chains might support subsidies to reduce "food deserts" in inner cities, as was the case in the Pennsylvania Fresh Food Financing Initiative. All of these stakeholders have a concentrated interest in the outcome of the policy debate on childhood obesity.

Put yourself in the position of as many stakeholders as you can. This will help you understand the complexity of the policy issue as well as areas of potential compromise later in the process, as well as levers for incentivizing cooperation rather than objection. Which of these stakeholders, or set of stakeholders, are the most critical for the particular childhood obesity policy being advocated?

Given the limitations of your time and resources, it will be impossible for you to develop an exhaustive list of all the stakeholders and complete an analysis of each of their strengths and weaknesses. However, going through the exercise of stakeholder analysis will provide you with insights to the coming political struggles. It is good to take one's best guess at the involved stakeholders in order to assist in constructing a childhood obesity policy that can not only be effective, but one that stands a chance in the political process. It is important to note that additional stakeholders might be added to your current list of stakeholders as the policy moves through the political process. Compromise is a core component of incremental policy making. New grassroots organizations may emerge and existing stakeholders may create new temporary coalitions. At this stage of the policy process, you might be able to estimate where support and opposition might rest.

Although not required, creating a stakeholder impact matrix might be useful in summarizing the power of major stakeholders, both those tending to favor and oppose a policy initiative on childhood obesity (see Table 5.1). This can also be done informally as part of your writing process, but not appear in the final document being submitted. To do this, you would first need to create a list of criteria to measure the political power of an organization. One could use the size of membership, the amount of financial resources, the level of intensity of the issue for the organization, the ability of the organization to rally its members (unity), its technology capability, the level of ongoing lobbying activity, its ability to inflict punishment on legislators, or other characteristics that you feel measure the power of a stakeholder. This matrix is to be used as a blunt tool, so the more honestly you construct the tool, the more useful it will be. Each measure would need to be scored, for example, on a scale of 1 to 10. So, for example, having more members would result in a higher membership score. Having a larger budget for lobbying or having a full-time lobbyist would give a higher score. Having other people in the policy field rate these groups according to your criteria will add some external validity to the index. Even with that, this will not be a precise measure and it will be based on many subjective judgments (e.g., ability to inflict punishment on legislators voting against their positions) as well as more objective facts (e.g., financial resources). For example, you could create categories for financial resources for lobbying with 1 representing $0 to $5,000, 2 representing $5,001 to $20,000, and so on. These lobbying resources would have to be adjusted based on the geopolitical unit; $5,000 for lobbying a local school board might be a great deal of money, whereas the same amount for lobbying Congress would not be significant. The intent is to take one's best estimate of the forces supporting and opposing your policy alternative and to measure them all by the same criteria.

Table 5.1 provides an example of a stakeholder impact matrix that can be used to evaluate stakeholders. Note that some of the criteria that are used are numerical and relatively objective (financial and number of members), whereas others are more subjective (intensity and unity). An

TABLE 5.1
Stakeholder Impact Matrix

| Organization | Financial | Members | Intensity | Unity | Total |
|:---:|:---:|:---:|:---:|:---:|:---:|
| A | 10 | 8 | 8 | 8 | 34 |
| B | 8 | 10 | 10 | 4 | 32 |
| C | 10 | 5 | 2 | 2 | 19 |
| D | 8 | 4 | 8 | 6 | 26 |
| E | 10 | 10 | 4 | 2 | 26 |

individual author or a group consensus model can be used to evaluate these. The intent is to construct a useful summary of the impact of stakeholders. One would list those that appear to be the most critical supporters or opponents and the most critical characteristics.

Notice in Table 5.1 that Organization A has the highest total score, because it has the highest level of financial resources (financial), a fairly large number of members (members), and feels relatively intense (intensity) about this issue area or values. You could also conclude by looking at the organization's history that it has been able to get its members to back its policy positions (unity) by getting members to directly contact legislators or the executive branch. Organization B has a large membership and it feels intensely about the issue/value. It also has relatively large resources, but has historically not been able to mobilize its resources for action. Organization C has a great deal of financial resources but scores poorly on other elements in the matrix. Although it has great financial power, it is not likely to engage in this particular issue, perhaps due to it having a low priority on its current legislative agenda. Therefore, it has the least political power of the stakeholders listed.

The above stakeholder impact matrix assumes that all of the elements of the political power index of stakeholders are of equal weight. However, one can construct the matrix so that financial resources weigh twice as much as membership, or membership is 1.5 the value of financial resources. One could also construct a resource-to-staffing ratio or resource–to–membership ratio as alternative criteria. One can do separate stakeholder impact matrices for likely supporting stakeholders and likely opponents. It is less important to have an exact measure of the power index of various stakeholders than it is to begin to evaluate where supporters and opponents of the policy are likely to come from and what general comparisons can be made.

Because this matrix is not an exact measure, the credibility of your analysis will rest in part on the attempt to provide information as accurately as possible. The intent of a policy analysis is to not only make a recommendation for a policy that is the most effective, efficient, or equitable in solving the policy problem, but to recommend a policy that also has some chance of political success. You may not wish to put this stakeholder impact matrix in the final document, but going through the exercise and evaluating the various stakeholders either subjectively or objectively is an important step in the analysis. It is important to identify potential organizations for developing a coalition or to understand the forces that will fight your proposal in the policy process. We will discuss this more in Chapter 8 on Recommendation and Strategy.

## SUMMARY

Politics revolves around values. Understanding the values that gird policy proposals is an important part of the policy analysis process. Because the political system determine winners and losers in the battle of values, it is important to understand how your policy will fit with different values. Despite the current trend of intense ideological positions, compromise on values becomes critical in any democratic system that rejects a winner-take-all orientation. Even the most simple of policy proposals has some kind of underlying values associated with it.

Understanding the value conflicts underlying your proposal will allow you to identify the major stakeholders for your policy proposal. Knowing the important stakeholders generally comes from political experience and knowledge. Much of this analysis is going to depend on your background and knowledge of the issue and the political power brokers within a particular political setting. Stakeholder analysis tends to be quite subjective. History of the political jurisdiction and knowledge of how other political jurisdictions have dealt with the issue will help considerably in gaining insight as to the important stakeholders. If you lack that knowledge directly, you can access participants in the political process that can assist your analysis.

In order to weigh the relative power of various stakeholders, you may wish to develop a stakeholder impact matrix for likely supporters and opponents. Although you may not want to include this matrix in your final report, it will assist you in writing your analysis and it will force you to compare stakeholders using the same criteria. Due to the nature of the political system in the United States, it is much easier to block legislation than it is to pass it. Therefore, an analysis of stakeholders, especially those who might oppose your policy proposal, will be critical in developing a strategy for implementation. We will discuss this in greater detail in Chapter 8 on Recommendation and Strategies. Sooner or later you policy proposal is going to have to test the political waters; it is important to understand what forces will help your policy and what forces will need to be overcome.

## SOME THINGS TO REMEMBER

- Understand the value conflicts of your policy/program proposal.
- Identify the major stakeholders for your policy proposal, and what resources (e.g., power, money, knowledge) they bring to the table. Make sure to consider stakeholders who may oppose your proposal, and whether compromises could be made.
- Identify stakeholders who may be missing from the process because they are not well organized or do not hold a lot of power (e.g., vulnerable populations). Will you make special efforts to reach out to them and include their perspective?
- Decide how you will organize the information about your stakeholders and which criteria you will use to compare them. You may use a stakeholder impact matrix like the one in this chapter to help you measure their strengths and weaknesses using the same criteria.

## KEY WORDS

Values
Compromise
Stakeholders
Advocacy

Coalitions
Deliberative democracy
Stakeholder analysis
Stakeholder impact matrix

# Six

# Criteria for Success

This chapter can normally be covered fairly briefly compared to other sections in your written policy analysis. However, brevity is not related to importance. The basic question that this section seeks to answer is, "What do you want to accomplish by this policy?" This will help you to later answer a corollary question, "How will you know if the policy is a success or a failure"? These considerations relate to policy evaluation, as illustrated in the policy wheel that we introduced in Chapter 1. It is important to remember that one should think about evaluation throughout the policy process, not just at the end. Policy should not be enacted for its own sake; policy is meant to solve a public problem, and policy outcomes that cannot be measured mean we have a policy that can never be deemed successful or unsuccessful. Statements of policy success in the absence of measurable outcomes open themselves to subjective interpretation and debate, often based on rhetoric rather than evidence. One should also plan to address factors related to why a policy may or may not have worked well.

Obesity in children will be a problem for years to come. Your policy proposal is not likely to eradicate obesity in children. At most, your policy will tackle one part of the childhood obesity problem, as shown in the Breakout Boxes in Chapters 5 and 6. If your policy is a success, what would you anticipate happening? What objective measures can you use over time to indicate whether the policy is having no impact, making things better, or making them worse?

## DEFINITION OF SUCCESS

One must always be careful in attributing causality when dealing with complicated social policies. The increase in obesity rates over the past few years may have been a result of the economic recession or an increase in the disparity of income, or perhaps some combination of the two, among other forces. An improving economy or a reduction in income disparities (which are not the same thing) may be the strongest contributors to improvements in obesity rates; these improvements may have little to do with the adoption of your particular policy. At this stage of the policy process, you are attempting to select a set of methodological tools that will help you to demonstrate the impact of your proposed policy.

Your proposed measures are not going to demonstrate causality; they are merely going to serve as guideposts for indicating change. One of the best ways to do this is to choose one or two measurable indicators to serve as the goals for your policy. You can also set subgoals to achieve; those might be specific to early stages of policy implementation. This serves two purposes. One is to demonstrate early success. The second is to facilitate buy-in by stakeholders and to facilitate implementation. If there is agreement on evaluative measures, it creates a potential for agreement on overall program goals.

One of the things that you need to take into account in selecting goals for your program/policy proposal is that policy makers are not known for having long-term perspectives. A politician's time frame tends to be less than 2 years from the last election. In actuality, given the need for fundraising and gearing up for primary and general elections, it can be less than 1 year. As elections get closer, a politician's time frame shrinks. Due to their 6-year term of office, U.S. senators are generally thought to have the luxury of being able to think further into the future and take more political risks. However, even if a particular politician is not up for re-election, adverse electoral results may result in the legislative branch changing control from one party to another and/or a politician losing or gaining the chairmanship of a critical legislative committee for your proposal. For example, although a governor or the President of the United States may not be up for re-election in a given year, he or she may lose or gain support in the legislative branch and thereby alter the chance of particular policies being adopted. The important thing to remember is that most policy makers do not have the luxury of time to get legislation passed or to benefit from the potential outcomes of any new policy. Short-term returns on policy become even more problematic as public problems get more and more complex and require a set of integrated actions over a long period of time.

Due to this short time-frame perspective, a policy that will demonstrate an outcome 10 years from the policy's passage is a harder political sell than one that demonstrates more immediate results. Enacted policies that show immediate positive results can be used to gain an advantage with voters (political capital) and help win re-election. Due to the complicated nature of health, health policies, in particular, may take many years to have an actual impact on the health of the population.

On the other hand, the inability to provide a short-term reward for a good proposal may not be its death knell; it may provide political space for the program to demonstrate its worth. This can also result in blame avoidance. This occurs when the impacts of the program are unclear or the initial costs lead to increased taxes down the road. Because the outcomes are delayed, the politician knows that he or she may no longer be in office when these effects become known.

What is important at this stage of the policy process is that you have an understanding of what is to be accomplished by your program/policy. It is unlikely that your program/policy will totally solve the problem as soon as it is passed. Indeed, will your policy proposal work? See Breakout Box 6.1 for a discussion of menu labeling. There needs to be an implementation phase of the policy that may involve writing new regulations, establishing a new set of institutions, and/or hiring additional personnel for enforcement. New regulations can take months and even years to pass. The Affordable Care Act (ACA) was enacted in 2010, and although some elements of the policy were implemented rather quickly after passage, the enforcement of the individual mandate and the insurance exchanges were designed to take effect 4 years later, in January of 2014. The actual impact of its major provisions to reduce the uninsured is not likely to be measurable for a number of years. The impact of the law in actually reducing mortality and disability is even further distant.

With respect to your policy proposal on childhood obesity, some impacts may not occur until adolescence, adulthood, or even old age. Yet you cannot necessarily wait 50 years to see the exact consequences of your policy proposal. This is especially true during difficult economic times, when attempts to cut programs that might be underperforming are high on the legislative agenda. Consequently, you need to be clear about what the objectives of the policy are in the short term, medium term, and the long term.

## BREAKOUT BOX 6.1

### Menu Labeling Example

Menu labeling has been a recent policy approach intended to help people make more informed choices about the foods they eat. But does it work? New York City implemented the first calorie-posting law in 2008. Philadelphia added a law in 2010 (the strictest to date), requiring sit-down chain restaurants to list saturated fats, trans fats, carbohydrates, sodium, and total calories beside every menu item. The restaurant industry initially fought hard against menu-labeling laws, but eventually backed a uniform national rule that would pre-empt all local ordinances. The federal calorie-posting rule, which was part of the 2010 Affordable Care Act, is weaker than what some states had proposed. Intense lobbying about which restaurants/products would be affected has since delayed a final rule. Several research studies have been conducted to evaluate the success of menu-labeling initiatives. For example, researchers in Washington state examined the impact of a menu-labeling regulation in King County, Washington, on calories purchased and awareness and use of labels at 6 and 18 months after policy implementation (Krieger et al., 2013). Although the researchers found no significant changes in calories purchased in the short term (e.g., 6 months after implementation), they did find a modest decrease in the calories purchased after 18 months, particularly among women and patrons of certain types of food chains. The researchers found that the average number of calories per purchase at chain restaurants fell by 38 calories, from 908.5 to 870.4 calories (at coffee chains, the average decrease was 22 calories, from 154.3 to 132.1 calories). After implementation of the policy, food chain customers who reported using calorie information purchased fewer calories (143 calories less) compared to those who reported seeing but not using the information and those who reported not seeing the information at all (135 calories less). Customer awareness of calorie information increased in food chains (18.8% to 61.7%) and in coffee chains (4.4% to 30%).

In another study, researchers assessed the impact of restaurant menu calorie labels on food choices and food intake (Roberto, Larsen, Agnew, Baik, & Brownell, 2010). They randomly assigned 303 participants in a study dinner to one of three conditions: (1) a menu without calorie labels ("no calorie labels"), (2) a menu with calorie labels only ("calorie labels only"), or (3) a menu with calorie labels and an informational

(continued)

## BREAKOUT BOX 6.1 (*continued*)

label stating "The recommended daily caloric intake for an average adult is 2,000 calories" ("calorie labels plus information"). Food choices and intake during and after the study dinner were measured. The researchers found that participants in both calorie-label conditions (Groups 2 and 3) ordered fewer calories than those in the "no calorie labels" group (Group 1). Groups 2 and 3 (combined) consumed 14% fewer calories than the "no calorie labels" group. However, individuals in Group 2 consumed more calories *after* the study dinner than those in both other groups. When calories consumed both during and after the study dinner were combined, participants in the "calorie labels plus information" group (Group 3) consumed an average of 250 fewer calories than those in the other groups. The researchers concluded that calorie labels on restaurant menus did affect food choices and intake, and adding a recommended daily caloric requirement label increased this effect.

A third study conducted by researchers in Philadelphia evaluated the nutritional content of menu offerings at nine fast-food chains from 2005 to 2011 (Namba, Auchincloss, Leonberg, & Wootan, 2013). Five of the fast-food chains had outlets in jurisdictions subject to menu-labeling laws, whereas four chains were located in jurisdictions that did not require menu labeling. The researchers used statistical models to assess whether chains in jurisdictions subject to menu-labeling laws increased "healthier" menu options or modified the nutritional content of their menu items relative to chains located in areas that did not require menu labeling. The researchers found that, after the introduction of labeling regulations, fast-food chains that were required to post calories increased the proportion of healthier entrées offered (from 13% before 2008 to 20% between 2008 and 2011). This was a statistically significant change relative to fast-food chains that did not post calories. However, the average calories for entrees remained the same overall (450 kcal) throughout the study period (possibly because although some restaurants added healthier items, the same restaurant [or other restaurants] countered by adding unhealthy items to the menu). The researchers concluded that menu labeling has thus far not affected the average nutritional content of fast-food menu items, but it may motivate restaurants to slightly increase the availability of healthier options.

(*continued*)

## BREAKOUT BOX 6.1 (*continued*)

**Thought Questions**

1. How do these examples use different study designs and research methods to study different parts of the policy process?
2. Think about the RE-AIM framework. To which of the RE-AIM functions (Reach, Effectiveness, Adoption, Implementation, Maintenance) does the information from these studies contribute, and in what ways?
3. How might a conservative policy maker frame these results differently from a liberal policy maker? You can see an example of how the media framed the issue at: http://articles.philly.com/2013-07-22/news/40709975_1_menu-labeling-fast-food-menus-fast-food-chains.

Short-term policy goals are often linked to "process" evaluation metrics or raising awareness in the population. For example, was the policy implemented as intended? Were all students really tested for obesity? Was a standardized protocol used for testing obesity? Was the test conducted by a trained person? If a menu-labeling policy was adopted, did the restaurants comply with posting the labels, and were customers aware of the labels when they visited a restaurant? These potential measures might be used to assess short-term policy goals. You might want to have 100% of elementary public schools covered by a nutrition program by 2020, or set a standard of fresh fruits and vegetables accounting for $x$% of the calories of school lunch programs in the United States by 2020. Alternatively or conjointly, a criterion might be to increase the efficiency of the same program by reducing the cost per meal by 10% by 2020. Your goal could also include the elimination of a program over a period of time. Again, what is important is that you have reliable, valid, and practical data (either available or its collection built into the policy) to indicate progress toward the policy/program's goals.

Medium-term policy goals are often linked to "impact" evaluation metrics that can include such things as changes in knowledge, beliefs, or attitudes (e.g., students reporting that they prefer fresh fruit over French fries, or customers reporting selections of healthier menu items and behaviors, such as students buying more fresh fruit compared to French fries in the cafeteria, or customers consuming more healthy food and changing caloric intake). Long-term outcomes refer to actual changes in health conditions (e.g., decreased obesity rates or decreased prevalence of diabetes).

There are a number of different criteria that you could use. Some of these are listed below:

- *Effectiveness*, for example, increasing the number of students covered or the comprehensiveness of interventions so as to lower obesity rates
- *Efficiency*, such as improving the ratio of input costs to outputs
- *Equity*, for instance, assuring that minority populations have the same or even more access to healthy food choices as more affluent populations
- *Practicality*, for example, allowing local variation in the administration of the program
- *Ideology*, such as supporting local and parental control or strict federal standards for local communities to follow
- *Sustainability*, for instance, focusing on programs that use ecological balance
- *Budget/Fiscal Principles*, for example, loss of revenue, cut program costs
- *Political*, such as gaining the support of a powerful stakeholder in order to score points against the other political party or politician and to gain political advantage for an upcoming election

This is not an exclusive list. However, you need to be explicit in terms of what you are attempting to accomplish with your policy proposal and how you plan on demonstrating that it is meeting its goals.

You can have more than one criterion for success. You can design a nutrition program for children that would be effective, efficient, equitable, and politically advantageous. One would want to have measures of success for each. However, your proposal might also increase the government's budget at the national, state, or local levels.

To maximize the reduction of obesity in children in the United States, effectiveness might be the major or only indicator of success. Cost, efficiency, and equity may be secondary. However, having the most effective program may also be very expensive. Where is the trade-off between cost and effectiveness? Alternatively, decreasing the disparity of obesity rates among various subpopulation groups in the United States might be your primary goal and other criteria might fall away. If maintaining the political support of a particularly powerful supportive stakeholder becomes a key criterion for success, then perhaps effectiveness and efficiency might become less important. Many policy/program compromises are made in the name of political acceptability. Because some policies/programs will be more successful in meeting our criteria than others, weighting these criteria may become important as you begin to evaluate alternative policies/programs.

These criteria for success should be established before you have completed your systematic review of policy alternatives, which is the next stage of your analysis. Your criteria for success should be front and center in terms of reviewing the various alternative policies/programs. You want to use the same set of criteria for evaluating all the various alternatives you are considering. You might have to revisit your criteria after you have completed your review, but using the same criteria for alternatives keeps your analysis more objective. Developing the criteria after you have selected your policy/program could be seen as stacking the deck in favor of a predetermined solution. Each policy/program is going to have both its strengths and weaknesses in meeting different elements of your criteria for short-, medium-, and long-term objectives. You are going to have to make a recommendation at the end of your systematic review of alternatives. Honestly appraising the alternatives gives your readers greater confidence in the selection of the alternative and developing appropriate arguments for the defense of your proposal.

## MEASUREMENT

Having criteria is only one step in the process. You will need to have data that are valid (an accurate measure of what you are attempting to measure), reliable (the ability to get the same measure time after time), and practical (a relatively inexpensive and easy set of data to obtain). One acronym that is frequently used is "SMART" goals, goals that are Specific, Measurable, Attainable, Realistic, and Timely (Centers for Disease Control and Prevention [CDC], 2012b).

Because you have selected the national level as your geopolitical unit, you have both complicated and eased your ability to obtain data. On one hand, you now need measures that reflect progress toward your goals in all 50 states. You need data that is collected the same way in all 50 states, or you could use a statically representative sample of the school-age population of the United States that reflects the nation as a whole. You will also need data that is collected and available over time so that you can measure progress in the short term, medium term, and long term.

You have also made your task easier by selecting the geopolitical unit of the United States, because the federal government is the largest collector of national health data. If your geopolitical unit was a particular state or local community, you might be more limited in the data that is available to you. States vary greatly in the amount and quality of their data. What is the reputation of your geopolitical system's data-collection efforts? If you were concerned with a particular region of the country, such as New England, the South, or the Mountain West, you would need to make sure that regional data was collected in the same manner by each of the states in that region, and/or that samples from smaller states or areas were sufficient so as to be representative.

We previously mentioned that there is a standard definition of obesity for children based on body mass index (BMI), as measured by the 95th percentile of the age group to determine childhood obesity (CDC, 2012a). Consequently, you have a fairly simple, valid, and reliable measure that requires only age, height, and weight to calculate a recognized measure of obesity. If you were to develop your own measure of obesity, it would be immediately challenged by opponents of your policy proposal as stacking the deck in favor of your proposal. This may or may not be true, but you have automatically tainted the credibility of your proposal by using your own measure of obesity instead of the accepted measure. Your measure might very well be a "better" measure of obesity, but if it has not yet been generally accepted, it is open to being challenged. In addition, because multiple sources of data and analytical studies use BMI, you have access to data from multiple locations and time periods all using the same measure of obesity.

Now the question of the frequency of data collection becomes critical. You want to use a measure that is collected frequently enough so you can demonstrate trends over time in a standardized manner. If data is only collected at the national level every 10 years (such as U.S. Census data), you will have to wait at least 10 years for your next set of data. Release of the census data may take an additional year or two before you actually can gain access to that new census data. Therefore, you want to make sure that measures are available that correspond to your policy proposal's short-, medium-, and long-term goals.

For obesity, there are several important national sources of information. One is the Behavioral Risk Factor Surveillance Survey (BRFSS; CDC, 2013a), and another is the National Health and Nutrition Examination

Survey (NHANES; http://www.cdc.gov/nchs/nhanes.htm). BRFSS is a nationally representative survey based on state data collection that is conducted yearly to reflect adult behaviors. However, BRFSS relies on a self-reported telephone-survey sample. Self-reported data for weight may be underestimated and self-reported height might be overestimated, leading to an underestimate of obesity. Despite this weakness, it does provide a yearly estimate and measure of change from year to year. Even better, the CDC has a Youth Risk Behavioral Surveillance System (YRBSS; CDC, 2013i) that collects data on a national sample of school-age youth for six risky behaviors, including:

- Unintentional injuries and violence
- Sexual behaviors
- Alcohol and other drug use
- Tobacco use
- Unhealthy dietary behaviors
- Inadequate physical activity

The YRBSS also measures the prevalence of obesity in youth and young adults. Notice that this measure is for school-based youth and young adults. In examining the methodology for the YRBSS you would find that it collects data from grades 9 through 12 in the United States. Will this fit your need in measuring success for your proposal? Could this be useful for the medium-term or long-term goals but not for the short-term goals of your program?

The NHANES is also a nationally representative sample-based survey that collects more specific information, but it does not collect data on children. The survey examines a nationally representative sample of about 5,000 persons each year. The NHANES survey includes demographic, socioeconomic, dietary, and health-related questions. This is supplemented with an examination component consisting of medical, dental, and physiological measurements, as well as laboratory tests administered by highly trained medical personnel. Knowing the strengths and weaknesses of your data sources is critical.

Many states and school districts have begun collecting their own obesity-related data. However, there are many different protocols used in doing the testing. In some jurisdictions a nurse might take the measurement of height and weight using a standard medical scale. In other jurisdictions a teacher may do the measurements using a bathroom scale and tape measure. When and how frequently the measurements are taken on children can also be important. If some data is collected in the fall and some in the spring, there is an 8-month difference in data collection. Does this matter? Unless there is some standardization of the process of measurement, it is difficult to determine whether a change is the result of the policy, better/poorer measurement, or merely maturation.

One could set up a nationally representative sample of schools (elementary and secondary) and have a standard yearly measurement of childhood BMI. That, however, takes additional money, staffing, protocols, and organization. It also requires a consistency in funding and state collaboration so that data is collected on a regular basis. Discontinuation of funding for data collection is frequently one of the first things to be cut during difficult budget times. New data sets that have not demonstrated their utility may be especially vulnerable.

For your childhood obesity policy you might state that one of the goals for the policy is to have a national sample of school-age children (ages 6 to 18) undergoing accurate obesity measurements within 2 years, and that by 2020 the obesity rate of this national sample will decline by 40%. This provides both short-term and medium-term measures for your policy. A long-term measure might be the reduction in the onset of type II diabetes in children.

However, your data task is not finished. Policies have both intended consequences (results that we anticipate and desire) and unintended or indirect consequences (consequences that are by-products of our policy and may not be initially intended). Unintended consequences can be both positive and negative. However, in the policy arena, they tend to be thought of more as the negative/adverse impacts that result from the policy.

Given your example of childhood obesity, an adverse consequence might be increased stigma of obese children and/or the increase in the incidence of eating disorders as a result of testing children's BMI. This is a real possibility given the serious consequences of eating disorders (e.g., bulimia nervosa and anorexia nervosa) in youth. On the other hand, potentially positive yet unintended consequences of your policy might be federal funding for bike and walking paths, similar to what is now done for highways. With increased bike paths, children as well as adults will have increased ability to exercise and use a mode of transportation that helps to control weight as well as protect the environment. Although this initiative would increase access to exercise, it may also result in more injuries both in the short and the long term. There will be bicycle collisions and falls. There may be collisions between bicyclists and joggers or bicyclists and cars. There may be increased wear and tear on joints that will lead to costly knee and hip replacements in 50 years.

Some of these adverse consequences could be avoided if bicycle/walking paths were made of composite materials that were more forgiving of falls than asphalt. In cities, one would want to assure that bicycle and pedestrian paths follow appropriate design guidelines, such as those developed by the American Association of State Highway and Transportation Officials (AASHTO). Some of these adverse consequences can be foreseen and some cannot.

You may decide to also have indicators for some of these adverse consequences. For example, you could systematically collect information about bicycle/auto accidents using estimates of the increase in bicycle traffic (Kerr, Rodríguez, Evenson, & Aytur, 2013). One might hope for a decrease in the number of automobile/bicycle accidents given the intentional design of the bike paths, but one would especially want to see a decrease in the rate of such accidents.

You may wish to consult with researchers at a local university as to how to identify and measure these potential intended and unintended consequences. The major advantage of beginning to think about the potentially adverse consequences of your policy proposal is that you can make modifications to it before enactment, so as to minimize adverse consequences. By thinking about these and measuring them, you can also deflect potential criticism of your policy.

This section of your policy analysis would offer a relatively brief discussion of the variables that one would use to measure the short-, medium-, and long-term success of your policy. This would include specific goals and time frames. You would identify measures that are available, valid, reliable, and accepted. This would also address the frequency of the data being collected. You would want to make sure that the data is available in sufficiently frequent intervals so as to demonstrate the policy's impact over time.

Ideally, such data sources should be respected public sources of data. The perennial problem is that such public data was probably collected for a different purpose than demonstrating the success of your particular policy or program. As a result, the variables may not precisely measure what you would ideally want to measure regarding your program's success. The best you can do is try to match the "ideal" data elements with those that are available.

## SUMMARY

Policies are generally enacted for multiple purposes. Policies and programs have both intended and unintended consequences. What we would like to do is advocate policies that have positive, intentional consequences and minimize adverse, unintended consequences. Be clear about what you wish to accomplish by your policy and what you and/or your readers might indicate as criteria for success. These might include measures of efficiency, effectiveness, equity, political expediency, and budgetary constraints, among others. Multiple criteria (reducing costs, improving health, or gaining political capital) are probably going to be used. Here you need to be explicit in terms of the criteria that are most important. Trade-offs will undoubtedly have to be made. These criteria should be established prior to the analysis of alternative policies so that you evaluate each policy alternative using a common set of expectations.

In addition to the criteria, one needs to have knowledge of and access to data that can help measure success. Data that is public and commonly accepted as valid and reliable are generally better indicators than new data created for a particular policy/program. Success will occur over time; policies/programs are not likely to have an instantaneous impact. Short-, medium-, and long-term goals with accompanying data points need to be identified. You also need to remember that most policy makers have relatively short time frames or perspectives as election and re-election are the primary measure of a politician's success.

## SOME THINGS TO REMEMBER

- Remember that policy makers tend to have short-term perspectives due to the effect of election cycles on the political process.
- Think about how you would measure the success of your program/ policy throughout the policy process; do not wait until the end.

- Establish clear criteria for success for your program/policy proposal.
- These criteria will be used for your Systematic Review of Policy Alternatives.
- Try to use measures that reflect short-, medium-, and long-term outcomes for your program/policy.
- Try to use measures that have been generally accepted, are available from standardized data-collection systems, and are supported by the scientific literature to gain as much synergy as possible from different sources.
- Try to take into account both intended and unintended consequences of your policy proposal.

---

## KEY WORDS

Evaluation

Effectiveness

Efficiency

Practicality

Ideology

Sustainability

Budget/fiscal principles

Politics

SMART (Specific, Measureable, Attainable, Realistic, Timely)

Behavioral Risk Factor Surveillance Survey (BRFSS)

National Health and Nutrition Examination Survey (NHANES)

Youth Risk Behavior Surveillance System (YRBSS)

Intended outcomes

Unintended outcomes

Short-term indicators (process measures)

Medium-term indicators (impact measures)

Long-term indicators (outcome measures)

# Seven

# Systematic Review of
# Policy Options

## INCREMENTALISM

Previously we discussed the concept of incrementalism in the political system in the United States. Here we need to pause to talk about the policy implications of incrementalism as well as its strengths and weaknesses. The person who popularized the concept of incrementalism in the U.S. policy process is Charles Lindblom (1980). He put forth this theory of the decision-making process as both a descriptive and normative good. Incrementalism is based on building marginally on policy that already exists rather than starting from scratch or dramatically changing policy direction. It involves small incremental steps from the status quo. One example of incrementalism tends to be a budgetary process. A budget is not normally built from scratch each year. There are other approaches (performance budgeting, mixed scanning, zero based, rational, etc.), but the one most commonly used is incremental budgeting.

One advantage of incrementalism is that the existing stakeholders are less likely to oppose a small change in the status quo as opposed to a major change. One can often avoid having to revisit large battles between stakeholders by only making small adjustments of the current policy. If a legislative defeat results in a catastrophic loss for a major stakeholder, the political tension is increased. Incrementalism tends to lower the cost of losing by using the previously agreed-upon solution as the basis of incremental change. As a consequence, there is an increased chance for agreement among major stakeholders. This brings political stability as well as predictability.

Any policy changes within the business environment (including health care) tend to realign factors that advantage some stakeholders and disadvantage others. Business organizations typically prefer predictable environments, even if there are some elements within that environment that are not particularly favorable to them. Existing stakeholders have survived and some have thrived within the status quo; disruption leads to uncertainty. Especially in areas where policies are synergetic and interconnected, a small change is more predictable and less threatening than a large change. A requirement for certain restaurants to post nutrition information becomes more acceptable, especially if it can deflect the call for more dramatic changes.

It is also normally argued that incremental policies are less likely to fail as only small changes are being made. By using incrementalism, one is merely tweaking the existing policy/program and the risk of failure is lessened. In addition, a small change can more easily be reversed if it appears as though that change has too many unintended adverse consequences. In addition, incremental changes tend to be less costly, at least in the short term, if not for the long term. The existing policy/program already has an organizational structure and staff; it merely needs some adjustment. It should also be remembered that politicians tend to have short-term perspectives. Incremental policy changes (even if small) may be more immediately visible and result in positive public reaction. If additional revenue is need, small tax increases are more tolerable than large ones.

With all of these advantages, it is sometimes hard to argue against an incremental policy/program. However, there are also disadvantages to incrementalism. One of the major criticisms of incrementalism is that it places a premium on coming to an agreement among existing stakeholders rather than solving the social problem. Getting existing stakeholders to reach a compromise is not necessarily the same as solving the problem. This is especially true since not all stakeholders have equal power. Those stakeholders with the most power may prefer the status quo. There are times when major policy changes need to be made and when incremental changes are not going to have a sufficient impact on the problem. Incremental policy changes are likely to result in small changes in the social problem. If a problem such as obesity is escalating very rapidly but the proposed solution is incremental, there is likely to be a widening gap between social/health goals and what actually occurs. Incremental solutions may not be sufficient to make headway in such instances. For example, as we saw in Chapter 5, getting restaurant chains to post the calorie content of their existing entrées (a relatively inexpensive policy option for restaurants to implement) has been shown to be only marginally effective in actually changing consumer product selection (Krieger et al., 2013).

Perhaps one of the most significant disadvantages of incrementalism is also one of its advantages; it protects the status quo. As a result, those who are disadvantaged by the current system (e.g., poor minority consumers living in food deserts) will remain disadvantaged, although perhaps marginally less so. One of the problems for inner cities is that there are areas where the only practical choice for inexpensive meals is a fast-food chain or readily available prepared foods. Mass transit often does not go to outlying inexpensive grocery stores. Making fresh and nutritious food available to those in such food deserts requires more than posting nutrition and calorie information. Eliminating food deserts is likely to require important zoning changes, supporting multimodal transportation or extending mass transit service, limiting the number of fast-food chains, developing farm-to-institution legislation, providing subsidies for vendors of fresh foods, changing restrictions on the use of food stamps, and allowing customers to use EBT (electronic benefits transfer) cards at farmers markets, among others. These are more comprehensive changes that will generally tend to be more politically controversial.

Nonincremental policies are certainly possible, as we saw with "Local Farms–Healthy Kids," and may be more effective in solving the public health issue. However, one must recognize that in many jurisdictions, such policies may also be more politically challenging to pass. We will talk about this further in Chapter 8 on Recommendations and Strategies. There is a common political aphorism stating that the perfect is often the enemy of the good (Redman, 2000). Sometimes striving for the ideal solution creates too many political enemies, and rather than having something less perfect enacted, nothing gets passed. There is a political trade-off here, doing what is more feasible rather than attempting to accomplish the ideal.

There is a political theory called the Overton Window, developed at the Mackinac Center for Public Policy, which maintains that there is a fairly narrow group of policy solutions that are politically viable at a given point in time (Russell, 2006). The political climate limits the number of acceptable policy choices along an ideological continuum that can be considered by policy makers and still win re-election. Policies outside this window may be more optimal in terms of solving the problem, but are not politically viable at the time. The political climate can be changed. This allows the window to be shifted to include other policy options that might not have been previously politically viable.

You can take studies from peer-reviewed literature and develop a totally new policy approach to the issue. Frequently, policy areas become locked into a particular paradigm or isolated in terms of the approaches considered, only using what has been used before. Sometimes you can take an approach used in another policy area and apply it to childhood obesity or another policy area. This is an opportunity to be creative and to shift the thinking about that policy issue. This creativity may open your policy proposal up to potential funding by a foundation that is looking for innovative policy approaches to a policy problem. Of course, you also have the task of demonstrating that this innovation may actually work. We will address this further in Breakout Box 7.2.

You are not limited to only recommending incremental policy proposals. Nonincremental policy proposals may well stimulate debate and move the political discussion in a different direction. Although a nonincremental policy/program may not be quickly adopted, it may lay the groundwork for eventual adoption. By advocating a major policy change, one is at least putting it on the legislative agenda for potential or future legislative action. Major change cannot come about without an advocate and a proposal. Compromises might have to be made to it in order to get your legislation passed, but a non-incremental policy proposal could provide a new framework for solving a public problem.

### EVIDENCE

At this point of your analysis, you should remember several things from Chapter 1. Type 2 evidence is very different in nature from the type 1 evidence you used in Chapter 3 to describe the policy background or in Chapter 4 to create the statement of the policy issue. For that you needed mostly descriptive data (type 1 evidence) such as incidence rates of childhood obesity to demonstrate that a problem existed. Now, however, you need to go beyond that and provide evidence to convince policy makers that a particular program or policy is associated with positive impacts on the obesity problem. This is a different level of evidence (type 2 evidence); it uses inferential data that relies on statistical modeling of associations between independent and dependent variables or case studies that demonstrate that a program has positive results. Refer back to Breakout Box 6.1 for examples.

Recall from your courses in statistics that an association between $x$ and $y$ does not necessarily mean that there is a causal relationship. There may be a number of confounding factors that influence the observed relationship between a policy change and obesity-related outcomes. For example, you could find a statistical relationship between childhood obesity and ethnicity (Messiah, Arheart, Lopez-Mitnik, Lipshultz, & Miller, 2013). However, that relationship is not causal but associational. Ethnic groups in the United States tend to have lower incomes, less education, and live in poorer environments; these are confounding factors for the relationship between childhood obesity and ethnicity.

Your political or lay audience may not have a great understanding of the importance and differences in the types of studies and methodologies that are used, so you must assist them in understanding what weight should be given to any individual study or group of studies. This is a heavy responsibility. Your understanding of statistics becomes important here because you are going to be making an assessment as to which program/ policy has the greatest level of evidence supporting that it is effective, cost-efficient, equitable, or whatever criteria of success you have earlier established. If you are not confident about your analytical skills, you need to seek out assistance.

Because obesity is a complicated problem and has many potential genetic, biological, and social causal factors, it is going to be difficult to determine the appropriate strategy to reverse the obesity trend in the United States. In fact, there is no definitive single solution to the problem. If there were, it would probably have been proposed and adopted in multiple communities or states with clear indicators of success. Consequently, your policy initiative is not likely to "solve" the problem of obesity in the United States, but it may provide a partial response to the growing obesity epidemic.

Because the success of your policy/program proposal is not a given, you will need evidence to support its adoption. You need to provide potential supporters with evidence to support their argument and you need to provide evidence to counter the skeptics. The evolution of evidence-based medicine/public health was discussed in Chapter 1. In this section of the policy analysis, you will focus on the development of a rational case for your policy on childhood obesity. Because policy is meant to address an existing social problem, you need to demonstrate that your policy proposal is likely to work in a given geopolitical system and will have favorable outcomes.

Here you should recall the difference between efficacy and effectiveness, as discussed in Chapter 1. "Efficacy" is basically whether the proposed policy or program can work at all; this typically occurs under ideal circumstances. Remember that a randomized clinical trial (RCT) is such a test of efficacy. However, whether or not the policy or program will work in a real setting is a much different question. There are issues of political acceptability, varying values and cultures, legal and ethical questions, or mere practicality that might undermine a potentially efficacious program. In policy we are more concerned about the "real world" with all its complications than we are in the ideal world. Therefore, external validity becomes very important in policy analysis (Rao & Anderson, 2012; Thomson & Thomas, 2012). This does not mean that internal validity (the degree of certainty that the intervention being studied is associated with the effect) is not important. However, if your policy proposal is unlikely to work in the real world, it has limited utility as public policy.

It becomes complicated and ethically problematic to do RCTs outside clinical settings, although group-randomized (quasiexperimental) designs are frequently used in public health (Hollar et al., 2010). A policy or program is usually developed for a particular geopolitical unit, and some type of formal or informal evaluation will be conducted to assess its impact. For example, if you are assessing a school nutrition policy intervention, sometimes there is a "before and after" evaluation in schools exposed to the intervention. Alternatively, there might be an evaluation comparing schools using the intervention against schools in which the intervention was not used. Sometimes there may be a "natural experiment" in which certain jurisdictions adopted a policy before others and you can compare the effects over time. Refer back to the menu-labeling policies described in Breakout Box 6.1. Sometimes there will be multiple cases with some type of random or nonrandom selection according to geography or setting. Sometimes there might be a rigorous qualitative evaluation of the policy development process. Refer back to the examples from Washington State in Chapters 4 and 5. Sometimes there will be no formal evaluation, but merely subjective opinions by participants as to how successful the policy/program was. Programs and policies funded by external sources (e.g., foundations or government agencies) tend to require formal evaluations. However, keep in mind that people/organizations do not like to be associated with a "failed" program or policy, so that any evaluation designed and conducted by the managers of a program may be slanted toward a positive outcome. Evaluations conducted by external evaluation experts tend to carry more weight.

The hierarchy of evidence discussed in Chapter 1 should not be taken too dogmatically. A well-designed, single-case study (which is at the bottom of the traditional hierarchy) may actually be the most useful study for a policy proposal because it might reveal details about the process of adopting or implementing a policy (as we saw in the Breakout Boxes describing the Washington State policies in Chapters 4 and 5). Such case studies are important to providing guidance as to which factors may be most important to policy work in the real world by examining the contextual factors of a policy's development (Yin, 2009). Qualitative research is a very valuable tool for policy analysis, especially for studying policy formulation and implementation (Sofaer, 1999). Cross-sectional studies can also be very useful, as the national data surveillance systems we mentioned previously (e.g., Behavioral Risk Factor Surveillance System [BRFSS], National Health and Nutrition Examination Surveys [NHANES]) lend themselves to this type of analysis. As mentioned previously, qualitative and quantitative data can be used in a complementary manner as part of a mixed-methods design.

For example, a study describing the implementation of a child nutrition program in an elementary school in New Jersey will tend to discuss in detail the types of things that worked well and those that did not work well. Of course, such single case studies suffer from a potential lack of generalizability or external validity, that is, the success of that program might be totally unique and not replicable elsewhere. The extent to which a policy can be replicated elsewhere is a critical issue. However, if you were developing a policy on childhood obesity for the state of New Jersey or a county in New Jersey, this single-case study might be very valuable because the case exists within the same value/political/legal culture of New Jersey. However, because your policy/program on childhood obesity is to be at the national level, the example from New Jersey provides some evidence but it is less persuasive that it will work in New Mexico, where a different set of value/political/legal variables will be at play. This does not mean that the case study in New Jersey is not important in your discussion for national policy on childhood obesity. The program may have been established as part of a demonstration program funded by a large organization and undergone careful external evaluation. For example, the Alliance for a Healthier Generation (2012) has done a study on its "healthy schools" program. A particular program might be very innovative and worth funding as a federal demonstration project in other states.

Another caveat is that many states have considerable "divides" in terms of their value/political/legal cultures, often along urban/rural or north/south or east/west geographic areas (e.g., northern and southern California). There are a number of states that have areas that wish to secede from the existing state because they feel they are so politically and culturally different.

What is important from the analytical side is that you are aware of the strengths and weaknesses of various types of studies supporting and opposing various policy options. Potential opponents to your policy proposal will indeed point to the weaknesses of the evidence that you select, so you need to be prepared to defend the evidence that you have.

This analytical process can be quite frustrating as the role of science has recently become politicized in policy debates. This is typically referred to as the need for "sound science." Advocates for "sound science" frequently point to one study or a few studies (no matter what their evidentiary strength) that raise questions as to the preponderance of evidence presented by the literature. Any evidence that something might not work is taken to mean that the policy should not be enacted because there is doubt. However, this argument is typically the result of a misunderstanding of the essence of science and becomes a political cover for disagreeing with the preponderance of available evidence. Unlike the laws of nature, there are few things in health and social science that can be demonstrated to hold true 100% of the time. Even within very successful clinical trials, the intervention rarely works 100% of the time.

Studies vary as to the populations covered, designs used, means by which they measured important variables, and statistical techniques applied—any or all of which might lead to differing results. There are well-designed studies and there are poorly designed studies. One has to be able to know the difference between the two. The relationship between tobacco and adverse health effects was debated for decades, resulting in policy delays on the regulation of tobacco. Differing results from studies do not mean that a relationship is not there. It is wise to be familiar with those studies that provide contrary evidence to your policy because opponents will quickly use those studies to attempt to discredit the evidence that you have presented.

Public health uses the precautionary principle as an important foundation for policy advocacy. This principle maintains that when the health of the public or the environment is at risk, it is not necessary to wait for scientific certainty before policy action is taken. Policy makers use this principle to justify decisions in situations in which there is the possibility of harm from not taking action. This principle maintains that there is a social responsibility to act if there is probable concern for people or the environment. Refer back to the Breakout Boxes in Chapters 4 and 5 to see how this was reflected in the policy examples from Washington State. The adopted policy can be changed if subsequent scientific studies reveal different outcomes or unintended consequences. As an example, public health programs/policies involving vaccination, quarantine, and other emergency measures can be implemented in conditions where an epidemic has serious potential consequences.

The important thing to remember here is to be honest and straightforward in the presentation of the evidence available. You always need to remember that you are preparing this analysis for someone else (e.g., a policy maker or organization). You do not want to have their credibility questioned or set them up for failure. You are collecting evidence and trying to assemble the best information available. No individual study is ever decisive, especially in a social/policy setting. If you rest your case on one study, opponents only have to find flaws in that one study to undermine your policy. What you need to do is decipher what the preponderance of the evidence shows and what the highest quality studies suggest regarding impacts and outcomes of your policy recommendation in a real-world setting. This is not an easy task.

## PEER-REVIEWED LITERATURE

Assuming your knowledge of obesity in children is limited, you will need to find innovative programs and evidence as to which programs have been demonstrated to be effective. Even though you might have multiple criteria for success, effectiveness is one of the major criteria that would be used to evaluate any policy. One would not wish to waste public resources by putting into place programs or policies that did not work. Therefore, what you first need to determine is what policy/program has a chance of working.

Peer-reviewed literature is one of the best sources of information on efficacy and effectiveness. However, there is a note of caution here in that there is a publication bias in favor of publishing studies that result in a positive outcome. Those studies that do not show a positive result (null studies) tend have a more difficult time being published, even though the lack of a relationship is just as important as the existence of a relationship.

Peer-reviewed studies are also one of the easiest sources to access due to the multiple centralized electronic databases that are readily available. If you are not familiar with the public databases, you should access a research university librarian to provide you with some initial assistance. They can ease your initial search and highlight major resources. In addition, research university libraries generally have free access to many of these databases as well as individual peer-reviewed journals. Many local hospitals have their own libraries that contain clinical journals. If you are located in Washington, DC, you can gain access to the Library of Congress (http://www.loc.gov/rr/readerregistration.html).

Because you are dealing with health, one of the most useful sources of peer-reviewed literature is the National Institutes of Health's National Library of Medicine's PubMed (http://www.ncbi.nlm.nih.gov/pubmed). This database catalogs most major peer-reviewed journals in the field of medicine, public health, and the environment. Although mainly covering U.S. peer-reviewed journals, this database also includes the more influential health journals in other countries. This is useful since obesity is not solely a U.S. problem. By entering the topic of childhood obesity in the PubMed database, you will be given citations for over 8,000 articles on childhood obesity as of 2013. That is probably more than what you wanted and more than will be useful for your analysis. Childhood obesity is such a common topic that it is one of the preset topics listed for PubMed. Because this is a very broad topic, the articles will cover all different aspects of childhood obesity in various countries. One can narrow the search by entering other characteristics into the search engine. For example, you could enter "school-based obesity prevention" (another PubMed preset topic), and you will then get more than 1,700 citations for different articles as of 2013. One can then scan those citations for the articles that seem to be the most current or relevant to your policy initiative. If you are covering a different policy area, you will probably need to access other major indices. For example, there are separate databases for law (Westlaw, www.westlaw.com) and business (Business Source Premier, http://www.ebscohost.com/academic/business-source-premier). Both of these indices may also be useful for health policy analyses, depending on the topic.

One of the things that you would want to look for within the PubMed citations is a systematic review article. These articles typically have "systematic review" in the title. See Breakout Box 7.1 for further details. They are particularly helpful because they summarize the findings of the published literature between given years for particular topics. By typing in "systematic review" after childhood obesity, PubMed gives you over 1,700 articles as of 2013. Some systematic reviews may be for minority populations; some may be for other countries; some may be more recent than others. You will want to scan this list for those systematic reviews that appear to be the most applicable to your policy topic or are the most recent. These systematic reviews will be helpful in highlighting the seminal works that you should examine. Systematic reviews tend to identify areas where there is basic consensus within the literature and where there are major or slight differences. They may point to especially innovative policies or programs. They will discuss important data and methodological differences among the studies. The bibliography of these systematic reviews will provide you with the ability to locate those critical studies that are most applicable to your policy interest. These studies might support your policy or support those who might challenge your policy proposal. Either way, you must understand what those articles contribute to the understanding of childhood obesity.

A similar type of study that you should attempt to locate is a meta-analysis. A meta-analysis combines data from multiple studies and then produces a summary statistical estimate of the overall statistical relationship among the variables. A meta-analysis is useful in examining the statistical strength of individual studies as well as coming up with one number

## BREAKOUT BOX 7.1

### Using Systematic Reviews to Inform Policy Analysis

Although one might think that there is a lot of evidence comparing various childhood obesity programs and policies, in reality, comparative effectiveness research is an emerging science, especially in community settings. An example of a systematic review of childhood obesity programs can be found in a recent article by Bleich, Segal, Wu, Wilson, and Wang (2013). The authors systematically reviewed community-based childhood obesity prevention programs in the United States and other high-income countries.

To find relevant studies, the authors searched databases, including MEDLINE, Embase, PsychInfo, CINAHL, clinicaltrials.gov, and the Cochrane Library. Only studies published in English were included. To be eligible for inclusion, obesity interventions had to have been implemented in the community setting; have at least 1 year of follow-up after baseline; and compare results from an intervention group to a comparison group. This yielded nine community-based studies for inclusion: five randomized controlled trials and four nonrandomized controlled trials with comparison groups. One study was conducted only in the community setting, three were conducted in the community and school setting, and five were conducted in the community setting in combination with at least one other setting (such as the home). Outcome measures included changes in body mass index (BMI) and health behaviors.

After synthesizing the data, the authors graded the quantity, quality, and consistency of the best available evidence by adapting an evidence-grading scheme recommended in the *Methods Guide for Effectiveness and Comparative Effectiveness Reviews* (Agency for Healthcare Quality and Research, 2012). Results showed that desirable changes in BMI were found in four of the nine studies. Two studies reported statistically significant improvements in behavioral outcomes (e.g., physical activity and vegetable intake).

The authors concluded that the strength of evidence is "moderate" that a combined diet and physical activity intervention conducted in the community setting with a school component is more effective at preventing obesity or overweight compared to other types of interventions or no intervention. A "moderate" rating indicates that

*(continued)*

## BREAKOUT BOX 7.1 (*continued*)

the authors had moderate confidence that the evidence reflects the true effect, and further research may change our confidence in the estimate of the impact over time. However, the authors emphasize that even if interventions have a modest effect on individual body weight, the cumulative population-wide impact has the potential to yield significant public health benefits. The authors also recommend more research using consistent methods in order to better understand the comparative effectiveness of childhood obesity prevention programs in community settings.

**Thought Questions**

Imagine that you are doing an analysis for a policy maker who is generally supportive of community-based childhood obesity programs and wants to continue dedicating funds to them. She is running against a conservative opponent who feels that tax dollars should not be used to fund programs of uncertain impact. How would you help your policy maker to:

1. Understand the evidence presented by Bleich et al., including its strengths and limitations?
2. Frame a message that aligns with her supportive stance for community-based obesity prevention programs, while not misconstruing the current state of the science?
3. Recognize how her opponent may frame the evidence presented above as indicators that these programs don't work, and how she might counter such an argument?

showing the effect size (generally a decimal from .00 to 1.00) of the variable under investigation. By combining multiple studies, a meta-analysis has the impact of expanding the size of the population represented by only one study (adding strength to the relationship) and potentially the inclusion of important subpopulations representing different ethnic groups, ages, and other variables. However, one must also be critical of such studies. One should examine the criteria used by the authors for including studies in their meta-analysis. The inclusion of poorly designed studies weakens any summary statement. If you search for a meta-analysis on childhood obesity on PubMed, you would find over 100 such studies as of 2013. An example of one such study would be "Childhood Obesity Prevention

Programs: Comparative Effectiveness Review and Meta-Analysis," a study conducted by Wang et al. at the Agency for Health Research and Quality (Wang, 2013). Some of these meta-analyses are more applicable to your potential policy concern than others, so again you will need to be selective. Meta-analyses tend to be statistically complex, so you might want to access someone who is comfortable interpreting the statistical analyses.

There are peer-reviewed journals covering both general and specialized medicine and public health. It is impossible to list all the sources, especially in all the health specialty areas. Among the more general policy and medical journals you should examine are such journals as *Health Affairs, Health Services Research, Environmental Policy Analysis, Inquiry, Journal of the American Medical Association, Journal of Community Medicine and Health Education, Journal of Health Politics, Policy and Law, Journal of Politics, Journal of Policy Analysis and Management, American Journal of Public Health, Journal of Public Health Policy, The New England Journal of Medicine, Preventing Chronic Disease, Preventive Medicine, Health & Place, Lancet, Nature, Pediatrics, Social Science and Medicine, Urban Studies,* and many others. Some of these journals are more theoretical and some of them are more practice oriented. Some specialize in rural health and some in urban health. Not all peer-reviewed journals carry the same weight. Each journal usually has an impact score (based on the frequency its articles have been cited in the literature) that is frequently located on the journal's web page.

Because you are focusing your policy research on childhood obesity, among the specialty journals that you would need to examine would be the *American Journal of Clinical Nutrition, Childhood Obesity, International Journal of Obesity, Journal of Endocrinology & Metabolism, Obesity Research, Diabetes, Pediatric Obesity,* and others. In addition, one would want to examine peer-reviewed journals in educational policy, the built environment, transportation policy, city planning, engineering, and other related areas to gain different perspectives on solutions to childhood obesity. One would use the bibliographies of accessed articles to find clusters of other research covering your topic.

The intent here is not to list all the journals that will be important for your policy analysis. It is to give you an idea as to the variety and richness of the information that is available to you through peer-reviewed journals.

## Grey Literature

Although peer-reviewed articles are an important source of policy information, they also have their weaknesses, especially for policy analysis. Peer-reviewed literature is developed by academics to promote general and applied knowledge and their careers as academics. Their personal research agendas may not match the policy needs of the country or region. This is especially true with a decline in the amount of sponsored research by state and national governments. Peer-reviewed journals also have their own interests and agendas and may not give precedence to articles that are policy or practice oriented and may not provide policy activists with the type of evidence that is needed for specific policies in a timely fashion.

Grey literature includes monographs, white papers, policy issue briefs, or technical reports that are not published by a general publisher. They might be policy issue briefs written by state or national private organizations. Grey literature tends to be written for specific audiences and has low print runs or may only be available in electronic format. Indeed, your own policy analysis will probably be an example of grey literature. Grey literature may go through some form of internal review process by the organization publishing the material, but it is generally not reviewed by an impartial panel of external reviewers. A document written by a state agency about its own programs is not likely to point out the shortcomings of its own programs, so one needs to be vigilant for self-serving content.

One of the places to look for policies/programs described by grey literature is to look at publications by geopolitical units (national, state, or local governments). State governments are frequently viewed as being a source of policy experimentation. Associate Justice Brandeis of the United States Supreme Court is generally attributed with calling states "the laboratory of democracy" in the United States (*New St. Ice Co. v. Liebmann*, 1932). The experience of a state or local obesity program is less likely to be published in a peer-reviewed journal due to its narrow or parochial reader interest. However, if the authors demonstrate that a state program/policy has potential national significance, it has a better chance of being published in peer-reviewed literature.

Accessing grey literature can be difficult. However, there are some useful sources. For example, The New York Academy of Medicine (http://www.greylit.org/reports/current) is an example of one organization that publishes a list of recently published state reports along with an electronic source to access the original report. One can use this site to search by author, title, publisher, or date of publication but not by topic. However, it is a very useful resource to keep abreast of what has been recently produced by state agencies throughout the country.

Because most grey literature ends up on agency websites, it can be searched on the web. However, such documents will not usually be the first page of a search engine's results unless you are very specific in terms of title and state. Consequently, the search for grey literature can be time consuming.

The World Wide Web is a great source for providing access to grey literature. However, that access creates its own problem, credibility. Some research groups have a particular ideological bias. One does want to get information reflecting different political ideologies such as a conservative perspective from the Heritage Foundation (http://www.heritage.org/) or a liberal perspective from the Center for American Progress ( http://www.americanprogress.org/) to learn of their differing perspectives of the issue. However, recognizing potential bias in websites is important in order to build a credible argument. It is also useful to gather information from such ideological sources in order to gain different particular perspectives on the issue. These organizations may have policy research-sounding names and a national board of advisors to add to their credibility. They may employ PhD fellows to write reports and briefs for them. Their publications are likely to be slanted to support their constituency's political positions. They are particularly helpful in warning you about the arguments that might be used to oppose your particular policy proposal. They may produce good-quality work. However, one must always be aware of their political agenda and be critical of the work produced. There are also private organizations that do a combination of writing policy white papers and legislative lobbying. They may have permanent paid lobbyists on staff. These typically have a very specific political/policy agenda. Make sure you find out the source of the grey literature that you access and examine what policy agenda the author/organization might have. This does not mean that you do not use such material; it only means that you should be cognizant of any potential bias it might have.

A major advantage of peer-reviewed publications is that the research has been blindly reviewed by a set of independent scholars who judge the validity of the methodology and the soundness of the findings of the

## BREAKOUT BOX 7.2

### The Evidence on Evidence: How Peer-Reviewed Findings Can Be (Mis)Translated by Publics and Policy Makers

*Newsweek*, September 9, 2009 online: The Daily Beast. The piece is titled "The Real Cause of Obesity." It is a short article on why the obese are often subjugated, unfairly it claims, because the real cause of obesity is not one's diet or environment, it is genetics. The article states: "Genetic studies have shown that the particular set of weight-regulating genes that a person has is by far the most important factor in determining how much that person will weigh" (Friedman, 2009). This is an interesting supposition in a popular news magazine. Although it may be true that those who are overweight and obese suffer from discrimination from others, the critical argument here is that people's actions by and large do not contribute to their obesity, but that it is primarily a result of their genetic makeup. How do we know, one might ask? The piece supposes that genetic studies have told us this— although those studies are not cited for verification.

All too often, evoking the name of "science" or "studies" is used as a proxy for truth and knowledge. The assumption, of course, being that science is always right. If anything, science is an imperfect set of enhanced but targeted guesses, that, if the studies are done well, produce findings with levels of certainty given a set of assumptions, be they accurate or not. The world and its workings are infinitely complex. No study can accommodate that level of complexity. One can only be as thorough in his or her reasoning and methods as possible within realistic parameters, given resources, access to study materials (people, places and things), and ethical and moral considerations. Does smoking cause cancer? We don't know . . . for sure. We are 99.9% sure, given experiments with rats and epidemiologic studies using humans. However, it is not ethically allowable to conduct a human experiment in which two people (preferably identical twins) are forced to live in an identically controlled environment for a good portion of their lives and where one was exposed to cigarette smoke and one was not. Ideally, we would have triplets so we could alter the dosage, or maybe septuplets to really get a sense of dose. Why? Because their genetic makeup would be identical, thus controlling for that effect in the causality equation. They would eat the same things, watch the same television shows, have the same furniture, follow the

*(continued)*

## BREAKOUT BOX 7.2 (*continued*)

same exercise routines, be exposed to the same access to sunlight, and every aspect of life would be the same to the smallest detail, aside from the exposure to cigarette smoke. Yet that study, and thus the evidence it would create, will never happen, and rightfully so.

As one reads the above-mentioned article, questions should immediately arise, such as: Who conducted this/these study(ies)? Where can I find it/them? The study or studies in the article are not referenced, therefore we cannot independently judge its/their empirical soundness. This is the worst form of "knowledge" transfer, for without references, this entire article becomes questionable.

A search of the peer-reviewed literature finds many articles linking genes to weight gain, but most of them identify the role of social and behavioral factors as well (Hewitt, 1997; Viguerie et al., 2012). The writer did not claim genetics was the ONLY factor related to obesity, just the most important. One study found in our peer-reviewed literature search a 2013 meta-analysis entitled "Genetics and Obesity," (apt) which examines the data to date on genetic variation and obesity. Some background is helpful here for those who are not geneticists. Biologically, there are two types of genetic variation (monogenic and polygenetic). The authors cite that there are currently 32 loci (genes) associated with weight gain and that the most recent evidence (2005 in this case) suggests that about 5% of severe obesity cases in children can be traced to monogenic polymorphism (mutations in the genotype) and fewer from polygenic polymorphism (Moleres, Martinez, & Marti, 2013). They conclude their review by stating that:

> despite the highly significant associations [between genetic mutation and weight gain/obesity] it has been demonstrated that the 32 loci identified for BMI account for only 1.45% of the phenotypic variation [21●], suggesting that new approaches such as the study of epigenetic mechanisms involved in obesity and a better knowledge of nutrient x gene interaction are needed. (Farooqi & O'Rahilly, 2005; Moleres et al., 2013)

This sounds complex, but despite an understanding of nutrient x gene interactions, the message is clear. Genetics seems to have a role in obesity, but we still don't know the extent. What is more important is that the authors critically discuss the measures and methods that the various studies used to conduct this work, that is, the parameters

(*continued*)

## BREAKOUT BOX 7.2 (*continued*)

around which this evidence was constructed. Although genes can be identified quite easily, what defines "obese" is subjective. They are critical of the BMI as an exact outcomes measure. Further, they suggest that more robust study designs should be used to better be able to account for the complexity of environmental factors and how they affect genetic expression and obesity, or what they call "epigenetic mechanisms."

Granted this is one review; however, it is a review of the current evidence found in a peer-reviewed scientific journal. It does not make bold assertions that obesity is all about genetics.

There is no binding rule that the news media be held to scientific standards. One would hope that policy makers would know the difference between science and the opinion of an online writer when constructing policy arguments, and that policy makers and those in the policy process would provide explicit links to the scientific evidence driving their proposals. The problem is that mass media may drive public opinion, despite the lack of scientific evidence or evidence to the contrary.

In a study published in 2013, Doctors Robert Badgett and Justin Hernandez found that politicians were significantly less likely than nonpoliticians to use citations when writing in or for journals (often in editorial or other nonresearch sections) such as the *New England Journal of Medicine* or the *Journal of the American Medical Association* (*JAMA*; Badgett, 2013). They state that this does not mean their proposals or assertions are not founded on evidence, just that it is not explicitly stated and verified. The problem is that when policy is not directly linked to evidence, it might as well be an online, unfounded statement. We can't really tell the difference.

The lesson here is that in the absence of evidence, policy is relegated to debate based on unfounded assertions and rhetoric.

paper. There is no such editor on the web and, therefore, by using the World Wide Web you have the extra burden of being that editor. As with anything on the web, there is high-quality and low-quality material. Citing questionable sources as your evidence in support of your policy undermines the credibility of your analysis. This does not mean that you should not use material from the web; it only means that you must be extremely careful of the material that you do use.

There are other disadvantages to using the web. A state's website may not have a very user-friendly search engine. Consequently, finding a particular article may be time consuming. In addition, articles may appear on a website and then be taken down and no longer be accessible. Using such data as a major source of information may be fleeting, and readers may not be able to actually access the original source.

Some policy papers blur the distinction between peer-reviewed and grey literature. The Rand Corporation (http://www.rand.org/) is one of the largest and most respected private research corporations that produces both grey literature and peer-reviewed publications. It produces very reputable research and has its own policy research PhD program. Federal government agencies frequently contract with it to do sophisticated analyses in a wide variety of policy areas. It publishes some of its own studies and also submits articles to peer-reviewed journals. The Henry J. Kaiser Family Foundation also falls into this area as well. It would be difficult to write a comprehensive review of Medicare, Medicaid, or health care reform policy without using analytical material and data from The Henry J. Kaiser Family Foundation (http://kff.org/).

Another important source for a variety of policy issues is The Brookings Institution (http://www.brookings.edu/). It publishes policy articles and books in a wide variety of areas. It includes blogs as well as articles by many distinguished authors. It also has a section devoted to public health issues.

Another important type of organization to access is private foundations that sponsor research and demonstration projects around the country or in specific regions. Within health care, there are many such foundations; one that is particularly notable is the Robert Wood Johnson Foundation (RWJF; http://www.rwjf.org/). It is the largest health-focused foundation in the United States and it is renowned for establishing model demonstration programs around the country that implement innovative solutions at the state and local level. Two RWJF programs, Active Living Research (www .activelivingresearch.org) and Healthy Eating Research (http://www .healthyeatingresearch.org), are particularly useful resources for finding obesity-related studies, including both peer-reviewed and grey literature.

RWJF publishes issue briefs that highlight successful programs it has funded around the country. For example, on the topic of childhood obesity there is an issue brief describing successful childhood obesity programs in Philadelphia, New York, Mississippi, and California (Robert Wood Johnson Foundation, 2012). Active Living by Design (ALbD), established by RWJF and the North Carolina Institute for Public Health at the University of North Carolina's Gillings School of Global Public Health, is also a good source of practical, community-level policy and environmental change initiatives across the country. Many of these community initiatives have been rigorously evaluated (http://www.activelivingbydesign.org/).

Although these tend to be local examples of policies/programs, they highlight potential solutions that could be taken to the federal level or expanded to other state/local areas by using federal funds. If, for example, an important aspect of your childhood obesity policy was to reduce disparities among populations, the previously mentioned issue brief cites Philadelphia as a place that has made progress in closing that gap (RWJF, 2012).

If you had decided to deal with state or local initiatives for your policy initiative instead of the federal level when forming the statement of the issue, you would want to be especially sensitive to what local foundations have established as priorities or funded demonstration programs in your geographic area. Many states now have relatively large state-/local-based health foundations as a result of the sale of their nonprofit hospitals to for-profit corporations. These foundations have become important sources for local experimentation and implementation of model programs in health care.

Another source of policy at the state level is the National Conference of State Legislators (NCSL; http://www.ncsl.org/). It is a bipartisan organization that conducts research and discusses policy issues. Its website is a great source for summaries of legislation introduced state by state on various topics with an electronic link to the bill in each state. The NCSL also conducts conferences for state legislative leaders to share information. It has a section on health care and provides a good source of information as to what is currently happening in individual states. An organization that has gained recent national attention is the American Legislative Exchange Council (ALEC; http://www.alec.org/model-legislation/). Although the ALEC often proposes model legislation, one must be aware that it has a political agenda favoring limited government, free markets, and state-based federalism.

Policy institutes in academic institutions are also an important source of policy ideas and evaluations of existing programs. They can also be advocates for certain policy initiatives. Some have close ties with state governments and others remain independent of political forces. Such institutes may focus on a particular topic such as early childhood development, and others might focus on regional or rural/urban areas. Some of these centers receive federal funds to serve as national or regional centers for expertise in policy development. These centers generally produce both grey literature and peer-reviewed literature.

There are also federal sources of grey literature that should be considered. We have previously mentioned the Congressional Budget Office (CBO). It provides studies on policies that have a budgetary impact (http://www.cbo.gov/). The CBO is a nonpartisan branch of the U.S. Congress that does research for members of Congress. The CBO is careful to protect its independence and be nonpartisan in its assessments. It also provides Congress with the official cost estimates for the costs or savings of any proposed legislation. Its estimates of the cost of legislative proposals can be critically important in Congressional debates on proposed legislation. Because its studies are nonpartisan, it has a great deal of credibility within and outside Congress. If one searches the CBO website for "childhood obesity," one will find studies of how obesity impacts spending on health care and federal budget or how budget sequestration will impact the Healthy, Hunger-Free Kids Act of 2010, or what will be the cost of reauthorizing a piece of legislation.

Another federal agency that is important to consult is the Government Accountability Office (GAO; http://www.gao.gov/). It too is a nonpartisan agency of the U.S. Congress that produces studies at the request of individual members of Congress. Being nonpartisan, the agency has credibility within and outside of Congress. It produces high-quality work. However, there are two things that must be considered in reviewing their reports. Although the agency is nonpartisan, the questions they are asked to examine may be quite partisan. Members of Congress may be looking for data to support their political perspectives and ask a question that is politically slanted. In addition, these studies are done at the request of a particular member of Congress looking for a timely response. The data available at the time may not be adequate to answer the question as completely as one might want if one had a couple years to study the issue, or there may not be sufficient time to do multiple sophisticated statistical analyses. In this respect, one must be careful to consider the nature of the requests for these data and, more important, the assumptions that were used in their development. Despite these limitations, GAO reports are respected and provide a useful resource for policy-specific areas.

GAO and CBO officials will testify before Congressional committees and their testimony will be contained in committee reports. Some of their reports may appear in the form of a letter of reply to a particular member of Congress. A search of the GAO website will reveal many reports on childhood obesity. If your policy proposal involves impacting (expanding, contracting, or eliminating) an existing federal program, the CBO and GAO are critical sources of information. The documents produced by these two agencies will be readily available to the staff of members of Congress and they will use them to support or oppose your policy initiative. As nonpartisan analyses, they will carry weight with members of Congress and their staff.

Another important federal source for policy alternatives is the Guide to Community Preventive Services (http://www.thecommunityguide.org/index.html). This guide is developed by the U.S. Preventive Services Task Force to make recommendations regarding the current body of evidence on different preventive health programs. It uses criteria to evaluate the level of evidence available for different preventive strategies. For example, it provides an assessment (High, Moderate, or Low) on the certainty of net benefit for a particular intervention strategy and then a letter grade (A, B, C, D, Insufficient Evidence) as to the magnitude of the impact of such a preventive strategy. Strategies graded A or B are generally recommended. Those with a grade of C are recommended if there are other considerations that support this strategy. A grade of D is given to those strategies it wishes to discourage for adoption. A grade of Insufficient Evidence is given if there is not a consensus among a panel of experts as to the benefit of such a preventive strategy. The Task Force has gained increased national significance in the implementation of the Affordable Care Act. Only those preventive procedures rated A or B can be cited by the Secretary of Health and Human Services as a required preventive procedure for health insurance policies.

If one looks at the Guide to Community Preventive Services for strategies for school-based obesity prevention programs, the score given is

"Insufficient Evidence" ("Healthy People 2020," 2010). This, of course, complicates your policy analysis in that there is no consensus among public health experts as to whether school-based obesity prevention programs are effective. This does not mean that such programs are ineffective. It merely suggests that to date there is a lack of consensus demonstrating that they are effective. If your policy proposal fit within a category that had a higher grade from the Guide to Community Preventive Services, this would bolster your argument for adoption.

It is also important to be aware of programs authorized by past legislation. For example, as a result of the American Recovery and Reinvestment Act of 2009, the U.S. Department of Health and Human Services (DHHS) received $650 million for a Prevention and Wellness Initiative (USDHHS, 2009). Part of this money was devoted to a competitive grant program for local communities to focus on programs leading to increased levels of physical activity, improved nutrition, decreased overweight/obesity prevalence, decreased tobacco use, and decreased exposure to secondhand smoke. Knowing what programs have been funded will provide you with examples throughout the country on different approaches that are being tried and evaluated.

Some laws have been passed but not yet fully implemented. For example, there is a DHHS advisory committee that will be established in 2015 that will make recommendations on dietary guidelines for Americans (Secretary of Health and Human Services, 2013). Although this does not indicate specific guidelines for children, legislation or a DHHS regulation could alter the committee's charter to develop specific guidelines for different age groups, including children or the elderly.

One would want to be familiar with efforts by the Institute of Medicine (IOM) to address the issue of obesity. Because obesity has become such a major health problem for a number of years, national resources such as the IOM have developed frameworks to address the problem. As mentioned earlier, the IOM has also published a major work entitled *Bridging the Evidence Gap in Obesity Prevention: A Framework to Inform Decision Making* (Kumanyika et al., 2010). In addition it has developed the L.E.A.D. framework, an approach to identifying, evaluating, and compiling evidence specific to obesity (Kumanyika et al., 2010). The L.E.A.D. framework calls for Locating evidence using a transdisciplinary systems perspective to understand obesity as a complex population-based problem, Evaluating evidence based on standards of quality of evidence, Assembling evidence that is relevant, and Informing Decisions by using the evidence in the decision-making processes.

Evidence-Based Practice for Public Health (EBPH) provides an electronic search engine to find the best evidence to support effective interventions (available through http://library.umassmed.edu/ebpph/index.cfm). It provides access to the Guide to Community Preventive Services, *Morbidity and Mortality Weekly Report (MMWR) Recommendations and Reports,* National Guideline Clearinghouse, as well as National Institute for Health and Care Excellence (NICE) Public Health Guidance from Great Britain. It also provides access to public health journals as well as databases. The Cochrane Public Health Group was established in 2008 to undertake systematic review of public health interventions (http://ph.cochrane.org/). A health impact assessment (HIA) is also a valuable tool for analyzing the health impact of policies outside the traditional health care sector, reflecting "the health in all policies" perspective (Fielding & Briss, 2006).

At this stage, we have really only evaluated policy/program alternatives from a perspective as to what would work. There are other methods of analysis that one might want to use. Because public programs involve monetary expenditures, cost–benefit analyses (CBA) and cost-effective analyses (CEA) are critical types of studies to include in your analysis. CEA studies measure the cost of policy or programs and compare that with the number of lives saved or some other measure such as the reduction in the number of obese children. One can compare one program versus another as to the number of dollars used to reduce childhood obesity. You should refer back to Chapter 1 to make sure you understand the difference between various economic analyses. You may also wish to analyze your policy/program alternatives based on other criteria, such as political acceptability or stakeholder support or opposition. These will certainly come into play when you make your recommendation.

## INTERVIEWS AND FOCUS GROUPS

You should consider interviewing a select number of key stakeholders. These might include other policy makers, officials within the bureaucracy, and other important stakeholders. (Refer to the examples in the Breakout

Boxes in Chapters 4 and 5). This type of qualitative information can be very valuable, either on its own or as part of a mixed-methods design. Interviewing experts in the field is also a way to access grey literature. Networking with experts in obesity, public health, and educational polices is a way to gain knowledge as to examples of policies that have been tried in different locations or that have gained national or regional notoriety. Contacting experts in state government, private organizations, or academe will provide you with a beginning knowledge of what experts in the field regard as innovative or successful efforts. These sources might also have knowledge of programs that have been tried in the past and failed.

Do not underestimate the expertise that is available within the bureaucracy of your own state government. Because many bureaucrats have continuous contact with federal officials through national or regional offices, they are valuable resources on national as well as state policy. These individuals are likely to be professionals who have dealt with nutrition, early childhood development, and educational issues over many years. They are familiar with or may be the creators of data that is critical for your analysis. They also attend national meetings where they learn from their counterparts in other states. You may be relatively new to the issue; they are not. You might hear, "We tried that 5 years ago, and it did not work." There may be some truth to that, or it may be an excuse for turf protection. Either way, these perspectives are helpful, especially if these are the same people who will be in charge of implementing your proposal after it has been adopted. They may be aware of some practical pitfalls that may undermine your policy's intent. These professionals are also sensitive to the political environment in which such policies have to be developed. The best-designed program can be a political failure because it does not account for the politics or value conflicts within a particular environment of a geopolitical system.

Another potential source of interviews would be stakeholders, such as those you listed in Chapter 5. These are people who are potentially positively or negatively impacted by the policy proposal and will devote resources to protecting their interests. As you learned in Chapter 5, some of these stakeholders have more resources and power than others; they will use those resources to either support or oppose policy changes. Choose those stakeholders who have the most relevance for your policy's success in being adopted and implemented. Consider how you may be able to address barriers, forge alliances, or find common ground with opponents.

Another group that is generally overlooked in policy analysis are those who are not organized into an interest group, but who might be the most impacted by the policy. This frequently means consumers and vulnerable populations. For example, if your policy included a proposed change in the Supplemental Nutrition Assistance Program (SNAP), important, organized stakeholders representing agricultural interests and grocery stores would have representatives who you could contact to obtain their perspectives. However, because any change in such a program would have a major impact on those actually using food stamps, you might also want to get input from them. Lower income persons using food stamps are generally not organized and lack a political advocacy group. There may be surveys of recipients available, but it is unlikely that there will be information on how your specific proposal might impact them. How will your policy change benefits or otherwise adversely affect them? Because policy is dealing with other people's lives, it is important to have an understanding of a policy proposal from their perspective. Too frequently, policy proposals ignore how policy will impact the most vulnerable because they are typically not represented in the political process. This is your opportunity to make their voices heard in your proposal. Qualitative methods can be very helpful here—you may need to go into neighborhoods and talk to people on their terms. You may not be able to do a rigorous survey, but insights obtained through interviews or focus groups (described next) can help to guide your policy. Policy analysts need to be able to walk in other people's shoes to be sensitive to equity concerns.

Interviews can be informal or structured. There are courses and texts in qualitative research methods to guide you in this process. You may have a set of questions that you ask of everyone. You may have structured interview questions for different types of contacts. You will want the results to be both informative and representative, following accepted standards for rigor in qualitative research.

Another qualitative method that is frequently used is the focus group. Focus groups, in which a small group of six to ten people are assembled to participate in a structured dialogue, can be more efficient in terms of time and resources compared to individual interviews (CDC, 2008; *Guidelines for Conducting a Focus Group*, 2005). The group needs to be large enough to generate rich discussion but not so big that some participants are left out. Focus groups require a skilled moderator who can effectively facilitate a group conversation. Do not try to conduct one of these yourself, unless you understand what it takes to moderate one or have some previous training. Determining which participants to include in the focus group is also an important part of gaining good information from a focus group. One must be sensitive to group dynamics in a focus group; for example, workers may not feel comfortable discussing safety or health-related issues when their supervisor is present in the group. People of very different political perspectives may not feel comfortable in the same focus group, so you may need to conduct several focus groups. Agency directors and government officials often prefer to be interviewed individually, both because of time constraints and confidentiality issues. Qualitative-methods texts, as well as online resources such as the ones cited here, provide information about conducting focus groups.

## WHEN TO CALL IT QUITS

As you can tell, there are a multitude of resources available to help you access and evaluate policy options. You will generally have an extensive resource base from which to pull. At some point, you will need to be sufficiently confident that you have covered the critical material that is necessary to conclude that you have not overlooked any major policy alternatives. You could probably spend 6 months or a year completing this analysis. However, practical time lines and resource constraints will come into play and you will need to draw a halt to your search for additional material. You will begin to recognize the point to quit when you keep seeing references to resources you have already accessed. This is not a guarantee you have exhausted resources, because you could just be locked into a particular paradigm of research. However, if you have made an honest attempt to access as many different sources as possible, you can begin to get a sense that you have covered the most important areas. Consultation with experts in the field will reaffirm whether there is further material to analyze.

You will now need to organize your material around the basic policy alternatives. Policies and programs will tend to cluster around specific strategies while differing on the details of such programs. Some may focus on school nutrition programs, some may focus on increased student activity, some may focus on the built environment to encourage healthy activity among children, some might focus on teacher education, and still others might focus on zoning changes to eliminate food deserts outside the school environment. You will want to consolidate the evidence and to present your decision maker with clear alternatives. This is difficult given that the topic of childhood obesity is multifaceted and interconnected. No one strategy/policy/program is likely to solve the problem of childhood obesity. However, given political realities you will need to make choices and not expect that the political process will accept a comprehensive, all-inclusive approach to childhood obesity. Given different political ideologies and values, along with multiple stakeholders with differing perspectives, you are going to have to choose.

Based on the evidence you select, you might reach a conclusion that one alternative is clearly superior to another. On the other hand, your analysis may lead you to conclude that certain policies/programs can be easily combined or that two are fairly equal in their impact and political acceptability. We will talk about this more in the final chapter. Presenting the trade-offs associated with several viable policy alternatives can be very important. There is no easy answer to this. You must build the best evidence you can from the material that you have accessed. People accessing the same information can come to very different conclusions.

What you need to remember in this section is to articulate what you have found as the supporting body of evidence for each alternative under consideration. Do the studies within the hierarchy of evidence tend to support each other, or do they differ? Do studies using different populations and methodologies come to essentially the same conclusion? Do more recent studies contradict or support older studies? Do respected journals, institutes, and foundations cluster around the same policies or programs? Do systematic reviews and meta-analyses reinforce a particular approach? Do states known for successful innovative programs tend to follow a particular path? Do CEA and CBA analyses favor one approach over another? Do your interviews and focus groups suggest a clear consensus for action or support? One should not try to force a consensus of the literature when one does not exist. There may indeed be no definitive policy response. Opponents to your policy proposal will quickly exploit discrepancies. This is where you are building an objective evidence-based case for one alternative over another.

## SUMMARY

This is going to be one of the longest sections to write in your analysis. Here is where you are going to be collecting evidence as to what might work or what has been tried in the past or in other geopolitical units. Depending on your expertise of the policy area, your search may require a great deal of effort and time. Accessing experts in the field, systematic reviews, and meta-analyses will help you get an overview of the important studies that have been completed. Accessing electronic databases for both peer-reviewed and grey literature (government and private organizations) will be critical in finding important policies and programs. Remembering the difference between efficacy and effectiveness in your appraisal of such policies and programs will also be important. You will need to be critical of the studies by examining the data and methodologies used, the logic of the conclusions derived from the data, and evaluating internal and external validity. Deciding when you have explored major alternatives and have sufficient evidence will be a key factor in terminating this portion of the analysis. This section will require the application of all the analytical skills that you have acquired and it will set you up for the remaining part of your analytical study.

## SOME THINGS TO REMEMBER

- Although incrementalism tends to dominate the political system in the United States, it has both strengths and weaknesses.
- You are not limited by incremental policy proposals; you merely need to understand the political trade-offs that are involved.
- Remember the difference between *efficacy* and *effectiveness* in a reality-based setting.
- Be honest and straightforward in your review of various policy alternatives. Seek alternative perspectives on alternatives.
- Use evidence-based peer-review and grey literature, along with qualitative methods, when possible, to evaluate the strengths and weaknesses of various alternatives.
- Seek assistance from librarians at research universities for accessing quality resources and data.

- Seek systematic reviews and meta-analyses as a place to begin your review of peer-reviewed literature.
- Seek assistance from political activists and bureaucrats in terms of what grey literature might be of assistance.
- Seek quality grey literature sources.
- Do not overlook the importance of state governmental professionals who have exposure to national and state policies and who might be responsible for implementing your policy proposal.
- Seek publications from well-respected foundations and research institutes.
- Use interviews of experts and stakeholders within the field.
- Remember that your policy analysis will be judged by the quality of the resources used.
- Recognize that many sources will have a policy bias.
- Know when it is time to quit—when you begin to see the same literature and arguments repeatedly and when a pattern starts to emerge.

## KEY WORDS

Incrementalism

Evidence

Type 2 evidence

Hierarchy of evidence

Sound science

Precautionary principle

Overton window

Peer-reviewed literature

PubMed

Systematic review

Meta-analysis

Grey literature

World Wide Web

National Conference of State
    Legislators

American Legislative Exchange
    Council (ALEC)

Henry J. Kaiser Family Foundation

Rand Corporation

Robert Wood Johnson Foundation
    (RWJF)

The Brookings Institute

Congressional Budget Office (CBO)

Government Accountability Office
    (GAO)

Institute of Medicine (IOM)

The Guide to Community Preventive
    Services

L.E.A.D. framework

Interviews

Focus groups

# Eight

# Recommendation and Strategies

These two parts of your analysis can be treated as one section or two different sections. Some might focus more on the recommendation than on the strategy, and others might see the two as inseparable. Some of your decisions might depend on the expectation of the policy makers. However you treat these topics, both should be covered. Here we have covered them together in the same chapter.

## RECOMMENDATION

This section of your report is the culmination of all your previous work. It is important at this stage to review your previous work to make sure that the recommendations are actually supported by each section of your analysis and that they tie together. For example, in the policy issue statement, you narrowed the area of concern to a specific policy topic within obesity and a specific geopolitical system. Are your potential recommendations consistent with that policy issue statement? In establishing your criteria for success, you attempted to define what a successful policy might look like and how you might be able to measure its progress. Do your recommendations align with those criteria? Your criteria for success might be more complicated than previously thought, or the data needed to measure success might have to change. In doing the systematic review of policy options, you may have evolved in your thinking from your original perceptions of the problem. That is a positive sign. Have you developed a solid evidence-based rationale for your recommendation? Your policy analysis is an iterative process. It is a living document. You will likely write and rewrite many of its sections, perhaps multiple times.

Certainly one of the measures of success you would want to use is the extent to which your policy proposal helps to improve the problem you have identified. Your systematic analysis has hopefully provided you with a good idea as to which proposal may work best in your geopolitical system.

In addition, your recommendation may also be influenced by the gain or expenditure of political capital. Remember that politicians want to gain political capital (public support, party leadership, major endorsements, or monetary contributions) for their re-election campaign or passage of additional pieces of legislation. They can then spend their political capital for re-election or for passage of other legislation now or in the future. Policy makers frequently trade favors with other policy makers on a quid pro quo basis in order to gain support for their own proposals. Which of these alternative proposals increases your policy makers' political capital? Alternatively, how much political capital do you think your policy makers are willing to spend in order to get this policy adopted?

Political ideology will also play a role in your recommendation. Given the ideological division in the United States in the past and current climate, it is important to be aware of important ideological and partisan divisions. Which is the most effective proposal in attaining success? Which is the most cost-effective proposal? Which proposal, for example, closes the equity gap in the incidence of obesity? This is where your analysis of the values undergirding the policy comes back into play. The section on systematic policy analysis could generally be very similar, whether it was written for someone on the political left or someone on the political right. The summary of the scientific evidence would probably be quite similar as well. However, the policy recommendation for these two different policy makers would be very different given the different value sets of these policy makers, the importance of political ideology in the political environment, political capital considerations, partisan concerns, and the different criteria for success for the policy proposal. All of these have to be understood and integrated to create a logical whole for your recommendation. This is also an opportunity for your own values (or those of the organization you represent) to play a role in the selection of the recommendation you make. You may wish to refer back to the Breakout Boxes in Chapter 5 for examples.

Explaining why you have chosen a policy option is more important than merely choosing A, B, or C. It is unlikely that there is one policy option that is so outstanding that it would be obvious to everyone. Because your policy makers are going to have to defend this alternative, you will need to provide them with what you believe are both the strengths and potential weaknesses of your recommendation. This section needs to not just sell the recommendation to your policy makers but also to warn them where the proposal is most vulnerable to attack. A recommendation that is overly or artificially positive may make it difficult for your policy makers to deflect criticisms brought up by opponents. Your policy makers need to be forewarned of what problems or issues might arise and where potential opponents may focus.

If there is evidence from your Systematic Review of Policy Options section that strongly supports one alternative over others, then that needs to be stated and reinforced in the recommendation section. If there is consistency of the evidence from your Systematic Review of Policy Options, you need to use that to make your case stronger. Hopefully, your Systematic Review of Policy Options section has revealed a pattern that demonstrates that studies with methodological rigor reinforce other studies using different methodologies and different populations. Do newer studies reinforce or contradict older studies? Do studies with different population samples lead to similar results? Does the evidence supporting your proposal rest on one major study for which results have not been supported by other studies? What you are looking for is a pattern within the evidence that tends to support one alternative versus the others. Remember that the policy makers may have skipped over or only skimmed your Systematic Review of Policy Options section. It is in the Recommendation section that you need to directly and concisely come to a conclusion as to the level of evidence regarding the various policy alternatives.

In reality, the current level of evidence for many policy interventions will be mixed (some studies may have found a positive impact in certain populations, but other studies may have found no significant impact). Different measures may point toward different levels of success, as we saw with the menu-labeling policies in Breakout Box 6.1. Furthermore, it may be difficult to find a randomized or group-randomized trial to inform your policy, for the reasons stated in previous chapters. In the past, this has frequently been used as a tactic to stall policy, by saying that we need more scientific evidence before a policy can be recommended. However, it is important to remember that we are unlikely to ever have absolute certainty about the impacts of many policies, making it necessary for policy makers to proceed with decision making in the face of uncertainty. Recall from our policy process diagram (Figure 1.1) that policy making is iterative.

As new data comes to light from the scientific community, policies can be terminated or revised. Due to the severity and complexity of many public health problems, we do not always have the luxury of waiting for more research to accumulate before taking action. It is also sometimes the case that although a policy maker may not be willing to make "big P" (legislative) changes, "little p" (organizational/institutional) changes may be feasible. Remember that when the consequences of inaction are great, action in the absence of perfect knowledge may be preferable.

Every policy choice has intended and unintended consequences. Those consequences that are intended will generally be clearly stated in your policy proposal, because those will align with your criteria for success. One should also provide an estimate as to the probability of these positive-intended consequences actually happening. Because positive results are not a given, what is the probability that they will actually materialize? To what extent will people and/or entities cooperate to self-regulate in support of the policy and thus avoid costly enforcement? What is the likelihood that business interests will not file suit to delay the implementation of your proposal? What must the 50 states do in order to implement your federal obesity proposal? Are the incentives for state action sufficient?

Intended consequences can be positive or negative, but hopefully the positive ones will outweigh the negative ones. A negative-intended consequence could be delaying the implementation of a proposal for a number of years, thus not impacting children during their critical developmental years and also potentially increasing the cost of the program due to inflation. Delaying implementation may also give opponents time to organize more resistance to the program before any positive outcomes can be achieved. Two points are important to note here. The first is that, as the policy analyst, you need to be clear on how you are determining these probabilities of success. Most likely, this will be a subjective assessment based on personal knowledge or the knowledge or your collaborators. This is fine, but know that areas of subjectivity are also areas where your analysis can and likely will be challenged on its assumptions. The second is that you should realize that, as your policy increases in scope, the likelihood of adoption and successful implementation might decline due to heightened opposition to anticipated large changes.

There are also unintended consequences to policy choices. These are less clear. These are things that will occur but are less predictable or may be unforeseen. Again, these may be positive or negative. For example, an unintended consequence of increasing exercise patterns in children to avoid obesity is the potential increase in physical injuries. Some could be minor scrapes and bruises and others could be life threatening. It is unknown what the extent of these injuries might be. However, one can use historical trends, published scientific studies, and other data to make some conservative estimates on what the impact might be. Steps might be taken to attempt to minimize these potential negative unintended consequences (e.g., increased adult supervision or building an environment designed with safety in mind), but some injuries will occur anyway. A positive unintended consequence might be the increased sale of athletic equipment, the development of new types of safety equipment, the development of child activity centers, the increase in construction of bike paths, or the increase in parental physical activity due to increased child activity. Of course, all of these in turn shift costs both to the individual and to society. Questions arise such as: Can families of lower means afford the costs of safety equipment or bicycles and thus be able to fully participate, or are disparities likely to arise? Further, will society be willing to shift resources from current needs to build and maintain bicycle paths, and what is the potential impact of doing so? One can never fully account for all the unintended consequences that will occur, but to the extent that one can be aware of potential adverse consequences, the less surprise there will be regarding the net impact of the program.

Due to these unintended consequences, it is good to have various checkpoints for the progress of the program/policy. Most programs/policies are not inherently perfect; they generally need some tweaking along the way. In fact, one type of evaluation, called "developmental evaluation," focuses on the developmental nature of the policy process by emphasizing that one should engage in evaluative thinking continuously during the policy process, not just at the end (Patton, 2010). You should attempt to estimate how long after the implementation of your policy you can start to measure progress toward its stated goals. Refer back to the study by Krieger et al. (2013) in Breakout Box 6.1 about the menu-labeling policy in King County for an example.

Sometimes goals themselves need to be adjusted as the context changes over time; this should also be documented. If your policy is not meeting its targets for specific time frames, it may be necessary to make some modifications in the program or alter the measures for determining progress.

In order to put this all into perspective, you could create a matrix that could be part of the document, compiled into an appendix, or left out of the printed narrative but used as a tool for your own clarification. As mentioned before, any matrix is merely a tool that can help you try to structure your own decision making. As such, it is only useful if you use it honestly. As in the matrix for the stakeholders, one could develop a scale (e.g., from 1 to 10, with 10 being the highest). Much of this will be somewhat subjective, but what the matrix forces you to do is to measure each of the alternatives using the same criteria. You gain nothing by not being forthright in your analysis. The following table is totally fictitious; it is not based on any actual analyses, and is intended to merely demonstrate how such a table might be developed. Other examples can be found in the health impact assessment (HIA) literature (Harris et al. 2009).

As seen in the recommendation matrix in Table 8.1, the various policy options have different strengths and weaknesses. Remember that these evaluations are fictitious and are meant only to illustrate the process. For example, the Healthy Kids Nutrition Program and the Federal Menu Labeling Requirements are evaluated as being the most incremental. The Federal Complete Street Funding option is evaluated as having the lowest political acceptability. One can change the criteria being used (the columns). One can total the rows to get a total score for each of the options. Table 8.1 treats all the criteria (Effectiveness, Incremental, etc.) as equals. However, you could weigh the criteria differently, with Effectiveness being 1.5 compared to 1 for Incremental. Since you only have data for one of the alternatives on the issue of cost effectiveness, you might want to remove that as one of your criteria. That would change the totals the last column. What is important is that you not treat the matrix as an absolute, but rather as a tool to help you think through how the various options compare.

Although the matrix will probably not appear in your report, developing it will help you write your narrative concerning the strengths and

## TABLE 8.1
## Recommendation Matrix

| Policy Alternative | Effectiveness | Incremental | Cost-Effective Analysis | Political Acceptance | Totals |
|---|---|---|---|---|---|
| Healthy Kids Nutrition Program | 6 | 9 | 6 | 8 | 23 |
| Federal Supplemental Physical Fitness Program | 7 | 5 | Not available | 4 | 16 |
| Federal Menu-Labeling Requirements | 4 | 9 | Limited cost data available in some states | 9 | 22 |
| Federal Complete Street Funding | 6 | 6 | Not available | 3 | 15 |

weaknesses of your recommendation. Given that most of the table is based on subjective evaluations, one would not want to interpret the numbers too literally. If one had a panel of experts judge the alternatives, the values might have more meaning. However, because this is just your opinion, you would not want the matrix to be misinterpreted by your reader to mean anything other than its representation of your evaluation. If one alternative is clearly a winner on one criterion, this might tip the balance in terms of your recommendation and be the focus of your narrative in defense of that alternative.

You should clarify with your policy makers from the beginning as to whether they prefer you to make a single recommendation or whether they wish to make the decision themselves and only want to be presented with multiple viable options. Policy makers who may be familiar with the HIA process may prefer a presentation of policy alternatives with qualitative and/or quantitative information about the pros and cons of each alternative (Cole & Fielding, 2007; Farhang et al., 2008; Human Impact Partners, 2008). As has been stated a number of times, you should have a clear understanding as to the expectations of the audience for whom your analysis is being written.

It may indeed be that you are torn between two policies or that you feel uncomfortable recommending one over the other, particularly when the underlying scientific evidence is mixed. As an alternative to providing one recommendation, you could list the alternatives in priority order. In this case, you are indicating that one alternative is better than the others, but you are leaving other options on the table. In this situation, you should probably explain the potential situations that would give rise to one alternative rising above the others. Under different circumstances, Policy Option B might supplant Policy Option A. For example, if an upcoming election has the potential to change control of one of the branches of government, then perhaps the whole political landscape might change after the election, thus making a different alternative more politically viable. To make your analysis more useful, you should be as direct and specific as possible.

## STRATEGIES

Your policy recommendation will have little impact unless you begin to think about how such a policy/program could be both adopted and then implemented by the political system. These are two separate but linked activities. The political process is largely concerned with what might be done (options, scope of policy, inclusions or exclusion of those impacted, cost, etc.), whereas the policy and implementation process is concerned with what can be done (who implements, what regulations are to be written, oversight, evaluation, budget, etc.).

The "best alternative" may not be actually politically viable. However, there are different strategies that can be used to increase the chances of success. The policy strategy that you recommend may actually be the most important factor in your analysis and determine its fate. Therefore, your recommendation has to take into account the political process that is most likely to lead to success.

### Legislative Strategy

Using the legislative process for policy approval is the typical strategy that one would follow to adopt a new program/policy. The legislative process contains two very separate processes (authorization and appropriation), both of which are critical and both of which involve different subsets of legislators. The authorizing legislative process is focused on the substantive portion of the proposal. It approves a particular legislative proposal to become law. Approval by both houses of the legislature and the executive provides the executive branch with the necessary legal authorization to set up the administrative structure to implement those policies and programs. For example, the Healthy, Hunger-Free Kids Act established the structure for the U.S. Department of Agriculture (executive branch) to develop regulations like Smart Snacks in School. Local school boards must now become involved in implementation functions, including enforcement mechanisms.

Particular legislative committees and subcommittees have jurisdiction over substantive policy areas such as health, nutrition, agriculture, and highways, among others. Legislators on those committees are a subset of legislators who tend to specialize in that particular policy arena and are very protective of their committee's jurisdiction. Depending on the particular focus of your proposal, your policy proposal could fall under the jurisdiction of the education committee, the health and human services committee, the agricultural committee, or perhaps two of those committees. If the committee has a wide jurisdiction there may be various subcommittees that will have initial jurisdiction over the legislation. Which of these committees or subcommittees might act more favorably on your proposal? Will writing your proposal with a targeted focus mean that a more sympathetic committee will have jurisdiction over the proposal? Does your policy maker have a good working relationship with the chair of a critical committee for passage? Who would be the best suited legislator(s) to sponsor your proposal? Is there a possibility to get legislators from both parties to sponsor your policy proposal? Is there a possibility for getting sponsors in each house of the legislature? You may find it helpful to review the Breakout Boxes in Chapters 4 and 5 for examples.

There are separate authorization processes and committees in each house of the legislature, so you will need to pay attention to each house, typically the House of Representatives and the Senate. They will have separate committees with different jurisdictions. They will have different rules and traditions in their authorization approval process. The majority leadership of each house might come from the same party or be controlled by different parties.

The second part of the legislative process is the appropriation process. This involves a very different subset of legislators who deal with the appropriation of funds and the budget. Both of these processes are critical, because it does indeed happen that a policy has been adopted through the authorization policy process and become law of the land, but it receives zero or $1 in the budget because its advocates have not paid sufficient attention to the appropriation/budgetary processes in both houses of the legislature. Such a situation mutes the authorizing process until funds can be allocated for implementation. This has happened with school-related wellness policies, whereby schools are required to form Wellness Councils, but often no additional resources are provided for the Councils to implement any recommendations (Boles et al., 2011). Sometimes legislatures will authorize a particular program but pass the responsibility of funding it to a different level of government, such as from the federal to the state level or the state to the local level. These are typically called unfunded mandates. Consequently, you will need to pay attention to the membership of budgetary committees in both houses of the legislature. Is there a member of the budget/appropriations committee who is sympathetic to your proposal and can cosponsor it?

The national and state governments (except for Nebraska) have bicameral legislatures. There is generally a House and a Senate that needs to pass the legislation in identical form. This means that your policy is going to have to be approved by at least four separate committees (authorization and appropriation committees) before even being voted on by the entire membership of the two legislative bodies. There are frequently other procedural committees (e.g., the United States House Ways and Means Committee) that can be stumbling blocks for your proposal. In addition, if there is a disagreement between the two legislative branches, it will have to be approved again by both houses after a conference committee has worked out the differences between the two houses. Other committees might be added depending on the particular legislative processes and specific legislative procedures. It is important for you to have an understanding of the legislative process that your policy proposal will have to go through.

Each of these committees and houses of the legislature have their own politics, perspectives, and personalities. One key legislator may be sufficient to prevent your proposal from going forward. Some legislatures require all bills to be reported out of committee with a recommendation for passage or defeat, whereas other legislatures allow committees to bury legislation, sometimes without a vote of the full committee. Some legislatures have powerful subcommittees. Some legislatures have very powerful chairs of committees who can singlehandedly bottle up legislation or impose their will on the rest of the committee. Some legislatures have relatively weak committee chairs but focus legislative powers in the leadership of the majority party in that chamber. Some legislatures have rules providing the minority party with significant powers and others have rules giving them very limited powers. No matter what legislative structure and processes are in place, it is incumbent on you to understand the peculiarities of the legislative body that your policy maker will be dealing with to get your proposal approved and funded.

In addition to the political structural requirements mentioned above, there are also numerous procedural rules and traditions that are followed in the legislative process. Each legislature will have its own set of rules that can be used to slow down or expedite legislation. It generally takes someone many years to understand all of these procedural rules. However, those who do understand them are at a decided advantage in getting legislation through the legislative process.

It is not expected at this stage of the policy analysis that you must determine all of this legislative strategy yourself. Much of the legislative strategy will shift as the policy works its way through the legislative process. Other members of your policy makers' staff may be responsible for legislative strategy. You may be able to reach out to legislative staffers, legal analysts, or some of your identified stakeholders to seek advice as to the best legislative strategy to pursue. However, to the extent possible, you should provide your policy maker with some idea as to how this policy could actually become law.

For example, because your policy proposal on obesity is at the national level, you will need to understand the dynamics of Congress. The role of committees in Congress has diminished in comparison to the norms in Congress 30 years ago. Party leadership positions (such as Speaker of the House, majority leader, or party whips) have gained increased control of the legislative process by lessening the importance of seniority for committee chair positions and reducing the size of committee staffs. The increased role of the filibuster in the Senate and the current need for 60 Senators to agree on proposed legislation rather than a majority of 50 has changed the dynamics of legislative approval in the Senate. The increased ideological division, especially in the House of Representatives with an increased number of gerrymandered "safe seats," makes standing on ideological principles rather than compromise more of the norm. These and other characteristics of the legislative climate need to be taken into account if you are to follow a legislative strategy and be successful. You need to understand the structure and policy processes of the governmental body with which you are dealing. It creates the rules of the road. To be successful, you need to understand those rules as much as possible.

Using the example of the obesity proposal, one would want to know who the chairs of the major committees are in the House and the Senate who will have initial jurisdiction of the proposal. What are their known positions on obesity? Health? Education? Who are their staff members that work on health issues? Has your policy maker worked with them in the past and built relationships based on trust and understanding? Are committee members or committee chairs open to compromise? Are any key committee members running for re-election and will they want to avoid taking any controversial positions, or do they want to establish a particular ideological track record? Are key legislative members preparing to run for another office and need to build a broad legislative record to run on? Has a powerful legislator announced that he or she is no longer running for office and is thus willing to expend all of his or her political capital for a worthy cause? Does a key legislator have a spouse who has diabetes? Is one of the legislators a physician or other clinician who can sell the policy to others on the committee or the floor of the chamber? Are there legislators whose spouses play an important role in health care or education? Knowing the background, career goals, personal interests, and family relationships of legislators, can all give you an inside track in building a legislative coalition?

Much of this legislative strategy will change as legislative sponsors come on board or lobbyists try to influence the content of the original proposal. At this stage, you merely need to be cognizant of the major political forces, personalities, and value orientations at play (Clark, 2002). Asking questions of people who have experience with the legislative process will assist you a great deal in understanding what might be possible.

This is also where your previous analysis of stakeholders becomes critical. From your list of stakeholders, you will find potential supporters and opposition to your proposal. Your policy maker will need to build a core group of stakeholders that he or she can begin to approach to support this policy. Because you have already weighted the stakeholders according to their relative strengths, you know which ones are critical for passage. You also know where opposition to your policy is most likely to emerge. As indicated before, some stakeholders may be able to supply money, some can provide assistance in writing the legislation, some can provide grass-roots testimony. Building such alliances with critical stakeholders is one of the first strategies in the legislative struggle for passage. Research on obesity policy suggests that if you can garner bipartisan support, your chances of success will improve (Dodson et al., 2009). If you have already contacted some of these stakeholders during your systematic review of the policy alternatives, you are much further along in this stage of getting their cooperation as the proposal moves forward.

In building potential alliances, you need to have an understanding of what is important to each of the stakeholders you are attempting to align in support of your policy. It is unlikely that every stakeholder supports all the elements of your policy proposal. Some stakeholders may support your policy for their own economic gain. Some may support it because it makes rational sense. Some may support it because your policy has less of an adverse impact than other options being considered. Some may not really be all that supportive of your policy but may be willing to vote for it in exchange for your policy maker's support for other legislation that is more important for them, a quid pro quo type of vote (I will vote for your proposal if you vote for mine). There may be as many reasons for stake-holders and other legislators to support your policy proposal as there are stakeholders/legislators. You may never know all the reasons some support or oppose the proposal unless a complete legislative history of that policy is written many years later by an objective party. At this stage, you are not going to actually build these alliances; you are merely preparing the groundwork for these to materialize and attempting to assess those that exist or have existed in the past.

In creating this coalition of interests, you might also begin to assess what you can give up and where compromise might be possible. Because your policy proposal has to pass multiple hurdles with different power-ful blockers, additional and different groups may have to be added to the coalition as you go from one committee to the next or from the House to the Senate. However, to get that additional group to support your policy, you might have to make an additional compromise. Will this additional compromise result in losing any stakeholders who were brought in earlier in the process? What in the policy is central and cannot be compromised? Are there aspects of the policy proposal that would be ideal to have but would not seriously weaken the impact of the policy if they were deleted? When is defeat preferable to further compromise? These are critical questions that will not be fully addressed until the process is over. However, knowing that these issues are coming and trying to lay the foundation for addressing them in the future are important aspects to consider in the policy process and in making your recommendation to your policy maker.

It should also be remembered that most legislative proposals do not become law. The legislative process is a long, circuitous, and frustrating process intentionally designed to weed out most legislative proposals. The political structure and processes were not designed to create an efficient decision-making machine. They were designed to divide political power, to give power to minority opinion, and to protect individual rights, even at the cost of frustrating majority rule. Frustration is part of the political process.

Some legislative proposals are designed not to pass. They may be introduced to merely keep the issue alive and before the public to prevent it from getting lost. The legislator may be biding time, knowing an issue can be addressed in the future, when the political environment is more favorable. At this stage in the policy analysis process, you should at least be clear as to whether your policy makers intend your policy to become law or whether they intend it to be a placeholder for future consideration. Again, how much political capital are your policy makers willing to expend for this proposal?

Passage of any legislative proposal will require your policy makers to expend both concentrated effort by staff and a portion of their political capital. If the prospects for passage are poor at the present time, one might introduce the legislation and allow it to percolate without expending a great deal of effort. Perhaps the political climate will change in 2 years or an incident will provide an opportunity for the issue to rise onto the active political agenda. On the other hand, your policy makers might wish to expend a great deal of their political capital in a losing cause in order to gain electoral or party support, and thereby make a net gain in political capital even though the policy proposal is likely to be defeated. Your policy makers' names may become publically attached to this policy issue or bill and give them increased political visibility. These are all legitimate strategies that have little to do with solving the policy issue. The point here is to engage in a strategy by intent and not by happenstance. You should have some idea as how your policy makers are viewing this issue and how the legislative process is likely to turn out. This may indeed influence your choice of alternatives and your choice of strategy.

One of the basic techniques of influencing the policy process is framing the policy issue. Legislation is complex. Any piece of legislation tries to do multiple things. To the public, the legislation is often confusing. Framing is basically a marketing tool for policy makers to get people to think about the legislation from a particular point of view, or "frame." It attempts to align a policy with an underlying value or emotion. For example, legislation to restrict fast-food chains within a given distance from a school, or limiting the number of fast-food chains in a particular neighborhood could be viewed through the "frame" of "keeping our children healthy." It is a simple phrase that can be repeated over and over as you attempt to add stakeholders and supporters to support your policy. On the other hand, because "Mom and Pop" stores and some fast-food chains are locally owned franchises and therefore "small businesses," your policy proposal could also be framed as "big government's overregulation" of small businesses with destruction of local jobs. The antismall-business frame can also be repeated over and over again. Small businesses in a particular state or house district can generate hundreds of letters to a targeted member of Congress in order to build a blocking coalition to stop your proposal.

The frame is likely to be a simplification of the policy and maybe even a purposeful distortion of the proposal. However, if the frame sticks in the public's mind, it will be the frame that influences the chances for the proposal's success or failure. The trick to framing is to be able to win the battle in how the legislation is to be perceived by the general public and other stakeholders. It will be repeated by news media to send direct and/ or subliminal signals to the public as to what the legislation is all about. The policy proposal can be perceived as "protecting children" or "big government." The side that wins in the framing battle has an advantage in the rest of the legislative struggle. Issues frequently get reduced to simple phrases such as "right to life," "choice," "pathway to citizenship," "clemency," "big government," "protecting our children," and "ObamaCare," among others. One of the major elements in a successful legislative strategy is to be proactive in framing the issue. You may find it helpful to refer back to the "Local Farms–Healthy Kids" (LFHK) policy in Washington State (Breakout Box 4.1). Notice how the Washington State legislature framed the issue, using language such as "The legislature intends that the Local Farms–Healthy Kids Act strengthen the connections between the state's agricultural industry and the state's food procurement procedures in order to expand local agricultural markets, improve the nutrition of children and other at-risk consumers, and have a positive impact on the environment."

When considering policy framing, the role of values becomes critical. Because you have already examined which values are at stake in this policy proposal, you already have an advantage in the framing process. Those attempting to frame the issue will focus on a set of core values in order to rally supporters to their side. What values can you build on? Which values will your opponents use to frame the issue differently? How can your policy issue be framed to draw the support of as many stakeholders as possible, or make it more politically difficult to oppose? The Pennsylvania Fresh Food Financing Initiative (FFFI; Breakout Box 8.1) provides an example of framing the issue of providing food access to low-income families as way to generate economic development. In framing the issue of childhood obesity, one could use the evidence that children who have more access to exercise have better learning outcomes (CDC, 2010). The frame becomes "academic improvement" rather than "reducing in-class contact time."

Thinking about framing at this stage of the policy process will also help as your policy maker starts to think about messaging and developing materials to market the proposal to various stakeholders. Political messaging has become quite sophisticated, often involving outside marketing and communications professionals, depending on the scope of the policy. Some of it may be very direct and some very subliminal in getting people to buy into your policy proposal. Stakeholders you previously identified as having deep financial pockets could be important in financing your messaging later in the policy process, because political messaging plays an important role in speech writing, press conferences, campaign strategy, website

## BREAKOUT BOX 8.1

### Framing the Issue: The Fresh Food Financing Initiative

In 1999, a nationally recognized nonprofit called The Food Trust partnered with the Philadelphia Department of Public Health and researchers at University of Pennsylvania to conduct a study on food access and found that low-income residents are less likely to live near a full-service supermarket and more likely to suffer from diseases related to a poor diet. The Food Trust is "Dedicated to ensuring that everyone has access to affordable, nutritious food and information to make healthy decisions" (The Food Trust, 2013). In 2004, the State of Pennsylvania allocated $30 million over 3 years to create the Fresh Food Financing Initiative (FFFI) to help lower the costs associated with opening and operating grocery stores in urban areas. The Reinvestment Fund (TRF), a Philadelphia-based community development financial institution, leveraged the state's investment with private funds and tax credits to build a $120 million fund. The FFFI became a collaboration among TRF, the Food Trust, and the Greater Philadelphia Urban Affairs Coalition. TRF manages the financing and grant program, distributing funds that can be used for predevelopment costs, land assembly and other capital expenses, preopening costs, and construction expenditures. Applicants are eligible if their project demonstrates a benefit for an underserved area (defined as a low- or moderate-income census tract), an area with supermarket density that is below average, or an area with a supermarket customer base with more than 50% living in a low-income census tract. The Food Trust coordinates with supermarket developers to match community needs with FFFI resources and promotes the fund through a statewide marketing campaign.

As of June 2010, FFFI had approved 93 applications for funding, totaling $73.2 million in loans and $12.1 million in grants since its inception in 2004. In addition to increasing access to healthy and fresh foods at affordable prices, the new and expanded stores have had a substantial economic impact on their neighborhoods. The funded projects created or retained 5,023 jobs throughout the state (TRF, 2006). A recent study of selected supermarkets in the Philadelphia region demonstrated that 75% of part-time jobs (84% of all positions)

*(continued)*

**BREAKOUT BOX 8.1 (*continued*)**

were filled by local residents who lived within 3 miles of their workplace (Goldstein, Loethen, Kako, & Califano, 2008). Furthermore, over 400,000 residents have benefited from increased access to healthy food (Giang, Karpyn, Burton Laurison, Hillier, & Perry, 2008).

The Chief Executive Officer (CEO) of TRF framed the issue in a way that appealed to many stakeholders: "These markets provide economic anchors for communities across Pennsylvania, attracting jobs to the community. These investments can drive the health and economic vitality of these communities, particularly during difficult economic times" (TRF, 2011). Framing the issue of food deserts as an opportunity for economic development and job creation broadens the potential coalition and prevents the issue from being framed as providing handouts of food for the poor.

**Thought Questions:**

1. Compare the initial framing reflected in the Food Trust's mission to the framing presented by the CEO of TRF. Which is likely to resonate with both conservative and liberal voters?
2. Although the FFFI is a success story, there are several characteristics of the Philadelphia context that helped to ensure success. In what ways might this serve as a national template? In what ways might it be unique?

design, e-blasts, and lobbying, among others. At this stage, you are not concerned so much with political messaging as with creating a frame for the issue. However, your policy maker's initial press release or news conference may take advantage of the your efforts at framing the issue and messaging.

## Administrative Strategies

Generally, when we think about the policy process, we think about the legislative process as described above. That is, indeed, where much policy is made. However, it is not the only place. The executive branches at the national and state levels have the ability to make policy through writing both executive orders and writing rules and regulations. As the chief executive officer, a president or governor can issue an executive order without gaining legislative consent. For a president or governor facing a less supportive legislature, this can be one way to change or influence policy without having to go through the legislative process. Executive orders cannot be contrary to existing law, but they can guide its interpretation and enforcement by agencies within the executive branch. As a result, getting your policy adopted may be as "easy" as getting the president or the governor to issue an executive order. Of course, this assumes that the executive supports your proposal.

However, the choice of issuing an executive order is not necessarily straightforward. One of the problems with an executive order is that the next executive can reverse it. An executive order has less permanence than legislation and is unlikely to have a sweeping policy impact. If an executive order is extremely controversial it can be overridden by the legislature, even though this may be very unusual.

When a legislature passes any public law, the bureaucracy within the executive branch needs to write administrative rules and regulations to clarify and guide the implementation of these laws. In writing these rules and regulations, bureaucrats within the administrative structure must follow a prescribed federal or state administrative procedures act to guarantee due process. Once adopted, these rules and regulations have the impact of law. An executive who is opposed to a given policy passed by the legislature may delay the writing of these rules and regulations, and, therefore, the implementation of the policy for years.

At the federal level, these rules and regulations appear in the *Federal Register* (https://www.federalregister.gov/). The *Federal Register* is a daily publication that includes both proposed and final rules and regulations for the federal government. Each state has its own administrative procedure law in effect, so if you are working at the state level, you will need to find what those procedures entail and where those rules and regulations can be found. Such administrative procedures generally have a period of time for open commentary where interest groups and others can raise objections and offer alternatives or amendments. This is a period of very intense lobbying by established interest groups to get their perspectives built into the law. Interest groups may have lost their battle in the legislature, but they still might be able to win in the rule-making process where there might be less visibility from the press and the general public. If the policy issue is contentious, adoption of the rules and regulations can take months or even years.

It could be that existing law is sufficiently broad to cover your policy proposal and no new legislation needs to be adopted. It could be that what is "merely" required to have your particular policy adopted is to change the rules and regulations of the Department of Education, the Department of Agriculture, or the Department of Health and Human Services. In such a case, your strategy recommendation may be to modify rules and regulations to permit your policy proposal to be implemented. However, as noted above, this is not always that easy, and doing so assumes that the executive branch is or will be sympathetic to your proposal.

Writing a new rule may also be problematic in that there may also be a question of funding. Although the Department of Health and Human Services might have the authority to modify existing regulations, there may not be discretionary funds available to actually implement the program. New rules and regulations may also be so politically contentious that it might be easier to go through the regular legislative processes of authorization and appropriation in order to give the policy/program the political support necessary for its success.

Executive orders and rules and regulations do not completely bypass the legislative branch. Legislative oversight allows legislators to hold public hearings on how an agency is administering any given program. Legislators can make their opposition to specific programs known through these hearings. In addition, executive agencies probably receive most of their funds from a legislatively approved budget and revenues. During the annual or biennial approval period for budgets, legislators can make their opposition known and refuse to provide money for implementation for any given program. Bureaucrats will be careful not to alienate powerful legislative committees that control their future budget requests.

## Litigation Strategy

There are other strategies that one might wish to consider. Rather than go the legislative or administrative policy route, another strategy is to pursue a litigation strategy. Existing laws may provide justification for a lawsuit and a legal remedy. Class-action suits or actions taken by the attorney general might be an alternative to get your policy implemented. If you are going to use the power of the attorney general, this generally means that you have that office's support. At the national level and in some states, the chief executive appoints the attorney general. In other states the attorney general may be elected by popular vote and could be of a different party than the chief executive. If you do not have the support of the attorney general, the cost of litigation will be borne by the litigants and may be prohibitive for a nonprofit public health organization.

The courts have been a very important policy actor in health care policy. The Supreme Court's decision on the Affordable Care Act is only one example in which the courts have played a decisive policy role in interpreting the appropriate use of governmental authority. However, the courts can also be used to force policy change when the legislative branch refuses to act. For example, the courts have been especially important in health policies regarding tobacco and behavioral/mental health issues at both the federal and state levels. The Tobacco Master Settlement Agreement (MSA) resulted in seven tobacco companies paying states $206 billion as a result of 46 attorneys general filing suit (Public Health Law Center, 2010). Some advocates see the tobacco settlement as a model for resolving other types of policy issues such as obesity (*Pelman v. McDonald's Corp.*, 2003). Below we will briefly discuss the advantages and disadvantages in taking the litigation route.

One of the major reasons to take a litigation strategy to policy is that the legislative and/or executive branches either refuse or are unable to make a policy decision when lives or important individual rights are at stake. Those subject to a policy may be powerless in the legislative process, even as their lives are being impacted by that policy. For example, in the not-too-distant past, people committed to mental institutions lacked political power and were deprived of their liberty without receiving appropriate mental health therapy that would allow them to regain their freedom. In many states, the courts stepped in to direct the political system (the legislatures and executives) to solve the policy issue. Sometimes the courts issued direct orders to administrative agencies. Patients' rights, deinstitutionalization of mental health, community mental health programs, and other policy changes emerged from these court orders. The courts became the stimulus for policy change when the political branches refused or were unable to act.

Another major advantage of taking the litigation route is that courts can issue an injunction to immediately stop further damage to potential victims until the issue has been resolved. The legislative process may take years; an injunction can prevent further injury from happening. The courts can force or prevent government or private groups from taking potentially harmful actions. For example, a court order could be used to prevent the government from instituting size limits on carbonated beverages.

Another advantage of a litigation approach is that the cost of solving the policy problem can be shifted from the general public's general tax base to those who are deemed responsible for the adverse impacts. As in the tobacco case, money is currently being paid to states by the tobacco companies as compensation for the past health impacts of smoking on their Medicaid programs. Some states have used this money to support new smoking-prevention activities and others have merely put the money back into their general funds. In either case, some of the costs of tobacco usage have been shifted from public treasuries to the tobacco companies.

This leads to another advantage of the litigation route; economic awards can create a deterrent effect in the private sector. Companies might change their behavior if there is a threat of civil or criminal litigation. Corporate public relations may also encourage a change in behavior in order to avoid lengthy and costly litigation or adverse publicity.

One of the major disadvantages of litigation is that the decision regarding a particular court case initially applies only to the specific litigants of the suit. Consequently, multiple lawsuits might need to be filed in multiple court jurisdictions (multiple states) in order to have a major policy impact. Winning one court decision may not lead to major policy changes. One way for litigation to have a larger policy impact is to file a class-action suit or to raise some constitutional or legal issue. Under a class-action suit, one of the litigants represents a class of people (e.g., consumers) and the resulting decision applies to all such litigants or consumers. However, the U.S. Supreme Court has made a number of recent decisions that have limited the ability to file a class-action lawsuit (*Am. Express Co. et al. v. Italian Colors Rest. et al.*, 2013; *AT&T Mobility v. Concepcion*, 2011). Another way for the lawsuit to have more of a policy impact is to have the case appealed to an appellate court (state or federal). If the case is accepted for appeal, a more general ruling may result in a wider application. For example, if the litigation is successfully appealed to a state or federal appellate court (such as the U.S. Supreme Court) it has potential to impact the entire country.

However, this brings up another problem with litigation; litigation takes a great deal of time and money with potentially limited results. Cases may take years to work through the system. Appellate courts such as the Supreme Court have discretion as to which cases they will review and which cases they chose to ignore. Litigation remains an important political strategy to change policy, especially if the political process appears to be a dead end. However, litigation should not be seen as a quick and easy strategy. Organizations with few resources are at a disadvantage compared to those organizations that can afford to hire the best legal advice for years of litigation. Is litigation a viable strategy for your proposal? What legal arguments are viable?

As described above, you have a number of different strategies available to you. At this stage, the strategy cannot be described in great detail because much of it will change as the political process begins to deal with your policy proposal. However, in making your policy recommendation to your policy maker, it is important for you to understand how strategy might influence your recommendation. You do not want to propose a policy that is dead in the political process from the very beginning. The most important element in terms of strategy is to gain a sense from your policy makers how much political capital they are willing to expend to make this proposal a reality.

## SUMMARY

This section is the culmination of all the other sections of your policy analysis. As such, it is the most important and visible section of your analysis. It is what most people will focus on when reading your analysis. However, its acceptance rests on how well the other sections have been developed. You need to understand what your policy maker wants in terms of a recommendation: one alternative, a list of alternatives in priority order, or just a list with the strengths and weaknesses presented for each alternative. You will need to ensure that the previous sections, such as your analysis of policy alternatives, support your policy recommendations. You may need to revisit some of those sections.

You will need to be clear as to the criteria you have selected to evaluate the alternatives. You will also need to be clear as to the trade-offs you have made in selecting one alternative over another.

Because your policy recommendation is unlikely to be universally acclaimed, you must provide the strengths, weaknesses, and trade-offs you have made in your recommendation. You cannot make a recommendation and then just let your policy makers ad lib a defense for the policy proposal. They need the details that will help sell the policy proposal to others and help to withstand counterarguments from likely opponents.

Remember that your recommendation is going to impact the lives of various stakeholders. Some of these people may be well represented in the political process and some may not be represented or be underrepresented. Some powerful stakeholders may be marginally impacted and some stakeholders may pay with their lives or livelihoods but have little influence in the political process. Remember that you are making a value-laden decision that has real and important consequences for a variety of people. In making your recommendation, put yourself in the position of multiple stakeholders. How would you feel about this policy if you were poor and had children? How would you feel about this policy if you were a child? How would you feel about this policy if you were an educator? How would you feel about this policy if you were governor of a state being impacted by federal policy? How would you feel about this policy if you owned a fast-food restaurant? How would you feel if you produced processed food? How would you feel if you were an organic farmer? Place yourself in as many positions as you can so that you can begin to see the real impact of the policy that you are proposing.

To make a recommendation on policy without thinking about the political process is irresponsible. Every policy proposal will have to go through some type of political process for its approval, funding, and implementation. Although you cannot control all the variables in the political process, you must understand the dynamics of what is likely to occur and to propose responsible strategies so that the policy can become law. In order for this proposal to gain traction, your policy maker will need to expend his/her political capital (time, money, staff, and political trades). Your policy makers may have to irritate powerful interest groups that have supported him or her (e.g., educators, unions, businesses) in the past. Your policy makers may gain public or stakeholder support. What is the political cost of this proposal? Are the costs outweighed by the benefits (votes for an upcoming re-election, campaign contributions, providing a partial solution to the problem)? Note that solving the policy issue is only one of the potential benefits to your policy makers; increased political capital, toward this or some other issue, may be even more important for your policy makers.

Particular aspects of the political process may determine the fate of your proposal. Therefore, you should begin to at least think about how to frame the policy proposal so that it attracts supporters and deflects opponents. Framing begins the marketing process of your policy proposal. It provides the frame from which the proposal will be perceived by the press and major stakeholders in the political process. In addition, you can start to think about messaging, the words and phrases that will be used to describe the proposal in press releases, press conferences, policy literature, advertising, and other documents. What would a press release look like for your proposal?

There are multiple strategies that can be used to turn your policy proposal into policy. Depending on your policy maker's position, an executive order or new rules and regulations may be sufficient to actualize the proposal. The use of litigation is also an alternative. Understanding whether or not these strategies are possible and what the strengths and weaknesses of each might be will add credibility to your proposal.

Developing a legislative strategy is the most common strategy for policy adoption. Here you must be cognizant of the intricate details of the legislative process as well as the personal dynamics involved among the various participants. Using your stakeholder analysis to begin a strategy for building a coalition of supporters will demonstrate external support and add strength to your proposal. You should think of who can help you in the legislative process and who is likely to be the largest roadblock. You will need to think of what trade-offs you are willing to make to gain additional support or prevent defeat in the legislative process. You will need to have a sense as to what is so critical that compromise is not an option to attain the core elements of the policy. Although the details of this strategy will change as the process proceeds, preparing for what lies ahead strengthens your analysis.

Finally, once you have completed this section, it is time to also develop the executive summary and complete the other elements discussed in Chapter 2 on Mechanics. It may be helpful to revisit that chapter.

Policy analysis is not for the faint of heart. It is a very difficult process that requires clarity of values, analytical capacity, imagination, empathy for those impacted, and clarity in writing. It can be very intimidating and challenging, but the reward of seeing a policy/program that can impact the lives of thousands or millions of citizens come to fruition becomes the ultimate reward.

---

## SOME THINGS TO REMEMBER

- Understand what type of recommendation your sponsor is looking to gain from your analysis (a single recommendation or multiple choices with strengths and weaknesses of all) and what its use will be.
- Calculate the political capital that will be gained and expended by your policy makers for this policy proposal.
- Determine the willingness of your policy makers to expend political capital for enactment of your policy proposal.
- Provide evidence-based material on the strengths and weaknesses of alternatives, not merely for the one(s) selected for your recommendation.
- Attempt to document intended and unintended consequences of the policy proposal.
- As an analyst, place yourself in as many stakeholders' positions as you can in order to understand their differing perspectives on the real impact of the proposal.
- Develop a matrix for helping you evaluate alternatives using the same criteria for success.
- Prepare for the evaluation of your policy proposal by setting timelines and specific benchmarks for success.
- Although strategies will evolve through the political process, provide a fundamental assessment as to the strategy that holds the most promise, whether it is legislative, executive, or litigation.
- Seek advice from people familiar with the political process to gain an understanding of the personalities and political processes that one must navigate.
- Begin thinking about how framing the issue in a particular way will attract stakeholder support throughout the political process.
- Through your stakeholder analysis, develop a list of those stakeholders who should be courted to build an alliance for support.

- Begin thinking about messaging for press releases and other publicity material that will be required as the political process moves forward.
- Develop a clear and concise Executive Summary that will focus your analysis in the most salient way.

## KEY WORDS

| | |
|---|---|
| Recommendation | Alliances |
| Intended consequences | Framing |
| Unintended consequences | Messaging |
| Health impact assessment (HIA) | Rule-making strategy |
| Recommendation matrix | Rules and regulations |
| Legislative strategy | Executive orders |
| Quid pro quo | Litigation strategy |

# References

Aday, L., Begley, C., Lairson, D., & Balkrishnan, R. (2004). *Evaluating the health-care system: Effectiveness, efficiency, and equity* (3rd ed.). Washington, DC: Health Administration Press.

Agency for Healthcare Quality and Research. (2012). *Methods guide for effectiveness and comparative effectiveness reviews*. Rockville, MD: Author.

Ainsworth, B. E., Haskell, W. L., Whitt, M. C., Irwin, M. L., Swartz, A. M., Strath, S. J., . . . Leon, A. S. (2000). Compendium of physical activities: An update of activity codes and MET intensities. *Medicine and Science in Sports & Exercise, 32*(9), S498–S504.

Alliance for a Healthier Generation. (2012, October). *Technical assistance matters: Schools need support to become healthier*. Retrieved from http://www.rwjf.org/content/dam/farm/reports/issue_briefs/2012/rwjf402203

American Express Co. et al. v. Italian Colors Restaurant et al. 133 S. Ct. (2013).

American Public Health Association. (2013a). *Toolkit for intervention of overweight children and adolescents*. Retrieved from http://www.apha.org/programs/resources/obesity/tacklingobesity.htm

American Public Health Association. (2013b). *Tracking childhood obesity: Vision and guiding principles*. Retrieved from http://www.apha.org/programs/resources/obesity/proresobesitykit.htm

America's Health Rankings. (2013). *Obesity (1990–2012)*. Retrieved from http://www.americashealthrankings.org/all/obesity#sthash.sbw1FOpM.dpuf

Anderson, L. M., Brownson, R. C., Fullilove, M. T., Teutsch, S. M., Novick, L. F., Fielding, J., & Land, G. H. (2005). Evidence based public health policy and practice: Promises and limits. *American Journal of Prevenative Medicine, 28*(5), 226–230.

Arnstein, S. (1969). A ladder of citizen participation. *Journal of the American Planning Association, 35*(4), 216–224.

Ascher, W., Blanck, H., & Cradock, A. (Eds.). (2012, September). Evaluating policies and processes for promoting healthy eating: Findings from the Nutrition and Obesity Policy Research and Evaluation Network (NOPREN). *American Journal of Preventive Medicine,* Suppl., S85–S152. Retrieved from http://www.cdc.gov/prc/program-research/research-in-brief/Nutrition-and-Obesity-Policy-Research.htm

AT&T Mobility v. Concepcion, 131 S. Ct. 1740 (2011).

Aytur, S., Rodriguez, D., Evenson, K., Catellier, D., & Rosamond, W. (2007). Promoting active community environments through land use and transportation planning. *American Journal of Health Promotion, 21*(4), 397–407.

Aytur, S., Rodriguez, D., Evenson, K., Catellier, D., & Rosamond, W. (2008). The sociodemographics of land use planning: Relationships to physical activity, accessibility, and equity. *Health & Place, 14*(3), 367–385.

Bacchi, C. (1999). *Women, policy, and politics: The construction of policy problems.* Thousand Oaks, CA: Sage.

Badgett, R. (2013). Are proposals by politicians for health care reform based on evidence? *Journal of the Medical Library Association, 101*(3), 218–220.

Barclay, E. (2013, July 30). *Despite legal blow, New York to keep up sugary drink fight* [Blog post]. Retrieved from http://www.npr.org/blogs/thesalt/2013/07/30/207026680/despite-legal-blow-new-york-to-keep-up-sugary-drink-fight

Bassett, M., & Perl, S. (2004). Obesity: The public health challenge of our time. *American Journal of Public Health, 94*(9), 1477.

Betancourt, J., Duong, J., & Bondaryk, M. (2012). Strategies to reduce diabetes disparities: An update. *Current Diabetes Reports, 12*(6), 762–768.

Bleich, S., Segal, J., Wu, Y., Wilson, R., & Wang, Y. (2013). Systematic review of community-based childhood obesity prevention studies. *Pediatrics, 132,* e201. Retrieved from http://pediatrics.aappublications.org/content/early/2013/06/05/peds.2013-0886.full.pdf+html

Boles, M., Dilley, J., Dent, C., Elman, M., Duncan, S., & Johnson, D. (2011). Changes in local school policies and practices in Washington State after an unfunded physical activity and nutrition mandate. *Preventing Chronic Disease, 8*(6), A129.

Bridging the Gap. (2012, December). *Child-directed marketing within and around fast-food restaurants.* Retrieved from http://www.bridgingthegapresearch.org/research/community_data/

Bridging the Gap. (2013, February). *Beverage availability in food stores nationwide.* Retrieved from http://www.bridgingthegapresearch.org/research/community_data/

Brownson, R. C., Chriqui, J. F., & Stamatakis, K. A. (2009). Understanding evidence-based public health policy. *American Journal of Public Health, 99*(9), 1576–1583.

Brownson, R. C., Royer, C., Ewing, R., & McBride, T. (2006). Researchers and policymakers: Travelers in parallel universes. *American Journal of Preventive Medicine, 30*(2), 164–172.

Buchbinder, R., Osborne, R. H., Ebeling, P. R., Wark, J. D., Mitchell, P., Wriedt, C., . . . Murphy, B. (2009). A randomized trial of vertebroplasty for painful osteoporotic vertebral fractures. *New England Journal of Medicine, 361*(6), 557–568.

California Executive Order No. S-04-10, Title 3 C.F.R. (2010 comp).

California Newsreel. (Producer). (2008). *Unnatural causes: Is inequality making us sick?* [Documentary]. Available for purchase at http://www.unnaturalcauses.org/

Centers for Disease Control and Prevention. (2008). *Evaluation briefs: Data collection methods for program evaluation: Focus groups* (Policy Brief No. 13). Retrieved from http://www.cdc.gov/healthyyouth/evaluation/pdf/brief13.pdf

Centers for Disease Control and Prevention. (2010). *The association between school-based physical activity, including physical education, and academic performance* (rev. ed.). Atlanta, GA: U.S. Department of Health and Human Services.

Centers for Disease Control and Prevention. (2012a). *Basics about childhood obesity.* Retrieved from http://www.cdc.gov/obesity/childhood/basics.html

Centers for Disease Control and Prevention. (2012b). *Develop SMART objectives.* Retrieved from http://www.cdc.gov/phcommunities/resourcekit/evaluate/smart_objectives.html

Centers for Disease Control and Prevention. (2012c). *Overweight and obesity.* Retrieved from http://www.cdc.gov/obesity/

Centers for Disease Control and Prevention. (2013a). Behavioral Risk Factor Surveillance System. Retrieved from http://www.cdc.gov/brfss/

Centers for Disease Control and Prevention. (2013b). *BMI percentile calculator for child and teen English version.* Retrieved from http://apps.nccd.cdc.gov/dnpabmi/Calculator.aspx

Centers for Disease Control and Prevention. (2013c). *Childhood overweight and obesity.* Retrieved from http://www.cdc.gov/obesity/childhood/

Centers for Disease Control and Prevention. (2013d). *Defining overweight and obesity.* Retrieved from http://www.cdc.gov/obesity/adult/defining.html

Centers for Disease Control and Prevention. (2013e). National Health and Nutrition Examination Survey. Retrieved from http://www.cdc.gov/nchs/nhanes.htm

Centers for Disease Control and Prevention. (2013f). *Obesity trends among U.S. adults between 1985 and 2010.* Retrieved from www.cdc.gov/obesity/downloads/obesity_trends_2010.ppt

Centers for Disease Control and Prevention. (2013g). *Obese youth over time.* Retrieved from http://www.cdc.gov/healthyyouth/obesity/obesity-youth.htm

Centers for Disease Control and Prevention. (2013h). Policy Research, Analysis, and Development Office. Retrieved from http://www.cdc.gov/policy/prado/

Centers for Disease Control and Prevention. (2013i). Youth Risk Behavior Surveillance System. Retrieved from http://www.cdc.gov/HealthyYouth/yrbs/index.htm

Centers for Disease Control and Prevention, Division of Community Health. (2013). *A practitioner's guide for advancing health equity: Community strategies for preventing chronic disease.* Atlanta, GA: US Department of Health and Human Services. Retrieved from http://www.cdc.gov/nccdphp/dch/health-equity-guide/

Citizens United v. Federal Election Commission, 568 U.S. 310 (2010).

Clark, W. (2002). *The policy process: A practical guide for natural resources professionals.* New Haven, CT. Yale University Press.

Clark, W. (2007). Sustainability science: A room of its own. *Proceedings of the National Academy of Sciences of the United States of America, 104*(6), 1737–1738.

Clark, W., & Dickson, N. (2003). Sustainability science: The emerging research program. *Proceedings of the National Academy of Sciences of the United States of America, 100*(14), 8059–8061.

Cole, B., & Fielding, J. (2007). Health impact assessment: A tool to help policy makers understand health beyond health care. *Annual Reviews of Public Health, 28*(3), 393–412.

Collins, J., & Koplan, J. (2009). Health impact assessment: A step toward health in all policies. *Journal of the American Medical Association, 302*(3), 315–317.

Committee on the Costs of Medical Care. (1932). *Medical care for the American people.* Chicago, IL: University of Chicago Press.

The Community Foundation for Greater Atlanta. (2008, summer). *How health affects our community: A community report on the healthcare needs of the homeless.* Retrieved from http://www.cjaonline.net/TechResources/HomelessHealth200807.pdf

Coveney, J. (2010). Analyzing public health policy: Three approaches. *Health Promotion Practice, 11*(4), 515–521.

Danaei, G., Ding, E., Mozaffarian, D., Taylor, B., Rehm, J., Murray, C., & Ezzati, M. (2009). The preventable causes of death in the United States: Comparative risk assessment of dietary, lifestyle, and metabolic risk factors. *PLoS Medicine, 6*(4), e1000058. Retrieved from http://www.plosmedicine.org/article/info:doi/10.1371/journal.pmed.1000058

Dannenberg, A., Bhatia, R., Cole, B., Heaton, S., Feldman, J., & Rutt, C. (2008). Use of health impact assessment in the U.S.: 27 case studies, 1999–2007. *American Journal of Preventive Medicine, 34*(3), 241–256.

Day, K. (2006). Active living and social justice: Planning for physical activity in low-income, black, and Latino communities. *Journal of the American Planning Association, 72*(1), 88–99.

Dodson, E., Flemming, C., Boehmer, T., Haire-Joshu, D., Luke, D., & Brownson, R. (2009). Preventing childhood obesity through state policy: Qualitative assessment of enablers and barriers. *Journal of Public Health Policy, 30*, S161–S176. Retrieved from http://www.palgrave-journals.com/jphp/journal/v30/nS1/full/jphp200857a.html

Easton, D. (1953). *The political system.* New York, NY: Alfred A. Knopf.

Evans, R., & Stoddart, G. (2003). Consuming research, producing policy? *American Journal of Public Health, 93*(3), 371–379.

Evenson, K., & Aytur, S. (2010). Policy for physical activity promotion. In B. E. Ainsworth & C. A. Macera (Eds.), *Physical activity and public health practice* (pp. 321–344). Boca Raton, FL: CRC Press.

Fakhouri, T., Ogden, C., Carroll, M., Kit, B., & Flegal, K. (2012, September). *Prevalence of obesity among older adults in the United States, 2007–2010* (Data Brief No. 106). Retrieved from http://www.cdc.gov/nchs/data/databriefs/db106.pdf

Falbe, J., Kenney, E., Henderson, K., & Schwartz, M. (2011). The Wellness Child Care Assessment Tool: A measure to assess the quality of written nutrition and physical activity policies. *Journal of American Dietetic Association, 111*(12), 1852–1860.

Farhang, L., Bhatia, R., Comerford-Scully, C., Corburn, J., Gaydos, M., & Malekfzali, S. (2008). Creating tools for healthy development: Case study of San Francisco's Eastern Neighborhoods Community Health Impact Assessment. *Journal of Public Health Management and Practice, 14*(3), 255–265.

Farooqi, I., & O'Rahilly, S. (2005). Monogenic obesity in humans. *Annual Review of Medicine, 56*(2), 443–458.

Field, M., & Lohr, K. (Eds.). (1992). *Guidelines for clinical practice: From development to use.* Washington, DC: National Academy Press.

Fielding, J., & Briss, P. (2006). Promoting evidence-based public health policy: Can we have better evidence and more action? *Health Affairs, 25*(4), 969–978.

Finkelstein, E., Fiebelkorn, I., & Wang, G. (2004). State-level estimates of annual medical expenditures attributable to obesity. *Obesity Research, 12*(1), 18–24.

Finkelstein, E., Trogdon, J., Cohen, J., & Dietz, W. (2009). Annual medical spending attributed to obesity: Payer-and-service-specific estimates. *Health Affairs, 28*(5), W822–W831. Retrieved from http://content.healthaffairs .org/content/28/5/w822.long

The Food Trust. (2013). Retrieved from http://thefoodtrust.org

Fradkin, J. (2012). Confronting the urgent challenge of diabetes: An overview. *Health Affairs, 31*(1), 12–19.

Freire, K., & Runyan, C. W. (2006). Planning models: PRECEDE-PROCEED and Haddon matrix. In A. C. Gielen, D. A. Sleet, & R. J. DiClemente (Eds.), *Injury and violence prevention: Behavioral science theories, methods, and applications* (1st ed., pp. 127–158). San Francisco, CA: Jossey-Bass.

Friedman, J. (2009, September 9). *The real cause of obesity.* Retrieved from http://www.thedailybeast.com/newsweek/2009/09/09/the-real-cause-of-obesity.html

Fuchs, V. (1974). *Who shall live? Health, economics, and social choice.* New York, NY: Basic Books

Fuchs, V. (1998). *Who shall live? Health economics and social choice* (2nd expanded ed.). River Edge, NJ: World Scientific.

Garber, A. (2011). How the Patient-Centered Outcomes Research Institute can best influence real-world health care decision making. *Health Affairs, 30*(12), 2243–2251.

Gawande, A. (2009). The cost conundrum. *The New Yorker.* Retrieved from http://www.newyorker.com/reporting/2009/06/01/090601fa_fact_gawande

Geiss, L., Li, Y., Kirtland, K., Barker, L., Burrows, N., & Gregg, E. (2012, November 16). Increasing prevalence of diagnosed diabetes—United States and Puerto Rico, 1995–2010. *Morbidity and Mortality Weekly Report, 61*(45), 918–921.

Giang, T., Karpyn, A., Burton Laurison, H., Hillier, A., & Perry, R. (2008). Closing the grocery gap in underserved communities: The creation of the

Pennsylvania Fresh Food Financing Initiative. *Journal of Public Health Management and Practice, 14*(3), 272–279.

Gielen, A., McDonald, E., Gary, T., & Bone, L. (2008). Using the PRECEDE/PROCEED model to apply health behavior theories. In K. Glanz, B. Rimer, & K. Viswanath (Eds.), *Health behavior and health education: Theory, research and practice* (4th ed., pp. 407–433). San Francisco, CA: Jossey-Bass.

Glasgow, R. E., Vogt, T. M., & Boles, S. M. (1999). Evaluating the public health impact of health promotion interventions: The RE-AIM framework. *American Journal of Public Health, 89*(9), 1322–1327.

Goldstein, I., Loethen, L., Kako, E., & Califano, C. (2008). *CDFI financing of supermarkets in underserved communities: A case study.* Philadelphia, PA: The Reinvestment Fund. Retrieved from http://www.trfund.com/wp-content/uploads/2013/06/Supermarkets_Full_Study.pdf

The Good Stewardship Working Group. (2011). The "top five" lists in primary care. *Archives of Internal Medicine, 171*(15), 1385–1390.

Govtrack.us. (2013). *Bills and resolutions.* Retrieved from https://www.govtrack.us/congress/bills/#statistics

Graham, J., Corso, P., Morris, J., Segui-Gomez, M., & Weinstein, M. (1998). Evaluating the cost-effectiveness of clinical and public health measures. *Annual Review of Public Health, 19*(1), 125–152.

Green, L. (1974). Toward cost-benefit evaluations of health education: Some concepts, methods, and examples. *Health Education Monographs, 2*(2), 34–64.

Green, L. (2006). Public health asks of systems science: To advance our evidence-based practice, can you help us get more practice-based evidence? *American Journal of Public Health, 96*(3), 406–409.

Green, L., & Kreuter, M. (2005). *Health program planning: An educational and ecological approach* (4th ed.). New York, NY: McGraw-Hill.

Grosse, S., Teutsch, S., & Haddix, A. (2007). Lessons from cost-effectiveness research for United States public health policy. *Annual Review of Public Health, 28*(2), 365–369.

*Guidelines for conducting a focus group.* (2005). Retrieved from http://assessment.aas.duke.edu/documents/How_to_Conduct_a_Focus_Group.pdf

Gutmann, A., & Thompson, D. (1996). *Democracy and disagreement.* Cambridge, MA: Harvard University Press.

Harris, E., Lindsay, A., Heller, J., Gilhuly, K., Williams, M., Cox, B., & Rice, J. (2009). Humboldt County general plan update health impact assessment: A case study. *Environmental Justice, 2*(3), 127–134.

Harvard School of Public Health. (2013). "Obesity." Retrieved from http://www.hsph.harvard.edu/obesity-prevention-source/obesity-definition/abdominal-obesity/

Health Impact Project. (2012). *National nutrition standards for snacks and a la carte foods and beverages.* Washington, DC: Pew Charitable Trust. Retrieved from http://www.pewhealth.org/uploadedFiles/PHG/Content_Level_Pages/Reports/KS_HIA_revised%20WEB%20FINAL%2073112.pdf

Healthy People 2000. (2009). Retrieved from http://www.cdc.gov/nchs/healthy_people/hp2000.htm

Healthy People 2010. (2000). *Understanding and improving health.* Washington, DC: US Department of Health and Human Services.

Healthy People 2020. (2011). Retrieved from http://www.cdc.gov/nchs/healthy_people/hp2020.htm

Healthy People 2020. (2013a). Retrieved from http://www.cdc.gov/nchs/healthy_people/hp2020.htm

Healthy People 2020. (2013b). Retrieved from http://www.healthypeople.gov/2020/default.aspx

HealthyPeople.gov. (2013). *Nutrition and weight status.* Retrieved from http://www.healthypeople.gov/2020/topicsobjectives2020/overview.aspx?topicid=29

Healthy Places. (2013). Retrieved from http://www.cdc.gov/healthyplaces/hia.htm

The Healthy Study Group. (2010). A school-based intervention for diabetes risk reduction. *New England Journal of Medicine, 363*(5), 443–453.

Hewitt, J. (1997). The genetics of obesity: What have genetic studies told us about the environment. *Behavior Genetics, 27*(4), 353–354.

Hollar, D., Messiah, S., Lopez-Mitnik, G., Hollar, T., Almon, M., & Aqatston, A. (2010). Effect of a two-year obesity prevention intervention on percentile changes in body mass index and academic performance in low income elementary school children. *American Journal of Public Health, 100*(4), 646–653.

Huang, T., Drewnowsksi, A., Kumanyika, S., & Glass, T. (2009). A systems-oriented multilevel framework for addressing obesity in the 21st century. *Preventing Chronic Disease, 6*(3), A82.

Human Impact Partners. (2008). *Health impact assessment guidebook.* Retrieved from http://www.humanimpact.org

Human Nutrition, Foods and Exercise. (2013). *Support and evidence of RE-AIM.* Retrieved from http://www.re-aim.hnfe.vt.edu/about_re-aim/FAQ/index.html#vicfit

Hunger-Free Kids Act of 2010, Pub. L. No. 111-296.

In re N.Y. Statewide Coal. of Hispanic Chambers of Commerce v. N.Y. City Dep't of Health and Mental Hygiene, No. 05505 (N.Y. App. Div. July 30, 2013).

Institute of Medicine. (2000). *To err is human: Building a safer health system.* Washington, DC: National Academy Press.

Institute of Medicine. (2001). *Crossing the quality chasm: A new health system for the 21st century.* Washington, DC: National Academy Press.

Institute of Medicine. (2012, September). *Best care at lower cost: The path to continuously learning health care in America.* Retrieved from http://iom.edu/Reports/2012/Best-Care-at-Lower-Cost-The-Path-to-Continuously-Learning-Health-Care-in-America.aspx

Ioannidis, J. (2005a). Contradicted and initially stronger effects in highly cited clinical research. *Journal of the American Medical Association, 294*(2), 218–228.

Ioannidis, J. (2005b). Why most published research findings are false. *PLOS Medicine, 2*(8), e124. Retrieved from http://www.plosmedicine.org/article/info:doi/10.1371/journal.pmed.0020124

Jilcott, S., Ammerman, A., Sommers, J., & Glasgow, R. (2007). Applying the RE-AIM framework to assess the public health impact of policy change. *Annals of Behavioral Medicine, 34*(2), 105–114.

Johnson, D., Cheadle, A., Podrabsky, M., Quinn, E., MacDougall, E., Cechovic, K., . . . Allen, D. (2013). Advancing nutrition and obesity policy through cross-sector collaboration: The Local Farms—Healthy Kids Initiative in Washington State. *Journal of Hunger and Environmental Nutrition, 8*(2), 171–186.

Johnson, D., Payne, E., McNeese, M., & Allen, D. (2012). Menu-labeling policy in King County, Washington. *American Journal of Preventive Medicine, 43*(3 Suppl. 2), S130–S135.

Jones, C. O. (1984). *An introduction to the study of public policy* (3rd ed.). St. Paul, MN: Brooks Cole.

Kaiser Family Foundation. (2011). *Snapshots: Health care spending in the United States & selected OECD countries.* Retrieved from http://kff.org/health-costs/issue-brief/snapshots-health-care-spending-in-the-united-states-selected-oecd-countries/

Kale, S., Bishop, T., Federman, A., & Keyhani, S. (2011). "Top five" lists top $5 billion. *Archives of Internal Medicine, 171*(20), 1856–1858.

Kallmes, D. F., Comstock, B. A., Heagerly, P. J., Turner, J. A., Wilson, D. J., Diamond, T. H., & Jarvik, J. G. (2009). A randomized trial of vertebroplasty for osteoporic spinal fractures. *New England Journal of Medicine, 361*(6), 569–579.

Kaplan, A. (1963). *American ethics and public policy.* New York, NY: Oxford University Press.

Kelley, R. (2009). *Where can $700 billion in waste be cut annually from the U.S. healthcare system?* Retrieved from http://www.ncrponline.org/PDFs/2009/Thomson_Reuters_White_Paper_on_Healthcare_Waste.pdf

Kerr, Z., Rodríguez, D. A., Evenson, K. R., & Aytur, S. A. (2013). Pedestrian and bicycle plans and incidence of crash-related injuries. *Accident Analysis Prevention, 50,* 1252–1258.

The Kids' Safe and Healthful Food Project. (2011). *Food for thought.* Retrieved from http://www.healthyschoolfoodsnow.org/foodforthoughtsource/

The Kids' Safe and Healthful Food Project. (2013a). *Calculating the cost.* Retrieved from http://www.healthyschoolfoodsnow.org/calculating-the-cost/

The Kids' Safe and Healthful Food Project. (2013b). *Financial impacts of nutrition standards for snacks sold in schools.* Retrieved from http://www.healthyschoolfoodsnow.org/financial-impacts-of-nutrition-standards-for-snacks-sold-in-schools/

King, D., Glasgow, R., & Leeman-Castillo, B. (2010). Reaiming RE-AIM: Using the model to plan, implement, and evaluate the effects of environmental change approaches to enhancing population Health. *American Journal of Public Health, 100*(11), 2076–2084.

Kingdon, J. W. (2003). *Agendas, alternatives, and public policies.* New York, NY: Addison-Wesley.

Kingdon, J. W. (2010). *Agendas, alternatives, and public policies* (updated 2nd ed.). London, UK: Pearson.

Klepper, B. (2004). *International Federation of Health Plans, 2010 Comparative Price Report: Medical and hospital fees by country.* Retrieved from http://careandcost.com/2010/12/04/international-federation-of-health-plans-2010-comparative-price-report-medical-and-hospital-fees-by-country/

Krech, R., Valentine, N., Reinders, L., & Albrecht, D. (2010). Implication of the Adelaide statement on health in all policies. *Bulletin of the World Health Organization, 88,* 720. Retrieved from http://www.who.int/bulletin/volumes/88/10/10-082461/en/

Krieger, J., Chan, N., Saelens, B., Ta, M., Solet, D., & Fleming, D. (2013). Menu labeling regulations and calories purchased at chain restaurants. *American Journal of Preventive Medicine, 44*(6), 595–604.

Kumanyika, S., Brownson, R., & Cheadle, A. (2012). The L.E.A.D. framework: Using tools from evidence-based public health to address evidence needs for obesity prevention. *Preventing Chronic Disease, 9*, 120157. Retrieved from http://www.cdc.gov/pcd/issues/2012/12_0157.htm

Kumanyika, S., Parker, L., & Sim, L. (Eds.). (2010). *Bridging the evidence gap in obesity prevention.* Washington, DC: National Academic Press.

Larson, N., Ward, D., Neelon, S., & Story, M. (2011). What role can child-care settings play in obesity prevention? A review of the evidence and call for research efforts. *Journal of the American Diet Association, 111*(9), 1343–1362.

Lasswell, H. (1936). *Politics: Who gets what, when, how.* New York, NY: Whittlesey House.

Lasswell, H. (1971). *A preview of the policy sciences.* New York, NY: American Elsevier.

Ledbetter v. Goodyear Tire & Rubber Co., 550 U.S. 618 (2007).

Leeman, J., Sommers, J., Leung, M. M., & Ammerman, A. (2011). Disseminating evidence from research and practice: A model for selecting evidence to guide obesity prevention. *Journal of Public Health Management and Practice, 17*(2), 133–140.

Leeman, J., Sommers, J., Vu, M., Jernigan, J., Payne, G., Thompson, D., & Ammerman, A. (2012). An evaluation framework for obesity prevention policy interventions. *Preventing Chronic Disease, 9*, 110322.

Lindblom, C. (1980). *The policy making process* (2nd ed.). Englewood Cliffs, NJ: Prentice Hall.

Lintelman, L. (2013). *Advocacy pulse: 2013 legislative wrap-up. June 2012–June 2013.* Retrieved from http://www.heart.org/idc/groups/heart-public/@wcm/@adv/documents/downloadable/ucm_446051.pdf

Longest, B., Jr. (1998). *Health policymaking in the United States* (2nd ed.). Chicago, IL: Health Administration Press.

Longest, B., Jr. (2009). *Health policymaking in the United States* (5th ed.). Chicago, IL: AUPHA/HAP Press.

Love, D., Custer, W., & Miller, P. (2010, September). *All-payer claims databases: State initiatives to improve health care transparency* (Issue Brief). Retrieved from http://www.commonwealthfund.org/~/media/Files/Publications/Issue%20Brief/2010/Sep/1439_Love_allpayer_claims_databases_ib_v2.pdf

Ludwig, J., Sanbonmatsu, L., Gennetian, L., Adam, E., Duncan, G., Katz, L., . . . McDade, T. (2011). Neighborhoods, obesity, and diabetes—A randomized social experiment. *New England Journal of Medicine, 365*(16), 1509–1519.

Lyn, R., Aytur, S., Davis, T., Eyler, A.,Evenson, K., Chriqui, J., . . . Brownson, R. C. (2013). Policy, systems, and environmental approaches for obesity prevention: A framework to inform local and state action. *Journal of Public Health Management & Practice, 19*, S23-33. doi: 10.1097/PHH.0b013e3182841709.

Madahian, B., Klesges, R., Kelesges, L., & Homayouni, R. (2012). System dynamics modeling of childhood obesity. *BMC Bioinformatics, 13*(12), A13.

Mays, G., & Smith, S. (2011). Evidence links increase in public health spending to declines in preventable deaths. *Health Affairs, 30*(8), 1585–1593.

McGlynn, E., Asch, S., Adams, J., Keesey, J., Hicks, J., DeCristofaro, A., & Kerr, E. (2003). The quality of health care delivered to adults in the United States. *New England Journal of Medicine, 348*(26), 2635–2645.

McLeroy, K., Bibeau, D., Steckler, A., & Glanz, K. (1988). An ecological perspective on health promotion programs. *Health Education Quarterly, 15*(4), 351–377.

Messiah, S., Arheart, K., Lopez-Mitnik, G., Lipshultz, S., & Miller, T. (2013). Ethnic group difference in cardiometabolic disease risk factors independent of body mass index among American youth. *Obesity, 21*(3), 424–428.

Michigan Cancer Consortium. (2012). *Policy, systems, and environmental change.* Retrieved from http://www.michigancancer.org/policy_systems_environchange.cfm

Moleres, A., Martinez, J., & Marti, A. (2013). Genetics and obesity. *Obesity Report, 2*(1), 22–31.

Namba, A., Auchincloss, A., Leonberg, B., & Wootan, M. (2013). Exploratory analysis of fast-food chain restaurant menus before and after implementation of local calorie-labeling policies, 2005–2011. *Preventing Chronic Disease, 10*, 120224. Retrieved from http://www.cdc.gov/pcd/issues/2013/pdf/12_0224.pdf

National Federation of Independent Business et al. v. Sebelius, Secretary of Health and Human Services, et al., 132 S. Ct. 2566 (2012).

National Heart, Lung, and Blood Institute. (1998). *Clinical guidelines on the identification, evaluation, and treatment of obesity in adults: The evidence report.* Washington, DC: National Institutes of Health.

National Institute for Health Care Reform. (2011, April). *Geographic variation in health care: Changing policy directions* (Policy Analysis No. 4). Retrieved from http://www.nihcr.org/geographic-variation

National League of Cities. (2013). *Local government authority.* Retrieved from http://www.nlc.org/build-skills-and-networks/resources/cities-101/city-powers/local-government-authority

National Parents' Rights Association. (2013). Retrieved from http://www.npra.info/

National Prevention Council. (2013). Retrieved from http://www.surgeongeneral.gov/initiatives/prevention/about/index.html

National Resource Center for Paraprofessionals. (2011). *CDC obesity maps.* Retrieved from http://www.slideshare.net/nrcpara/cdc-obesity-maps

Nestle, M., & Jacobson, M. (2000). Halting the obesity epidemic: A public health approach. *Public Health Reports, 115*(14), 12–24.

New St. Ice Co. v. Liebmann, 285 U.S. 262 (1932).

Newhouse, J. (1993). *Free for all? Lessons from the RAND health insurance experiment.* Cambridge, MA: Harvard University Press.

Ogden, C., Carroll, M., Kit, B., & Flegal, K. (2012, January). *Prevalence of obesity in the United States, 2009–2010* (Date Brief No. 82). Retrieved from http://www.cdc.gov/nchs/data/databriefs/db82.pdf

Ogden, C., Curtin, L., Lamb, M., & Flegal, K. (2010). Prevalence of high body mass index in US children and adolescents, 2007–2008. *Journal of the American medical Association, 303*(3), 242–249.

Organization for Economic Co-operation and Development. (2010). *Executive summary: Obesity and economics of prevention: Fit not fat.* Retrieved from http://www.oecd.org/dataoecd/52/4/46044572.pdf

Parental Rights Organization. (2013). Retrieved from http://www.parentalrights.org/

The Patient Protection and Affordable Care Act of 2010, Pub. L. No. 111-148, §1312, 124 Stat. 182 (2010).

Patient-Centered Outcomes Research Institute. (2012, January). *Draft national priorities for research and research agenda, version 1.* Retrieved from http://pcori.org/assets/PCORI-Draft-National-Priorities-and-Research-Agenda1.pdf

Patton, M. (2010). *Developmental evaluation: Applying complexity concepts to enhance innovation and use.* New York, NY: Guilford.

Pelman v. McDonald's Corp., 237 F. Supp. 2d 512, 519 (S.D.N.Y. 2003).

The Pew Charitable Trusts. (2013). *7 Questions about smart snacks in school standards.* Retrieved from http://www.pewhealth.org/other-resource/7-questions-about-smart-snacks-in-school-standards-85899491414

Pomeranz, J. (2011). The unique authority of state and local health departments to address obesity. *American Journal of Public Health, 101*(7), 1192–1197.

Preamble to the Constitution of the World Health Organization as adopted by the International Health Conference, New York, 19–22 June, 1946; signed on 22 July 1946 by the representatives of 61 States (Official Records of the World Health Organization, no. 2, p. 100) and entered into force on 7 April 1948.

Public Health Law Center. (2010). *Master settlement agreement.* Retrieved from http://publichealthlawcenter.org/topics/tobacco-control/tobacco-control-litigation/master-settlement-agreement

Rajotte, B., Ross, C., Ekechi, C., & Cadet, V. (2011). Health in all policies: Addressing the legal and policy foundations of health impact assessment. *Journal of Law, Medicine, & Ethics, 39*(Suppl. s1), 27–29.

Rao, J., & Anderson, L. (2012). Examining external validity in efficacy and secondary articles of home-based depression care management interventions for older adults. *Preventing Chronic Disease, 9,* e172. Retrieved from http://www.ncbi.nlm.nih.gov/pmc/articles/PMC3523890/

Redman, E. (2000). *The dance of legislation.* Seattle, WA: University of Washington Press.

The Reinvestment Fund. (2006). *The economic impact of supermarkets on their surrounding communities* (Issue Brief No. 4). Retrieved from http://www.trfund.com/wp-content/uploads/2013/06/supermarkets.pdf

The Reinvestment Fund. (2011). *Healthy food retail financing at work: Pennsylvania fresh food financing initiative.* Philadelphia, PA: Author. Retrieved from http://www.cdfifund.gov/what_we_do/resources/Healthy%20Food%20Retail%20Financing%20102411.pdf

Robert Wood Johnson Foundation. (2012, September). *Declining childhood obesity rates—Where are we seeing the most progress* (Issue Brief). Retrieved from http://www.rwjf.org/content/dam/farm/reports/issue_briefs/2012/rwjf401163

Robert Wood Johnson Foundation. (2013a). Retrieved from http://www.rwjf.org/

Robert Wood Johnson Foundation. (2013b, February 12). New Orleans, Louisiana: 2013 Roadmaps to Health Prize. Retrieved from http://www.rwjf.org/en/about-rwjf/newsroom/newsroom-content/2013/02/new-orleans--louisiana--2013-roadmaps-to-health-prize.html

Robert Wood Johnson Foundation. (2013c, July). *Declining childhood obesity rates.* Retrieved from http://www.rwjf.org/en/research-publications/find-rwjf-research/2012/09/declining-childhood-obesity-rates.html

Roberto, C., Larsen, P., Agnew, H., Baik, J., & Brownell, K. (2010). Evaluating the impact of menu labeling on food choices and intake. *American Journal of Public Health, 100*(2), 312–318.

Rose, G. (1992). *The strategy of preventive medicine.* Oxford, UK: Oxford University Press.

Russell, N. J. (2006). *An introduction to the Overton Window of political possibilities.* Retrieved from http://www.mackinac.org/7504

Sabatier, P., & Jenkins-Smith, H. (1993). *Policy change and learning.* Boulder, CO: Westview Press.

Sassi, F. (2010). *Obesity and economics of prevention: Fit not fat.* Paris, France: Organization for Economic Co-operation and Development.

Satcher, D. (2001). *The surgeon general's call to action to prevent and decrease overweight and obesity, 2001.* Washington, DC: U.S. Department of Health and Human Services.

Schattschneider, E. (1960). *The semi-sovereign people.* New York, NY: Holt, Rinehart, and Winston.

Schenck v. United States, 249 U.S. 47 (1919).

Schifferdecker, K., & Reed, V. (2009). Using mixed methods research in medical education: Basic guidelines for researchers. *Medical Education,* 43(7), 637–644.

Schmid, T. L., Pratt, M., & Witmer, L. (2006). A framework for physical activity policy research. *Journal of Physical Activity and Health,* 3(Suppl. 1), S20–S29.

Secretary of Health and Human Services. (2013). *Charter 2015 dietary guidelines advisory committee.* Washington, DC: Department of Health and Human Services.

Singh, A., Mulder, C., Twisk, J., van Mechelen, W., & Chinapaw, M. (2008). Tracking of childhood overweight into adulthood: A systematic review of the literature. *Obesity Review,* 9(5), 478–488.

Smedley, B., Smith, A., & Nelson, A. (Eds.). (2003). *Unequal treatment; confronting racial and ethnic disparities in health care.* Washington, DC: National Academies Press.

Sofaer, S. (1999). Qualitative methods: What are they and why use them? *Health Services Research,* 34(5), 1101–1118.

Starr, P. (1982). *The social transformation of American medicine.* New York, NY: Basic Books.

Steinberg, E., & Luce, B. (2005). Evidence based? Caveat emptor! *Health Affairs,* 24(1), 80–92.

Stokols, D. (1992). Establishing and maintaining healthy environments. Toward a social ecology of health promotion. *American Psychologist,* 47(1), 6–22.

Stokols, D., Allen, J., & Bellingham, R. L. (1996). The social ecology of health promotion: Implications for research and practice. *American Journal of Health Promotion, 10*(4), 247–251.

The Strategic Growth Council. (2013a). *Health in all policies task force.* Retrieved from http://sgc.ca.gov/hiap/

The Strategic Growth Council. (2013b). *Health in all policies task force—About us.* Retrieved from http://sgc.ca.gov/hiap/about.html

Swinburn, B., Gill, T., & Kumanyika, S. (2005). Obesity prevention: A proposed framework for translating evidence into action. *Obesity Review, 6*(1), 23–33.

Taber, D., Chriqui, J., Perna, F., Powell, L., & Chaloupka, F. (2012). Weight status among adolescents in states that govern competitive food. *Pediatrics, 130*(3), 437–444.

Tatsioni, A., Bonitsis, N., & Ioannidis, J. (2007). Persistence of contradicted claims in the literature. *Journal of the American Medical Association, 298*(21), 2517–2526.

Thaler, R., & Sunstein, C. (2008). *Nudge; improving decisions about health, wealth and happiness.* New Haven, CT: Yale University Press.

Thomson, H., & Thomas, S. (2012). External validity in healthy public policy: Application of the RE-AIM tool to the field of housing improvement. *BMC Public Health, 12,* 633. Retrieved from http://www.ncbi.nlm.nih.gov/pmc/articles/PMC3481477/

Thorpe, K., Florence, C., Howard, D., & Joski, P. (2004). The impact of obesity on rising medical spending. *Health Affairs, 23,* W4-480. Retrieved from http://content.healthaffairs.org/content/early/2004/10/20/hlthaff.w4.480.long

Thorpe, K., Florence, C., Howard, D., & Joski, P. (2005). The rising prevalence of treated disease: Effects on private health insurance spending. *Health Affairs, 5,* W5-317. Retrieved from http://content.healthaffairs.org/content/early/2005/06/27/hlthaff.w5.317.citation

Tresandre, L., & Chatterjee, S. (2009). The impact of obesity on health services utilization and costs in childhood. *Obesity, 17*(9), 1749–1754.

United States Department of Agriculture. (2013). *Agriculture Secretary Vilsack highlights new "Smart snacks in school" standards; will ensure school vending machines, snack bars include healthy choices* (Report No. 0134.13). Washington, DC: Author. Retrieved from http://www.usda.gov/wps/portal/usda/usdahome?contentid=2013/06/0134.xml

United States Department of Health and Human Services. (2009). *American Recovery and Reinvestment Act summary of the prevention and wellness initiative-community component.* Washington, DC: Author. Retrieved from http://

www.cdc.gov/chronicdisease/recovery/PDF/PW_Community_fact_
sheet_final.pdf

United States Institutes of Health, National Cancer Institute. (2013). Accessed
September 20, 2013, from http://seer.cancer.gov/

U. S. Government Printing Office. (2013). National school lunch program and
school breakfast program: Nutrition standards for all foods sold in schools
as required by the healthy, Hunger-Free Kids Act of 2010; Interim final
rule (7 CFR Parts 210 and 220). *Federal Register.* Vol 78, no. 125, p. 39068.
Retrieved from http://www.gpo.gov/fdsys/pkg/FR-2013-06-28/pdf/2013-
15249.pdf

Viguerie, N., Montastier, E., Maoret, J.-J., Roussel, B., Combes, M., Valle, C., . . .
Langin, D. (2012). Determinants of human adipose tissue gene expression:
Impact of diet, sex, metabolic status, and *cis* genetic regulation. *PLOS Genetics.*
Retrieved from http://www.ncbi.nlm.nih.gov/pmc/articles/PMC3459935/
pdf/pgen.1002959.pdf

Virginia Commonwealth University. (2013). *Place matters.* Retrieved from
http://www.humanneeds.vcu.edu/Page.aspx?nav=200

Wang, C. (1999). Photovoice: A participatory action research strategy applied
to women's health. *Journal of Women's Health, 8*(2), 185–192.

Wang, C., Orleans, T., & Gortmaker, S. (2012). Reaching the healthy people
goals for reducing childhood obesity: Closing the energy gap. *American
Journal of Preventive Medicine, 42*(5), 437–444.

Wang, Y., Wu, Y., Wilson, R. F., Bleich, S., Cheskin, L., Weston, C., . . . Segal, J.
(2013, June). *Childhood obesity prevention programs: Comparative effectiveness
review and meta-analysis* (Report No. 13-EHC081-EF). Rockville, MD: Agency
for Healthcare Research and Quality (United States). Retrieved from http://
www.ncbi.nlm.nih.gov/pubmed/23865092

Ward, D., Hales, D., Haverly, K., Marks, J., Benjamin, S., Ball, S., & Trost, S.
(2008). An instrument to assess the obesogenic environment of child care
centers. *American Journal of Health Behavior, 32*(4), 380–386.

Ward, D., Vaughn, A., & Story, M. (2013). Expert and stakeholder consensus
on priorities for obesity prevention research in early care and education
settings. *Childhood Obesity, 9*(2), 116–124.

Washington Environmental Council. (2013). *Local farms, healthy kids.* Retrieved
from http://wecprotects.org/issues-campaigns/local-farms-healthy-kids

Washington State Department of Health. (2013). *"Local Farms–Healthy Kids Act"
passed by WA State Legislature.* Retrieved from http://depts.washington.edu/
waaction/action/n1/c2.html

Washington State Legislature. (2008). The Local Farms–Healthy Kids Act; SSB 6483.PL.

Weiss, R., Dziura, J., Burgert, T., Tamborlane, W., Taksali, S., Yeckel, C., . . . Caprio, S. (2004). Obesity and the metabolic syndrome in children and adolescents. *New England Journal of Medicine, 350*(23), 2362–2374.

Weissert, C., & Weissert, W. (2006). *Governing health: The politics of health policy* (3rd ed.). Baltimore, MD: Johns Hopkins Press.

Wennberg, J., & Gittelsohn, A. (1973). Small area variations in health care delivery: A population-based health information system can guide planning and regulatory decision-making. *Science, 182*(4117), 1102–1108.

Westlaw Professional Legal Research. (n.d.). *How to find statutes.* Retrieved from http://lscontent.westlaw.com/images/content/FindStatutes10.pdf

Whitaker, R. C., Wright, J. A., Pepe, M. S., Seidel, K. D., & Dietz, W. H. (1997). Predicting obesity in young adulthood from childhood and parental obesity. *New England Journal of Medicine, 337,* 869-873. doi: 10.1056/NEJM199709253371301

Whiteman, H. (2013, August 8). U.S. child obesity rates are dropping, says CDC. *Medical News Today.* Retrieved from http://www.medicalnewstoday.com/articles/264548.php

Work Group for Community Health and Development. (2013). Other models for promoting community health and development, Section 2: PRECEDE/PROCEED. In *The community tool box* (Chap. 2). Retrieved from http://ctb.ku.edu/en/table-contents/overview/chapter-2-other-models-promoting-community-health-and-development/section-2

World Health Organization. (2010, April). *Adelaide Statement on health in all policies.* Retrieved from http://www.who.int/social_determinants/hiap_statement_who_sa_final.pdf

Wulff, K., Miller, F., & Pearson, S. (2011). Can coverage be rescinded when negative trial results threaten a popular procedure? The ongoing saga of vertebroplasty. *Health Affairs, 30*(12), 2269–2276.

Yin, R. K. (2009). *Case study research: Design and methods* (4th ed.). Thousand Oaks, CA: Sage.

# Index

AARP, 106

AASHTO. *See* American Association of State Highway and Transportation Officials

abbreviations, 48–49

ACA. *See* Affordable Care Act of 2010

accountability care organizations (ACOs), 37

ACOs. *See* accountability care organizations

Active Living by Design (ALbD), 149

Active Living Research, 148

Adelaide Statement 2010, 7

adjusted relative risk (ARR), 49

administrative strategies, 178–180

advocacy coalitions, 98–99

Affordable Care Act of 2010 (ACA), 23, 31, 68, 81, 85, 91, 95, 99, 109, 117, 118, 151, 181

Agency for Health Care Policy and Research (AHCPR), 21

Agency for Healthcare Research & Quality (AHRQ), 21–22, 28, 31, 142

AHCPR. *See* Agency for Health Care Policy and Research

AHRQ. *See* Agency for Healthcare Research & Quality

ALbD. *See* Active Living by Design

ALEC. *See* American Legislative Exchange Council

alliances, 173

allocative efficiency, 14

all-payer claims databases (APCDs), 30, 37

American Association of State Highway and Transportation Officials (AASHTO), 126

American Heart Association, 56, 68

*American Journal of Clinical Nutrition*, 142

*American Journal of Public Health*, 142

American Legislative Exchange Council (ALEC), 149

American Public Health Association, 109

American Recovery and Reinvestment Act of 2009, 152

*Am. Express Co. et al. v. Italian Colors Rest. et al.*, 182

analytical studies, 34–38

APCD. *See* all-payer claims databases

appendices, 49

appropriation, 168, 170

ARR. *See* adjusted relative risk

Association of University Centers on Disabilities, 25

*AT & T Mobility v. Concepcion*, 182

CPSIA information can be obtained
at www.ICGtesting.com
Printed in the USA
LVHW03s1721270818
588278LV00010B/98/P